ArtScroll Series®

Rabbi Nosson Scherman / Rabbi Meir Zlotowitz

General Editors

מצפים ◆ לישועה

Yearning

Longing for
the *Geulah*
and enhancing
your life
in the process

INCLUDES 7 STRATEGIES FOR HASTENING THE GEULAH

Published by
Mesorah Publications, ltd

With Fire

A 5-Minute Lesson-A-Day

Rabbi Heshy Kleinman
Author of *Praying With Fire*

Foreword by Rabbi Mattisyahu Salomon

FIRST EDITION
First Impression … June 2010

Published and Distributed by
MESORAH PUBLICATIONS, LTD.
4401 Second Avenue / Brooklyn, N.Y 11232

Distributed in Europe by
LEHMANNS
Unit E, Viking Business Park
Rolling Mill Road
Jarow, Tyne & Wear, NE32 3DP
England

Distributed in Australia and New Zealand
by **GOLDS WORLDS OF JUDAICA**
3-13 William Street
Balaclava, Melbourne 3183
Victoria, Australia

Distributed in Israel by
SIFRIATI / A. GITLER — BOOKS
6 Hayarkon Street
Bnei Brak 51127

Distributed in South Africa by
KOLLEL BOOKSHOP
Ivy Common
105 William Road
Norwood 2192, Johannesburg, South Africa

ARTSCROLL SERIES®
YEARNING WITH FIRE
© *Copyright 2010, by* MESORAH PUBLICATIONS, Ltd.
4401 Second Avenue / Brooklyn, N.Y. 11232 / (718) 921-9000 / www.artscroll.com

---

ISBN 10: 1-4226-0996-0 / ISBN 13: 978-1-4226-0996-5

Typography by CompuScribe at ArtScroll Studios, Ltd.
Bound by Sefercraft, Quality Bookbinders, Ltd., Brooklyn N.Y. 11232

בס"ד

שמואל קמנצקי
Rabbi S. Kamenetsky

Study: 215-473-1212
Home: 215-473-2798

2018 Upland Way
Philadelphia, Pa 19131

בס"ד ג' מטות ומסעי ונשמחה לפ"ק

למע"כ הרה"ג וכו' מוה"ר אברהם צבי הכהן
קליינמאן שליט"א

אחדשה"ט דהדרג"ת שלום כמשפט,

בעוונות דורנו צפיית לישועה נתמעטה שאין מרגישים
בחסרון שמחסרים ישראל השלמות כי מצבם בו הם
במצב מנותק מאור ה' אלוקים להשלמות של מה שחסר
בעולם בזה מחשבת הש"י.

כי בזה הפרקה של צפיית לישועה שכל מה שחסר
בעולם ובפרט עם כל יחיד בזה מושג הקב"ה ואי"כ כל
אדם שחוטא לפני הקב"ה ומודה על כל שעה ושעה וצפה
צפיית לישועה.

ובודאי מה' לפני מה שמעורר כל יחיד ומעורר לבני
אדם כל כי בזה צפיית לישועה ויזכה הכלל להשלמת
ממצבי את הרדיפות שבזמננו ומצב לשלם.

מוקירו
שמואל קמנצקי

RABBI YAAKOV PERLOW
1569 - 47TH STREET
BROOKLYN N.Y. 11219

יעקב פרלוב
קהל עדת יעקב נאוואמינסק
ישיבת נאוואמינסק - קול יהודא
ברוקלין, נ.י.

בס"ד יום ד' דבהעלותך, י"ג סיון תשע"ג

הרב היקר והנעלה מוה"ר אברהם צבי קליינמאן שליט"א מוציא כעת
לאור חיבור אשר פרי יגיעו הוא בפינת לימודו, ובמיוחד לספריו
הקודמים ועתה ספר נחוץ ומועיל בלימוד פרקי הדרכה ביסודי
הדת ודרכי העבודה התמימה, להבין את אורח חיינו על המסלה
הגדולה בית א-ל ונלמדנו סלה ומוסר בהם חיים של יום יום, איך
להתקרב אל הבורא ית' באמונה ובבטחון ואיך לעבור את פני ועדו
בעולם הזה בשובה ונחת, בהשגה ודעת, להגיע אל תכלית החיים
ע"י התורה והמצוות וההליכה בדרכיו, יתברך שמו. ובודאי ספר
זה יביא תועלת גדולה לרבים, ובפרט בדור הזה ובשנה המבורכת,
ויפתח לנו את הדרך שלפנינו להכניס ולהנציל דבורו של אמונה
ישראל ובדרכם דרכי הבקשות להתקרב אל מרומי התורה ולבחור
החיים על מסילת חיינו. והנני מברך אותו בכל חותמי ברכות להרבה
סייעתא לראות מעשיו מתנוססים ורוב פירות עד ביאת הגואל
הגדול בברכה ומברכו כטוב

יעקב פרלוב

בס"ד

אור ל' חקת תש"ן לפ"ק
פה לייקוואד יע"א

[גוף המכתב בכתב יד:]

אשר ונפלאתי על כ[...] הצזילות אשר זכה יב"ג [...] אגוד[...] לכ: הלשומען [...]

זהול ספרי כדרכו מ[...] חמצוה בכל דרכי דעהו ועל כו50 אל מצות תפלה אשר

תוד ערץ בסית 6&2 ויחן לשתוך את לבם אל אחב' לקק"י מצות ולעגדו בכל לבבכם.

האל והאהבת [...] כי לו הצלחת מהומה לעצה ראש להות מקבה את הרבי'.

כגח ונשו לגו לטטיה ולעודד על יסף היסודות אשר לני [...] וחיל לקק"י את תקוה

אוי יתמהאת חכה לו לכלמית לאשעה להיות מתניך לנשאת השאלה בכל יום שלגבאו.

העי אפרן כאלו כבה עד עעד לצבות את הרבין בס"זקא [...] לשאיר כן עבד עוד

ספרבי ושמו מאמ-נועין הלהודי' כל עספרו בי תעקמו נ[...] לשאנה כי כל מימ[ו]

לאהבינ מפאר איד חיק על תולהך לאקמ 3 [...] קדושי לעוות הדרך.

כן נכבה כלנו לראות אחפה התמאות צ[...]

אאנ הכוה בכפוד ובת[...]

ידידות נאמנ[ה]

אאמ חיש סולמן

Table of Contents

Chapter 3: A Priceless Relationship

STRATEGY 1: LONGING FOR THE GEULAH

Chapter 4: Metzapim L'Yeshuah

Chapter 5: Kiddush Hashem in Everyday Life

STRATEGY 2: CREATING A PEOPLE UNITED

Chapter 6: The Problem — Hatred, Hurt, and Hostility

Chapter 7:
Solution I: Living With Emunah and Bitachon
Solution II: Internalize Gratitude

Chapter 8:
Solution III: Ending Jealousy and Hatred

Chapter 9:
Solution IV: V'ahavta L'rei'acha Kamocha

STRATEGY 3: HONOR SHABBOS PROPERLY
STRATEGY 4: PRAY FOR THE GEULAH
STRATEGY 5: THE POWER OF TZEDAKAH

Chapter 10: Revealing Hashem's Presence: Shabbos, Tefillah, and Tzedakah

STRATEGY 6: INCREASE TORAH STUDY

Chapter 11: The Uniqueness of Torah

STRATEGY 7: TESHUVAH: THE ANTIDOTE TO OUR EXILE

Chapter 12: Teshuvah: In Our Times

Chapter 13: A New Dawn

FOREWORD: LONGING FOR JERUSALEM

by HaRav Mattisyahu Salomon

When we leave a house of mourning, we speak the famous words of consolation, "May God comfort you among the rest of the mourners for Tzion and Jerusalem." Who are these mourners for Jerusalem? Who among us mourns for Jerusalem? Who among us appreciates what we are missing? Who among us pleads with God for a rebuilt Jerusalem because he feels an aching need for it? Who among us exclaims in complete sincerity, "If I forget you, O Jerusalem, may my right hand forget its power"?

The Jerusalem for which we long so desperately and whose loss we have mourned for thousands of years — it is not the land and the buildings of Jerusalem that we miss. It is the supreme connection with God that Jerusalem represents. Recreating Jerusalem in our imaginations as a conduit for our prayers is the best available to us right now, but it is no comparison to a rebuilt Jerusalem, crowned with a shining Temple in which the Divine Presence will dwell forever. Only when we appreciate what Jerusalem represents and what we have lost can we grieve over its destruction.

We are all familiar with the words of the prophet (*Yirmiyah* 2:2), "Go call out in the ears of Jerusalem: So said God, 'I remember for you the care of your youth, the love of your betrothal, when you went after Me into the desert, into a land that was unplanted.'"

Adapted from *With Hearts Full of Faith* (ArtScroll/Mesorah Publ., 2002).

R' Chaim Volozhiner wonders about the reference to Jerusalem in this prophecy. Since when does Jerusalem have ears? And when was Jerusalem in the desert? And why should he call out only to Jerusalem and not to the rest of the Jewish people?

Jerusalem, says R' Chaim Volozhiner, is a name given to the Jewish people united in the quest for perfection. Corresponding to the terrestrial Jerusalem, he explains, there is the celestial Jerusalem that is described in the mystical terms of the Kabbalah as *"makom kenisas hisklalelus neshamos shel Klal Yisrael."* Here on this earth and in Heaven above, Jerusalem is the name given to the unifying force within the Jewish people.

God tells the prophet, "Go call out in the ears of Jerusalem." Go to the Jewish people when they are united together to strive for perfection, when they deserve to be called collectively by the name Jerusalem. And what is the prophet to say to them? How is he to help them in their common quest for spiritual perfection? He is to remind them of their first steps as a nation. He is to say to them in the Name of God, "I remember for you the care of your youth, the love of your betrothal, when you went after Me into the desert, into a land that was unplanted."

How do we understand this? How does the recollection of the desert in particular help the Jewish people rise to higher levels?

The Torah tells us (*Bamidbar* 14:4) that when things became difficult in the desert some people said to each other, "Let us appoint a leader and return to Egypt." The Steipler Gaon, in *Chayei Olam*, finds this absolutely astonishing. Surely they could not have already forgotten the unspeakable misery and suffering they had endured in Egypt. How could they want to return? Could we imagine someone saying, "Things are so difficult for me here, I would rather return to Auschwitz"?

The answer, says the Steipler Gaon, is that the Egyptian land, fertile, beautiful, blessed with a temperate climate, was the most desirable in the world. "Like the garden of God," the Torah tells us (*Bereishis* 13:10), "like the land of Egypt." The problems the Jewish people had were not with the Egyptian land but with Egyptian society. But at this time, when the Jewish people were struggling through the desert, Egyptian society lay shattered by the devastation of the Exodus. Egypt was desolate, depopulated, defenseless, and vulnerable. It was the weakest among the nations. A walkover.

After receiving the Torah, the Jewish people could easily have turned around and conquered Egypt. They could have settled down on its fertile plains to live a comfortable Jewish life in accordance with the Torah, just as Jews would do in many places in the Diaspora over the centuries. In the other direction, they faced the hardships and tribulations of the bleak desert, dependent every day on God's miraculous support, always afraid that they might slip and transgress and be left in the desert to their own devices. And what would happen if they managed to survive the journey through the desert? What awaited them beyond? The powerful kingdoms of the seven Canaanite nations awaited them on their steeds and chariots at the borders of the Holy Land. And what if God deemed them unworthy of miraculous intervention? How would they fare on the battlefield against such fierce enemies? Hunger, thirst, war, these were the prospects they faced if they pushed on to Eretz Yisrael. Comfort awaited them in Egypt.

So the Jewish people were faced with a dilemma. What should they do? Should they go establish a Jewish country on the ruins of old Egypt? Should they opt for a life of comfort and safety in a land that would provide all their needs with relative ease and allow them to spend their time learning Torah and fulfilling its mitzvos? Should they forgo the fulfillment of the *mitzvos hateluyos ba'aretz*, the commandments relating to the Holy Land, and the higher levels of sanctity that can be attained only in Eretz Yisrael, for the sake of security and comfort in Egypt? Should they opt for a Torah life on a lower standard in Egypt or struggle through the desert and fight wars in the Holy Land in order to achieve Torah life on a higher standard?

The Jewish people united and chose the more difficult path for the sake of an extra closeness to God that can be found only in Eretz Yisrael, in Jerusalem, in Tzion. Therefore, it is not surprising that in moments of weakness, when things were difficult, some elements would grumble about the decision that had chosen Eretz Yisrael over Egypt. It is not surprising that some people would say, "Let us appoint a leader and return to Egypt."

Every step the Jewish people, united in their supreme devotion to God, took through the broiling desert was a reaffirmation of this critical decision. Every step confirmed the willingness of the Jewish people to give up comforts for the sake of spiritual achievement, to give up worldly success for the sake of coming closer to God.

And so whenever the Jewish people unite in this same spirit, whenever we coalesce into an entity that can be called Jerusalem, God recalls for our sake the dedication that characterized the early steps of the Jewish nation when they "went after Me into the desert, into a land that was unplanted." He joins us together with our gallant ancestors who were prepared to walk through the desert and fight wars for the sake of being close to Him.

After the Holocaust, the Jewish people had to reach in, to focus on rebuilding the internal institutions of the communities, the synagogues, the schools, the communal charities. When this was done successfully, we reached out to those of our brothers and sisters who had wandered from the warm embrace of the Torah. Now the time has come to reach up, to rise above the preoccupation with comfort and security and seek higher levels of spiritual achievement for the Jewish people as a whole.

So when we hear the sad news that all too often emanates from Jerusalem, when we feel an instinctive pang and a yearning in our hearts, we must stop and think. For what do we yearn? What does Jerusalem mean to us? Deep in our hearts, we must recreate the exalted idea of Jerusalem, of unity among all Jews in the quest for ever greater closeness to God. If only we can do this, God may just decide to let us see Jerusalem rebuilt speedily in our days.

PREFACE: YEARNING FOR ISRAEL

by Rabbi Yisroel Reisman

A *study of "Metzapim L'Yeshuah," Longing for the Geulah,*
would be incomplete without an appreciation of the yearn-
ing of the Jewish People for a return to the Land of Israel.
In our day, Torah learning and institutions have blossomed there,
numerous Jews have made it their home, and it is in fact visited by
many Jews. At the same time, we are still very much in the throes of
our Galus experience. Certainly, the nature of our yearning for Israel,
as part of our Galus experience, needs a special appreciation.

ISRAEL, THE LAND

The Land of Israel and the Jewish people are intertwined in a most mysterious way.

We know Eretz Yisrael as our home. Jews have continued to live there, often with great sacrifice, for all but 52 years of our exile. Yet, historically, the overwhelming majority of Jews who have ever lived, included many of our greatest Rabbis and teachers, never set foot in the Holy Land. It was only for an 850-year period that the majority of the Jewish people lived in Eretz Yisrael. For the rest of our 3,300 year existence, most Jews have been dispersed throughout the many lands of our exile. This realization leads to some confusion as to our fundamental relationship with the Holy Land.

Is Yiddishkeit dependent on a relationship with our homeland? Is the Land of Israel an essential part of our faith or merely the place of our history? If so, why is it that our People have spent far more time outside of Eretz Yisrael, than we have spent living there?

THE MYSTERY

The mystery is not new. As a matter of fact, the Torah hints at it, at the very birth of our People. It is something we allude to at the Pesach Seder. During the Seder, we drink four cups of wine. The *Yerushalmi* explains that this is based on the four Biblical expressions of redemption (*v'hotzeisi, v'hitzalti, v'ga'alti, v'lakachti*) which are mentioned in *Parashas Va'eira*. We drink four cups of wine, representing four levels of redemption. These four words refer to our Exodus from Egypt, without any reference to the destination of the Jews who left that land.

There is a fifth expression of redemption in this *parashah*. *V'heiveisi*, and I will bring you (to Israel). This word refers to our entry into Eretz Yisrael. Is this an essential component of our redemption, as a people? Or is it simply a location on the globe, our destination, when leaving Egypt?

A place — or a purpose? A destination — or a destiny?

At the Seder table, there is uncertainty as to how to deal with *V'heiveisi*. Is this a fifth expression of redemption, which would obligate us to drink a symbolic fifth cup of wine? Or, is it just a physical fact of our travel, not fundamental enough to be part of the Seder?

We don't know. We can't figure it out. The place of Eretz Yisrael in the story of our redemption is a mystery. We leave a fifth cup of wine as the "Cup of Eliyahu." At the time of the *Geulah* the prophet Eliyahu will decide this question.

It has been said that an essential component of romance is mystery. Indeed, the mystery of our relationship with the Land has not lessened our love for it.

In our hearts, Jews are absolutely certain that Israel is intimately tied to our People, even as we may find it difficult to define that relationship. In the Torah world, different factions have different ways of relating to the Government of Israel. For all of us, though, the romance with the Land continues.

HARAV SHIMON SHWAB'S TWO ISRAELS

Our appreciation of Eretz Yisrael is greatly enhanced by the teachings of Harav Shimon Schwab. Often, in his published works, Rav Schwab returns to a concept of dual visions of Eretz Yisrael in general and Jerusalem in particular.

At the end of *Parashas Va'eira*, we read of our forefather Avraham's first visit to the mount upon which Jerusalem would be built. Rav Schwab (*Maayan Beis HaSho'evah*, p. 324) relates the conversation that took place, as our forefather Avraham and his entourage approached the site of Jerusalem.

Avraham sees the mountain from the distance. It appears to be different than the adjacent mountains; Avraham can see a holy cloud, a sign of the Divine Presence upon this mountain.

Avraham turns to his son Yitzchak, and asks, "What do you see?"

Yitzchak responds, "I see a holiness hovering over the mountain, a sign of Divine Presence."

Avraham then turns to Yishmael and Eliezer, and asks, "What do you see?"

They look at the mountain and respond, "We see trees and stones."

Abraham tells them, "If so, stay here with the donkeys. They too, see only trees and stones. Yitzchak and I will ascend the mountain."

It has remained this way for all time. Two people can look at the same spot. One sees holiness and spirit. The other sees nothing more than the physical world before him.

THE SPIES

After leaving Egypt, the first Jews to enter Canaan are the *meraglim*, the Spies sent to scout the land. They return with different messages. Ten of them are pessimistic about the Jewish future in Israel; only Yehoshua and Calev speak warmly of the Land.

HaRav Schwab explains that they, too, had looked at the Land from different perspectives. The ten *meraglim* viewed Eretz Yisrael from a physical perspective, gazing at the land as a spot on the globe, a geographic location. They saw nothing inviting, they saw "a land that consumes her inhabitants."

Yeoshua and Calev looked upon the Land with the eyes of Avraham and Yitzchak. They looked for spirituality; they saw the Divine Presence on the mountain.

As it was then, in the very beginning of our relationship with the Land, so it remains for eternity. There are two Eretz Yisraels: the Eretz Yisrael of trees and stones and the Holy Eretz Yisrael, the seat of the *Shechinah*.

Four hundred people board a flight to Israel. For some, it is a wonderful destination, a place with Mediterranean beaches and plenty of Jewish shopping. For others it is our destiny, the Land of our spiritual glory, the seat of our Sanhedrin, the birthplace of our prophets, a place of connection for our souls.[1]

---

1. How ironic that the ads of the Israeli Tourism Office, touting Mediterranean beaches and the Tel Aviv nightlife, use as its logo, an image of the *meraglim*, carrying giant grapes. How appropriate!

IN OUR PRAYERS

Our daily *Shemoneh Esrei* includes a prayer for the rebuilding of Jerusalem.

In his *Iyun Tefillah* (p. 362), Rav Schwab explains the opening words of this blessing. *V'li'rushalayim ircha b'rachamim tashuv, And to Jerusalem, Your city, may You return, in compassion.* This prayer, alone among the eighteen original prayers of *Shemoneh Esrei*, begins with the letter *vov*, a prefix indicating connection, "*And.*"

HaRav Schwab[2] explains that the *vov* is meant to hint at the dual Jerusalem, the physical Jerusalem **and** the spiritual Jerusalem. For millennia, we have been praying for a return to Jerusalem. We have not been praying for a return to the physical spot known as Jerusalem. This is merely a geographic point, a place on the globe, a destination. Our prayers are for a return for the double-faceted Tzion, the city of our destiny.

Indeed, the final syllable of the Hebrew name Yerushalayim, is "*ayim,*" which is typically reserved for expressions of a pair, as in *yadayim* (hands), *raglayim* (feet), or *oznayim (ears).* Jerusalem, too, has a duality.

ZION

"Tzion" is a term in *Tanach.* To what does it refer? Where is Tzion?

In one of the ironies of modern Hebrew, Zionism is used to refer to the desire for a Jewish homeland in the Land of Israel. Yet, in its Biblical use, "Tzion" does not refer to the Land of Israel, nor to a Jewish homeland.

Again, we look to HaRav Shimon Schwab, in his *Iyun Tefillah* (p. 381): "Tzion, in *Tanach* and in our prayers, most often refers to the Beis HaMikdash, the Holy Temple, as in *Tzion mishkan k'vodecha, Tzion, the resting place of Your Glory* ...Tzion is a description of the Beis HaMikdash because (the Beis HaMikdash) is the most outstanding spot for the Jewish People."

HaRav Schwab is not alone in this definition.

She'arim Metzuyanim BaHalachah (Succah 41a) writes: "The expression 'Tzion', as found in *Tanach* and in our prayers, is the Beis HaMikdash. The verse in the Book of *Melachim I* (referring to) the City of Tzion. . .was actually a reference to the Beis HaMikdash."

Rav Tzadok HaKohen (*Pri Tzaddik, Shemos* 118), writes simply, "Beis HaMikdash, this is Tzion."

---

2. The synopsis of Harav Schwab's words, presented here, hardly does justice to the beautiful essay presented in his *sefer*. We have only presented the brief point relevant to our current discussion.

How puzzling! A study of our prayer book seems to contradict this definition!

Each Shabbos, in the section added to *Bircas HaMazon*, we pray, *V'hareinu b'nechemas Tzion irecha*, *And show us the consolation of Tzion Your city*.

In our Yom Tov Mussaf prayers, we ask, *V'havi'einu l'Tzion ircha b'renah*, *bring us to Tzion, Your city, in celebration*.

Also: *Hasheiv shecinascha l'Tzion irecha, return Your Divine Presence to Tzion, Your city*.

On Shabbos, in the *Tzur MiShelo* poem, we sing, *Ir Tzion temalei, the City of Tzion replenished*.

Indeed, we find that the *Rosh* (to *Berachos* 48b) writes: "Tzion and Jerusalem are the same." These sources lead us to conclude that Tzion is a name for the city of Jerusalem.

If we are to accept our teachers' definition of Tzion as a reference to the Beis HaMikdash, how are we to understand these numerous references to "*Tzion, Your city*"?

A DIFFERENT ZION

A closer examination of HaRav Shimon Shwab's words resolves this contradiction and leads us to a new appreciation of Tzion.

The word Tzion, is related to the Hebrew word *metzuyan*, meaning outstanding or excellent. Thus, Tzion is a reference to the most outstanding part of Jerusalem, what HaRav Schwab refers to as the *neshamah*, the "soul" of the city. This is the Beis HaMikdash, the seat of the Divine Presence.

(The lesson is the same as HaRav Schwab had made in his teachings, referenced earlier.)

Jerusalem exists on two levels. As a physical city, a point on the map, Jerusalem is hardly worthy of the name Tzion.

Tzion, the outstanding city, is the location of the Beis HaMikdash. In physical terms, the Beis HaMikdash was a small part of the city. In spiritual terms, it is the *neshamah*, the soul of the city. Physically, the human being may be two hundred pounds of flesh and blood. In the spiritual realm, though, the person is his soul, his spirit, that which makes him special.

There is therefore no contradiction between Tzion, Your city, and Tzion, the Beis HaMikdash, the seat of the Divine Presence.

As it turns out, we have it both ways; Tzion does refer to the city of Jerusalem, but more specifically, to the most spiritual component of the city. The physical location of Tzion is the Beis HaMikdash, the soul of Jerusalem.

MYSTERY SOLVED

The mystery of *v'heiveisi* is thus solved. Is Israel our place or our purpose? Is this a physical homeland or an essential part of our destiny?

It all depends which eyes read the word *v'heiveisi*. If you see Israel through the eyes of Yishmael and Eliezer, or through the eyes of their donkeys, you see nothing in *v'heiveisi*. The eyes of the ten *meraglim*, too, see only a point on the map.

Israel is what we make of it.

Seen through the eyes of Avraham and Yitzchak, the eyes of Yehoshua and Calev, *v'heiveisi* becomes our destiny, our purpose. Indeed, this is our test, our struggle, to yearn for the heavenly Jerusalem.

Today, we struggle to appreciate Israel and Jerusalem. The fifth cup sits on our Seder table, not fully appreciated.

In the words of HaRav Schwab (*Iyun Tefillah* p. 363): "We speak of these concepts in a manner similar to one who describes the various colors to one who is blind from birth... it is in this manner that we, too, talk about concepts of a spiritual Beis HaMikdash."

The fifth cup sits on our table. It awaits the era of Eliyahu, a time of clarity Then, we will all drink the cup of *v'heiveisi*.

YEARNING FOR ISRAEL

We return to our initial question:

We have come to understand that when the Jewish People relate to Israel as a spiritual place, we connect to our destiny; we gain from our association to Israel. The distraction of an attraction to the physical beauty of Israel threatens our dream, distracts us from our destiny.[3]

A physical attraction to a land requires that one be there. This is not necessarily so, if we speak of a spiritual attraction.

For 2,500 years, the majority of Jews have lived outside of Israel. Each day, we have turned in prayer, facing Jerusalem and praying for its redemption. After each meal, we've recited the Grace After Meals, in which two of the four blessings refer to Israel and Jerusalem. During the High Holy Days, the *Yomim Nora'im*, our prayers and thoughts constantly reference Tzion and Jerusalem.

Even when we were far away, the spiritual Jerusalem was always on our

---

3. Indeed, the Gemara (*Pesachim* 8b) relates that the hot springs of Teveria are not located in Jerusalem, "lest one say that if I had traveled to Jerusalem for the springs alone, it would be worthwhile."

national consciousness. From a distance, we connected to Israel on a daily basis.

The spiritual Israel knows no borders. It has always existed in the soul of the Jewish People, wherever we may be. From the distance, our yearning has been our connection.

Today, things are different. We visit Eretz Yisrael and cannot help but take pride in the great achievements of the *Yishuv*. We marvel at a Land that has welcomed back her children, by giving forth her bounty, where only desert existed for millennium. We thank God for a country where Jews are the majority; where the street signs are in the letters of our alphabet; where, after 2,500 years, Jerusalem has once again become the center of Torah scholarship. None of these things have happened for thousands of years!

Be careful! What do these observations do to you? Do they satisfy your yearning for Jerusalem? Many Jews feel content with their connection to Israel. They visit Israel to see the sights, enjoy the beauty, and (like the *meraglim*) partake of the foods.

They have failed the test of our generation's connection to Eretz Yisrael. They yearn for the spiritual Israel far less than their forefathers who lived far away.

Can it be that Jews have merited a return to the Land of Israel, only to appreciate it less???

METZAPIM L'YESHUAH

We are challenged. Let us yearn for the spiritual Israel as never before. Let us pledge, together, to yearn for Godliness in God's Land.

Let those of us who live in the Diaspora visit the land to grow from its spiritual wealth.

Let our visits to Israel include hours of intense Torah study in one of Israel's citadels of Torah.

Let's visit the yeshivos of *baalei teshuvah*, sit among them, get to know them, and thereby grow from their examples of extraordinary sacrifice and devotion.

Let's undertake to visit Jerusalem and pray among Jerusalem's Jews and to walk among them.

Let us truly yearn for the rebuilding of the Heavenly Jerusalem, swiftly and in our day.

PROLOGUE: YEARNING WITH FIRE — BEING "METZAPIM L'YESHUAH"

INTRODUCTION

In *Praying With Fire*, I quoted Rav Pam, who wrote in his *sefer, Atarah L'Melech*:[1] "Do not read this *sefer* as one reads a newspaper, superficially and without a sense of purpose. The masters of *mussar* would say that one who seeks to be influenced and inspired by something he learns must review the subject matter again and again, and most importantly, he must ponder it well." *Baruch Hashem*, thousands took that message to heart.

The same request is applicable regarding this *sefer*. The purpose of *Yearning With Fire* is not to say *"vertlach"* (brief insights that do not impart any real lesson); rather, it is to inspire all of us toward repairing what is amiss in our *avodas Hashem*, which is central to clearing the pathways between us and the Divine Presence. By longing for the *Geulah* we not only bring redemption closer, thereby generating abundant blessings for everyone, we also enhance and improve our lives *today*, achieving the ultimate relationship with Hashem.

Using the lessons of *Chazal*, through highly practical, doable strategies, *Yearning With Fire* will inspire any and every Jew to a *revitalized, more purposeful* approach to life. When that vision is our focus, it serves to guide us joyously along our path in life.

NO PREDICTIONS

Yearning With Fire is *not* a sefer about *when* the *Geulah* will arrive. As the Rambam states:[2] "A person should not occupy himself in the words of *Aggados* (concerning these matters), nor spend excessive time in the

---

1. *Rav Pam*, Rabbi Shimon Finkelman (ArtScroll/Mesorah Publ.), p. 110.
2. *Hilchos Melachim* 12:2.

Midrashim on these and similar matters, and should not regard them as primary. For they lead neither to love (of God) nor to fear (of God). Thus, although awaiting Mashiach is a bedrock belief of Judaism, predicting when it will occur is *not* a fundamental Jewish principle.

Even before the nightmare of the Holocaust had occurred, the Chofetz Chaim, among others, had stated that all the signs for the coming of Mashiach had already come true.[3] Yet, in a discussion of the Chofetz Chaim's assertion, Rav Elchonon Wasserman[4] clarified that the Chofetz Chaim had only observed that the signs of Mashiach's coming had been fulfilled, but, "We do not know how long the *chevlei Mashiach* will last."[5]

This sense of imminence, the certainty that the time for the Final Redemption has surely come, is by no means a new phenomenon. More than the Rambam's[6] statement, that spending excessive time in the Midrashim on these and similar matters leads neither to love (of God) nor to fear (of God), from time to time, our long history of personal and national suffering has turned our legitimate — and mandatory — spark of hope into a ravaging blaze of false Messianic fervor.

FALSE HOPES

While many previous generations harbored an intense longing for the *Geulah* in their hearts, it has often been in response to horrendous persecution and poverty, for which redemption was the only foreseeable relief.

Perhaps the most infamous of these periods began in 5335 (1574 C.E.), when Shabbetai Tzvi began to cast his spell over large segments of the Jewish world. To the beleaguered Jews of the time, who had known nothing but persecution, massacre, and exile, the promise of redemption was too glorious to resist. Throughout the Diaspora, communities rejoiced with celebratory processions, purified themselves with acts of mortification, and sent innumerable delegations to behold the so-called Mashiach.

The sheer power of the movement eventually alarmed the ruling Ottoman authorities, who summoned the Mashiach. to appear before them. Given the choice of conversion or death, Shabbetai Tzvi shocked his followers by choosing to convert to Islam.[7]

---

3. *Beis HaSho'evah*, p. 20.
4. Adapted from *Selected Speeches,* Rav Shimon Schwab (CIS Publ., Abridged Edition), p. 17.
5. However, see *Even Sheleimah*, Ch. 11, fn. 4.
6. *Hilchos Melachim* 12:2.
7. Adapted from *A Historical Atlas of the Jewish People,* Edited by Eli Barnavi (Published by Schocken Books).

Despite this crushing disappointment, the continued persecution of the Jews kept their burning desire for redemption alive. With each new disaster, the certainty that "this is it," arose, only to be suffocated by further travails.

With the Holocaust, many great Torah leaders, including Rav Yechezkel Levenstein,[8] the Steipler Gaon,[9] and Rav Eliyahu Lopian[10] believed that they had witnessed the final stages of pre-Messianic turmoil. Rav Levenstein stated:[11]

> It seems to me that many of the details [that apply to the End of Days] have already occurred during the Holocaust...it was an eis tzarah, a time of suffering [of a magnitude] that previously had not existed until our time...

In 1967, nineteen years after the founding of the Jewish state, the nation once again experienced the sense that their moment had finally arrived. Rav Schwab recounts: [12]

> Then came the Six Day War and almost everybody believed that this was it. Lost territories were retaken in just six days — wonder of wonders! The boundaries of Eretz Yisrael were once again the boundaries described in the Tanach. The enemies were beaten. Millions of Arabs and Moslems had been subjugated by a handful of Jews. The euphoria was enormous. [13]

All of the disappointments, born of sincere hope in the Redemption, leave the believing Jew to wonder how we should interpret these confusing signs. There is Jewish sovereignty over a large part of the Land of Israel, and yet, we remain in a terribly dark *galus*. Are the many setbacks and troubles besetting us truly disappointments, reflecting false hope? Or are they, on the contrary, exactly the signs *Chazal* have designated as landmarks for recognizing the proximity of our destination?

> A man sets out on a long trip to visit a friend who lives far out in a rural area. The friend has provided the man with directions: "It's a rough road, with a lot of ruts, some foggy stretches, and one part that gets washed out in the rain," he tells him. "But it gets even rougher toward the end. Just keep going. Stay alert and go slowly. When you get to a

8. *Ohr Yechezkel, Emunah*, p. 313.
9. *Orchos Rabbeinu*, Vol. 1, p. 287.
10. *Lev Eliyahu, Parashas Va'eschanan*, p. 187.
11. *Ohr Yechezkel* loc. cit.
12. *Selected Speeches*, Rav Shimon Schwab (CIS Publishers, Abridged Edition), pp. 18-19.
13. See *Taam V'Daas on Chamishah Chumshei Torah, Parashas Vayigash*, pp. 248-249.

part that is completely impassible, you'll see a fork in the road. Bear right, and you're there."

STAYING AWAKE

How, then, does one interpret the sense of imminence described by the Chofetz Chaim in his time, and the post-World War II Torah figures in their time? Does it spring from a true vision of the forces afoot in the world, or does it reflect nothing more than the hopeful dreams cradled in the hearts of leaders who bore their generation's unbearable sorrows?

How could they be nothing more than dreams, when the precise depictions given in the Torah and Talmud of pre-Messianic times have become an unthinkable reality? As *Yearning With Fire* will show, it is not the perceptions of the Torah luminaries that are in any way flawed, but rather, the flaw lies in our own grasp of how to fulfill the obligation to "await" the *Geulah.*

> *A traveler set out on the road in a wagon. Fearful of nighttime marauders, he chose to sleep during the day and remain awake at night. He would awaken just as the moon began to rise, and fall asleep with the first glimmer of sun. When he arrived at his destination, he asked the wagon-driver why his route, which was known for its scenic beauty, had been so dark and dismal. The driver answered, "The scenery was beautiful. The sun shone every day, but you never saw it, because you slept through it all."*

Like this traveler, the Dubno Maggid[14] expounds, the Jewish people have many times throughout history "slept through" a potential time of redemption. As many commentators describe,[15] there are times when Mashiach can arrive in a moment — *achishenah*, suddenly. There is an "illumination" up above in Heaven for redemption. However, we, on earth, did not prepare the "receptacle" to receive the great "light" from above.[16] Had the Jewish people remained "awake" and vigilant, they could have brought Mashiach during those times.

---

14. As cited in *Ohr Gedalyahu, Vayikra,* p. 82, fn. 8. See also *Ohel Yaakov, Parashas Emor,* p. 116.
15. *Sanhedrin* 98a. See *Abarbanel,* in *Sefer Yeshuos Meshicho,* Part 2, *Iyun* 1, Ch. 1, p. 39; *Turei Even,* on *Rosh Hashanah,* 11b, s.v. *B'Tishrei;* and the *Chasam Sofer* in *She'eilos U'Teshuvos Chasam Sofer,* Vol. 6, *Siman* 98, s.v. *Vehinei.*
16. *Ohr Gedalyahu, Bereishis,* p. 129, s.v. *V'inyan zeh.*

AT ANY TIME

Mashiach can come *any* day, even before the predetermined date: *As Tehillim declares:*[17] *"This day* if you will listen to His voice!" Every generation has a special *keitz* (designated time) of its own, for, as stated, Mashiach is alive and present in every generation, albeit concealed.[18] He is ready to be revealed at a moment's notice.[19] In the course of history prior to "its time," there are especially auspicious times to affect his coming.

That fact is that Mashiach will come, and can indeed come, at any time. According to all the signs that our Sages have given us listed at the end of Gemara *Sotah*[20] regarding *ikvesa* d'*Mashicha*, everything has already occurred. Nothing is missing. The rest is up to us!

---

17. 95:7.
18. See *Even Sheleimah* 11:9, which states that every generation has its own special *keitz*, subject to Israel's merit . However, see *Pesach Einayim* on *Sanhedrin* 98a.
19. See *Sanhedrin* 98a.
20. 49a.

HOW TO USE THIS BOOK

ONE DAY AT A TIME — 5-MINUTE LESSON

Chazal teach that *"maaseh avos siman lebanim*[1] — the actions of our Patriarchs are a model for the children." Yaakov Avinu, a paradigm of truth, was shown "a ladder stationed on the ground[2] with its head (the top rung) reaching the heavens" as a symbol of his life's task, to demonstrate that one cannot successfully ascend the spiritual ladder in one stride.[3] In our service of Hashem as well, we must complete the tasks required by each level of growth; it is not possible to reach the top rung in one huge leap.

In this vein, Rav Pam[4] cites a teaching from *Mishlei:*[5] *Wealth gained by vanity* [i.e., dishonesty] *will diminish, but what one gathers by hand will increase.* Our Sages explain: If a person studies a great deal of new material at once, he will not retain his knowledge, but if one *gathers by hand*, meaning that he studies small quantities at a time, he will thereby increase his knowledge.[6]

CALENDAR

To facilitate daily learning, this book features a learning calendar displayed on the margin of each day's lesson. While keeping to this calendar can strengthen one's sense of purpose in undertaking this daily learning, the more important goal is to learn each day in sequence.

---

1. See *Ramban, Bereishis* 12:6.
2. *Michtav MeEliyahu*, Vol. 1, p. 25.
3. It is for this reason that Yaakov Avinu, upon awakening, immediately began to pray to Hashem.
4. *Rav Pam*, Rabbi Shimon Finkelman (ArtScroll/ Mesorah Publ.), p. 102.
5. 13:11.
6. *Avodah Zarah* 19a.

If one begins learning this *sefer* on a later date or misses a day of learning, he should resume with the next consecutive day rather than seek to stay with the calendar. In this way, the logical progression of the learning will be maintained.

TAKE IT WITH YOU

To assist the reader in internalizing the message of each lesson, we have provided a brief summary of the main points of each section in "Take It With You." While these will assist in integrating and retaining the information in the day's lesson, they cannot impart the total depth and nuance of the main body of the text.

LEARN EACH DAY AS A MERIT

Before beginning the **YEARNING WITH FIRE'S** 5-minute daily lessons, one can say:

יְהִי רָצוֹן מִלְּפָנֶיךָ שֶׁלַּתַּלְמוּד שֶׁאֲנִי לוֹמֵד (לוֹמֶדֶת) הַיּוֹם יִהְיֶה לִזְכוּת לִישׁוּעַת כְּלַל יִשְׂרָאֵל בְּעֵת צָרָה וְלִזְכוּת _____.

May it be Your will that my study today be a merit for the salvation of Klal Yisrael in a time of distress and as a merit for (name) _____.

The merit can be applied to any of the following: *refuah sheleimah* (complete recovery), *zivug hagun* (*shidduch*), *zera shel kayama* (to have children), *parnassah* (livelihood), *shalom bayis* (peace in the home), or any other need. See **Praying With Fire 2**, Day 112, page 369, for how to say the name when praying for another.

CONCLUSION

Read one day at a time — or more if you choose — of the teachings of the Gemara and the great *Rishonim* and *Acharonim* from whose reservoirs of Torah wisdom we will learn. You are sure to find inspiration. Ultimately, however, the objective of this book will be realized through the desire it engenders in the reader to hasten the *Geulah*.

In *Michtav MeEliyahu*,[7] Rav Eliyahu Dessler writes that a person who is inspired regarding an important task should know with certainty that it is incumbent upon him to fully accept the assignment. Hence, our role is merely that of one inspired from Heaven, who has gathered the wisdom of

---

7. Introduction, p. 17.

others and feels compelled to share these treasures with all who are interested.

May it be Hashem's will that our modest attempts to gather these meaningful teachings will inspire you, the reader. May the merit bring strength and comfort to Klal Yisrael in the time of crisis in which we live, and hasten the Redemption.

ACKNOWLEDGMENTS

The first place in the Torah where the Hebrew word for "thanks" appears is when Leah gave birth to her fourth son, Yehudah. She said, "This time I will thank Hashem." Rashi comments that Leah felt grateful to Hashem for each of her children. However, when she gave birth to Yehudah, she recognized and admitted to Hashem that she had been granted sons beyond her fair share. True thanksgiving occurs when people feel they have been given more than they deserve.

To have had the *zechus* (merit) to author the **Praying With Fire** series (**Praying With Fire 1 and 2**) was more than I ever dreamed. To have even imagined that I would have the opportunity to author **Yearning With Fire** is truly beyond contemplation. Once again I thank Hashem for giving me the opportunity. The only possible explanation is that *all* this happened because of great *siyata d'Shmaya*, Heavenly Help.

In the *Modim* blessing of *Shemoneh Esrei*, we exclaim: "We shall thank You and relate Your praise — for our lives, which are committed to Your power, and for our souls ... that are entrusted to You..." Every moment of life is ours only because God gives it to us. We normally take our existence for granted. Thus, with these words we admit to Hashem that every moment of our lives is a gift that He has granted us.

I thank *Hakadosh Baruch Hu* for providing me with life and its numerous gifts. These include providing me with health, the means, the knowledge, the ideas, the people from whom I have learned, and the time necessary to undertake this endeavor, along with countless other remarkable gifts too numerous to mention.

HODAAH

The Hebrew word for thanksgiving is *hodaah*. This word also means "to admit." Rav Hutner comments that when one person gives thanks to another he is really admitting that he needed the other person.

The Gemara teaches us the extent of our requirement to show *hakaras hatov* by informing us that one should not throw a rock into a pit from which he draws water. At first glance, the duty to thank the water appears odd. Water is an inanimate object, it has no feelings, nor did it intend to help us.

Rav Dessler explains *Chazal's* profound lesson, that our need to show thanks is not because the giver bothered or was inconvenienced on our behalf, or that he intended to perform a service for us. Our requirement to express thanks is solely because we were the recipient of good that should cause our hearts to swell with positive feelings toward the giver. This should compel us to reciprocate and give back even more than what we received, the least of which is to first express our sincere heartfelt thanks.

Many heartfelt thanks are in order to those whom I needed and who were instrumental in the writing and completion of **Yearning With Fire**.

I thank **HaRav Mattisyahu Salomon,** *shlit"a, Mashgiach* of the Lakewood Yeshivah, Beis Medrash Govoha, and **Rabbi Yisroel Reisman,** *shlit"a*, Rav of Agudath Israel of Madison, for graciously taking the time to prepare a foreword and a preface, respectively, for this book.

Much thanks to **Rabbi Meir Zlotowitz** and **Rabbi Nosson Scherman** of Artscroll, who graciously gave me the opportunity to write **Yearning With Fire**. We are all indebted to them for having provided us with the opportunity to learn about so many vital topics affecting our spirituality.

Thanks to **Avrohom Biderman** and **Mendy Herzberg** for coordinating all the aspects of the project at ArtScroll until its completion. Thanks to **Gedaliah Zlotowitz** for his sage advice. Many thanks to **Eli Kroen** for producing the all important book cover, and to **Chanah Finkelstein** of Masterpiece Design for the concept

Thanks to **Rabbi Sheah Brander,** ArtScroll's master craftsman, whose indelible fingerprint is on every page. Thanks to **Mrs. Reizy Ganz** for skillfully paginating each page and for its aesthetics. Thanks to **Mrs. Esther Feierstein** and **Mrs. Toby Goldzweig** for their typesetting expertise.

Mrs. Mindy Stern's devoted attention to every word and nuance in this book has added immeasurably to its quality. A master of her craft, her contributions are highly valued and deeply appreciated.

Great thanks to **Mrs. Judi Dick** of ArtScroll who selflessly gave of her editing talents, experience, and dedication in bringing this work to its completion. The largesse of her dedication, selflessness, and expertise is surpassed only by her heart.

Once again, I offer a special note of thanks to the principal editor of the book, **Mrs. Chana Nestlebaum** — not just from myself, but on behalf of the readers of this book who will benefit most from her words of passion, expertise in editing, and ability to "keep it flowing." May Hashem shower her with great merit for all she has done.

I would also like to thank **Rabbi Ezra Bloch** of Lakewood, New Jersey, for reviewing the manuscript and the many footnotes. I pray that the footnotes will enable the scholar to take a more enlightening approach in understanding this book. Thanks to **Dov Finkelstein,** LCSW for writing the "You Can Do It" section in the chapters on *Achdus* and *V'ahavta l'rei'acha kamocha*.

With all the issues facing individuals, communities, and Eretz Yisrael, over the past several years, ***Yearning With Fire*** was a project whose time had come. After Pesach 5769 a group of Toronto *askanim* (Eli Bienenstock, Menachem Brown, Ittamar Janowski, Michael Kuhl, Ronen Lazar, Michael Mills, and Moshe Sigler) asked me to come to Toronto to speak and give *chizuk* to the Toronto community on the topic of *achdus* and *tefillah*. It was there that Ittamar Janowski urged me to do something to help galvanize Klal Yisrael for *achdus*. Be"H, may this *sefer*, along with many other remarkable efforts launched in Klal Yisrael, help bring the *Geulah Sheleimah*. I thank Ittamar for giving me the *chizuk*.

I am deeply grateful to **Mrs. Sharon First** who has served the V'Ani Tefillah Foundation with true dedication and zeal for the last few years. Under pressure and on short notice, she has been able to accomplish the task of a team of others. She has played a key role in spreading the Foundation's message to shuls, schools, and communities not only nationwide, but across the globe. May Hashem give her the abilities to continue to help Klal Yisrael grow in spirituality and to hasten the *Geulah*.

The Gemara advises: "Go up a step to choose a confidant." Rashi explains that it is advisable to attach oneself to people who are of greater distinction than himself so that he will come to emulate them.

I am truly blessed to have "attached myself" to **Rabbi Mordechai Gelber**. His *tzidkus* and compassion for the individual as well as for the *tzibur* is well known by all in Flatbush, Brooklyn, New York. **Rabbi Gelber** is co-founder of Hakhel, a not-for-profit volunteer organization formed in Flatbush in 5755 for the purpose of uniting our communities through the study of Torah, acts of *chesed*, and the proper performance of mitzvos. He is author of the daily "Hakhel E-Mail Community Awareness Bulletin" that reaches thousands each day. He also publishes the annual "Hakhel Master Gemach List." In the course of these and the many other community projects with which he is involved, he has enlightened many and enabled countless people to grow spiritually. All that he does is without fanfare and the recognition that he so justly deserves.

Chazal teach that one's wife is called the "home." Special thanks to my wife **Bruria**, a true *eishes chayil,* for creating a home in which the learning and teaching of Torah and the doing of *chesed* is paramount. Because of her selfless support, I was able to disappear for hours on end in order to undertake the writing of this book. May Hashem bless her with great merit for all she does.

I apologize to anyone who assisted in this book in any way, whose name I have inadvertently omitted. To **all** who have assisted with **Yearning With Fire,** may Hashem shower you with the great merit that accrues to those who enlighten and uplift the public.

Finally, I thank you, the reader, for your desire to help Klal Yisrael to hasten the redemption by improving our *avodas Hashem.* I pray that each day of learning brings each of us a step closer to the day when the prayers, tears, and longings for the redemption uttered by Jews throughout the centuries will be answered by our loving Father in Heaven.

CHAPTER 1:
THE ULTIMATE VISION

ACHIEVING THE ULTIMATE

DAY 1

1
Tishrei

1
Teves

1
Nissan

1
Tammuz

*T*hroughout the world, thousands of men spend hours each day and night, poring over the sacred words of the Talmud. Every Shabbos, Yom Tov, and even during the week, thousands of individuals have opened their hearts and homes to anyone in need: in need of a warm nutritious meal; a warm, caring word; and a warm, welcoming heart. During the week, from the wee hours of the morning till long after midnight, thousands of Jews learn the daily daf (folio of Talmud) in the many shuls that dot the landscape. Tehillim groups are proliferating in every neighborhood.

In the morning and the afternoon, streets are clogged with traffic as an army of buses transport thousands of Jewish children to and from Jewish schools. The broad spectrum of religious Jews strives to enhance their day-to-day existence with a myriad of good deeds and stellar behavior. Jews of all ages are engaged in bikur cholim, seeking shidduchim for others, kiruv, harbatzas Torah, tzedakah, and in sharing their God-given bounty with others in all areas. There is more Torah learned, more chesed performed, more charity dispensed, and more emphasis on growth in Yiddishkeit than at any other time in our long and difficult exile.

If there were a "Torah-meter" that could measure all the learning, *shiurim*, yeshivos, shuls, and mitzvah observance occurring around the globe during the past seventy years, it would surely soar right over the top. The rebirth of Torah Judaism that began after World War II has been nurtured by the explosion of new technology and media, enabling Torah learning and inspiration to reach every corner of the globe.

Several hundred new *sefarim* each year add to this vigorous flow of Torah learning. Organizations seeking elevated levels of mitzvah performance abound. Shabbos, *tzenius, tefillah, shemiras halashon, shaatnez, shemittah,* and more have taken root and blossomed. Talented, charismatic speakers carry the Torah's message to the masses of Jews in communities around the world.

Yet, we still find ourselves in exile, longing for the Ultimate Redemption. With each passing day we perceive that we still have a way to go. It's time to examine why; what stands between our hearts and the purifying power of the Torah we embrace?

As we prepare to examine this question and strive to remedy the situation by removing the final roadblocks to the *Geulah,* let us revitalize ourselves to the task by attempting to comprehend the world of *Geulah* in all its material and spiritual splendor.

Take It With You

▸ *Torah learning and inspiration have proliferated in the past seventy years as never before.*

▸ *We must strive to remove the final roadblocks to the Geulah.*

1 Tishrei — For continued strength and good health for

חיה מרים בת רחל

our dear mother-in-law and grandmother
Pam Leitman and Melanie Leitman

1 Teves — לע"נ הרב בצלאל מרדכי ב"ר אהרן זצ"ל

1 Nissan — לזכות הגאולה השלמה ובנין בית המקדש במהרה בימנו

1 Tammuz — In memory of our friend, teacher and inspiration Reb. Zlata Geisinsky
Dedicated by Bob & Nancy Weissman

UTOPIA

DAY 2

*L*et's look for the good in what happened," Zev's wife encouraged him when he lost his job. "You'll have a little time for yourself and the grandkids, now. You can spend more time learning Torah while you look for another job. Think of it as an opportunity!"

"If I knew I'd have another job a month from now, I'd see it that way. But right now, I'm just scared. How will I support our family if nothing comes through soon? I'll be sunk!"

In the world we inhabit now, where God's presence is hidden, Zev faces a tremendous challenge. The mitzvah of *emunah*, belief in God, requires that Zev instill in himself a conviction that even if the situation looks bad, it has been planned by God for his ultimate good.

The world redeemed, however, operates in perfect harmony. Pain and suffering no longer play a role, for the inherent good in all God does is no longer hidden. Yeshayah paints the Messianic era as a time of ultimate bliss:[1] "The eyes of the blind shall be clear-sighted, and the ears of the deaf shall be opened…the lame shall leap as a hart and the tongue of the mute shall sing…"[2]

The Gemara[3] describes the Messianic era as a time of extraordinary fertility. Trees will grow ripe fruits every day, and Eretz Yisrael's wilderness will be "like Eden, and her desert like the garden of God."[4] Even the burdens of earn-

---

2
Tishrei

2
Teves

2
Nissan

2
Tammuz

---

1. 35:5-6.
2. See *Bereishis Rabbah* 95:1; *Tanchuma, Vayigash* 8 and *Metzora* 2.
3. *Shabbos* 30b; *Kesubos* 111b.
4. *Yeshayah* 51:3. See *Yechezkel* 36:29-30, also *Rambam, Hilchos Melachim* 12:5: "At that time there will be neither famine nor war, neither envy nor strife. All good things will be bestowed in abundance, and all delicacies will be accessible like dust." *See,* however, *Midrash Tehillim* 87:3.

ing a livelihood will be relieved, as "Strangers shall stand and feed your flocks and aliens shall be your plowmen and your vinedressers." [5] As the Rambam states:[6] "In those [Messianic] days it will be so much easier for people to earn a livelihood up to the point that one will work very little in a business and will achieve great profit."[7]

In the Messianic era, anti-Semitic incidents, including attacks on individual Jews and on Jewish properties, will cease. The Jewish people will have the opportunity to rise to the status of sages,[8] for they will come to know their Creator to the utmost capacity of human beings. As Yeshayah describes: "The earth shall be full of the knowledge of God as the waters cover the sea."[9]

This is not a fantasy world; it is *our* world — redeemed. Throughout that world, the overwhelming preoccupations with politics, wars, scandals, and headlines will simply vanish, to be replaced by one intense passion — to know God.[10]

At that time, our spiritual sensitivity will be so exquisitely refined that we will perform the Torah's commandments motivated solely by the deep spiritual euphoria they engender. No one will have to compel us, nor will we have to compel ourselves to fend off laziness or distraction, for there will be no greater source of satisfaction than to do God's will.[11]

---

5. *Yeshayah* 61:5; see also ibid. 49:23 and 60:10-12.
6. *Peirush HaMishnah, Sanhedrin* 10:1.
7. However, see *Shabbos* 63a, where it states that there will be poor people, "For the poor shall not cease from the land" (*Devarim* 15:11). See *Ritva* on *Shabbos* 63a, s.v. *Ein bein,* which states that although there will be poor people they will not have a longing for material things. See *Meshech Chochmah, Devarim* 19:8; *Michtav MeEliyahu,* Vol. 3, pp. 353-354; *Sifra D'Tzniusa (Gra),* Ch. 1, p. 10; *Gra* on *Berachos* 34b, for additional explanations. Also see *Kesef Mishneh* on *Rambam, Hilchos Teshuvah* 8:7.
8. See *Michtav MeEliyahu,* Vol. 5, p. 163, s.v. *V'yoseir mizeh,* which states that they will have *ruach hakodesh.*
9. 11:9. See *Rambam, Hilchos Melachim* 12:5. *See also Netzach Yisrael,* Ch. 42.
10. *Rambam,* ibid.
11. See *Rambam, Peirush HaMishnah,* Introduction to *Sanhedrin* Ch. 10, which states that the Divine blessings that will come with Mashiach's arrival are not an end in themselves. Our longing for the

▸ *Several sources describe the Messianic era as a time free of illness, strife, and sorrow, filled with spiritual clarity and material abundance.*

▸ *The Rambam states that the main feature of Messianic times will be the Jewish people's freedom from foreign powers, which will enable us to devote ourselves totally to serving God.*

▸ *In either scenario, the primary trait of the Time to Come is the Jewish people's total attachment to God, and the vast euphoria that state will engender.*

In the Rambam's view,[12] the main difference between the present world and the Messianic days is "delivery from servitude to foreign powers."[13] Yet, that one transformation will be enough to free us to become completely absorbed in Torah and mitzvos,[14] opening an era ruled by goodness, kindness, wisdom, knowledge, and truth. Therefore, even though the world will continue to function in its normal manner, human society will be so exalted that "there will be neither war nor hunger, nor jealousy nor competition."[15] The natural outcome of that state will be a perfect world, where one will bask in the glow of the *Shechinah*'s presence, his every need fulfilled. Even the common man will have perfect faith that God provides for him, freeing him from his struggle for sustenance and his inner struggles with jealousy and hate.

Thus, the magnificent vision of the era of Mashiach's time is the ultimate prospering of a partnership between God and the Jewish people. Just as God "suffered" together with us as we were persecuted through the centuries, when the time comes for rejoicing, God will revel with us when we experience the glory of the *Geulah*.

Messianic era is *not* for the sake of dominating the world. Nor is it so that we "have much produce and wealth, ride horses, and indulge in wine and song, as is thought by some confused people."
12. *Hilchos Melachim* 12:1-2; see *Hilchos Teshuvah* 9:2.
13. See *Berachos* 34b. See also *Ohr HaChaim* on *Shemos* 21:11.
14. *Hilchos Teshuvah* 9:2.
15. *Rambam, Hilchos Melachim* 12:5. See *Lechem Mishneh* on *Hilchos Teshuvah* 9:2, which states that when the Rambam writes, "There will be no difference between the current age and the Messianic era except [the emancipation] from our subjugation to the [gentile] kingdoms," he did so only to support his point that the laws of nature will remain in effect.

2 Tishrei — By Cory and Jonathan Glaubach in honor of their children, בתיה פסיה, אברהם לייב, רחל דבורה

2 Teves — Dedicated to the Woolf And Fortinsky Families by Dr. David and Tovit Fortinsky and family

2 Nissan —

2 Tammuz — לע"נ הרה"ג ר' פלטיא-ל בן ר' דוד ישעי-הו ז"ל Dedicated by his family

EARNING REWARD

DAY 3

I n our world today, good and evil, with the consequences of reward and punishment, are the opera-
tive systems of the world in which man finds himself.
Throughout the Torah, reward and punishment encourage the Jewish people's adherence to the mitzvos.[1] God
promises abundant sustenance, political sovereignty,
honor and security among the nations of the world, clarity
and purpose to those who adhere, and the opposite —
war, famine, humiliation at the hands of enemies, confusion and despair — to those who do not.[2] From the time of
Adam, man has been engaged in a struggle with his own
evil inclination[3] in order to earn reward for the right choice
and to avoid punishment for the wrong one.[4]

Nevertheless, the rewards and punishments that play out
in the physical world are not the ultimate consequences of
our actions. The definitive reward is reserved for the spiritual realm, for our lives in the World to Come. Service to
God in this world is the means to earn merit for that eternal
reward; the material rewards and challenges of the physical
world are given only as tools with which to earn that merit.[5]

The Messianic era, besides bringing us great blessings in
this world, will provide us with a vastly heightened ability
to earn eternal merit, since all the obstructions that stand
between us and God will have vanished. It is for that rea-

3
Tishrei

3
Teves

3
Nissan

3
Tammuz

---

1. *Hilchos Teshuvah* 9:1.
2. *Vayikra*, Ch. 26.
3. As the Torah (*Devarim* 30:6) states: "Hashem, your God, will circumcise your heart and the heart of your offspring, to love Hashem, your
God, with all your heart and with all your soul, that you may live."
The word "circumcise," usually referring to *bris milah*, here refers to
the heart, for just as the foreskin is a barrier to holiness, so is the evil
inclination a barrier between a Jew's heart and his pure soul.
4. *Ramban* on *Devarim* 30:6.
5. See *Rambam, Hilchos Teshuvah* 9:1; *Michtav MeEliyahu*, Vol. 1, p. 5.

▸ *The Torah
promises
reward for
performing
mitzvos and
punishment
for trans-
gressing.*

▸ *The ultimate
rewards are
not in this
world, but
rather, in
the World to
Come.*

▸ *A person's
struggle
against the
yetzer hara
is a factor
in earning
his eternal
reward.*

▸ *In Messi-
anic times,
there will no
longer be
a struggle
to perform
God's will.
There will,
however,
be another
means to
merit one's
eternal
reward.*

son, says the Rambam,[6] that "the Sages did not yearn for the Messianic age so [the Jews] can have dominion over the gentile kingdoms … rather [they desired] to be free [to involve themselves] in Torah and its wisdom without any disturbances in order to merit the World to Come."

In view of the above, the Rambam's assertion leaves a question. If the basis of one's reward is choosing good over evil, and "according to the struggle is the reward,"[7] what reward can one earn when there is no longer a struggle? What choice can one make other than the joyous performance of the mitzvos when God's presence is manifest to all? Rav Chaim Friedlander[8] asks this question, pointing out that the Talmud advises us to pursue merit while it is still available:[9]

Shlomo HaMelech advises:[10] "So remember your Creator in the days of your youth, before the evil days come, and those years arrive of which you will say, 'I have no pleasure in them'"; these are the days of Mashiach, when there will be no opportunity to acquire merit or liability.[11]

Does the perfection of the redeemed world, then, impinge upon that which we will experience of the eternal world? This obviously cannot be the case, for if it were, no one would wish to forfeit a glorious eternity for 70, 80, or 120 sublime years on earth. The answer to this conundrum is rooted in a better understanding of the purpose the Messianic era serves for the Jewish people and for mankind, for as we will see, there can be no "down side" to the revelation of God's glory in our world.

---

6. *Hilchos Melachim* 12:4.
7. See *Avos* 5:23: "Ben Hai Hai said: According to the struggle is the reward." See also *Tzlach* on *Berachos* 5a, s.v. *Rashi*, s.v. *Yissurin shel ahavah*.
8. *Sifsei Chaim, Pirkei Emunah U'Bechirah*, Vol. 2, p. 137, s.v. *Amnam*.
9. *Shabbos* 151b.
10. *Koheles* 12:1.
11. However, see *Rashi, Shabbos* 151b, s.v. *Lo zechus*.

3 Tishrei —
3 Teves —
3 Nissan —
3 Tammuz — In memory of Trudi and Irwin Kabak
Dedicated by their loving children and grandchildren

ANOTHER ROAD
TO REWARD

DAY 4

Every Torah Jew is familiar with the concept of struggle — struggling to learn Torah, working hard every day to raise a family, dealing with setbacks and obstacles in performing mitzvos. As we gather our strength to meet each challenge, we are reassured by Chazal's words: "According to the struggle is the reward."[1] What, then, will pave our path to our great reward when Mashiach arrives and struggle ceases to exist?[2]

Rav Friedlander[3] asserts that even when Mashiach arrives, challenges to our spirituality will not disappear, but rather, the *yetzer hara* will gradually release its hold on man's heart. Eventually, the *yetzer hara* will exist outside of man's nature,[4] and "Man will return to the state that

4
Tishrei

4
Teves

4
Nissan

4
Tammuz

---

1. See *Avos* 5:23.
2. See ibid. 2:1: "Be careful to perform a minor mitzvah in the same manner as a major one, for you do not know the reward for each mitzvah." It seems, therefore, that a mitzvah's reward might be measured with two separate yardsticks — one that measures the effort expended and the other the value of the mitzvah itself. Which is the true measure? According to *Derech Hashem* (*Cheilek* 1, 4:7), each mitzvah has a twofold purpose: first, to fulfill Hashem's desire that man perform His will, and second, to achieve the degree of perfection in the individual and in the world inherent in the performance of the mitzvah itself. This is the effect known only to Hashem.

When one considers the first purpose of a mitzvah — fulfilling Hashem's will — it is clear that if one has difficulty he is richly rewarded for his great effort in overcoming obstacles to fulfill Hashem's desire. The reward for the mitzvah itself, which is the effect of the actual mitzvah on the person and on the world, may be large or small, and it is regarding that aspect that the Mishnah states, "We do not know the reward for each mitzvah." Thus, his reward will be great because of the great effect of the mitzvah on himself and on the world.

3. *Sifsei Chaim, Pirkei Emunah U'Bechirah*, Vol. 2, p. 137, s.v. *Amnam*.
4. See *Tzipisa L'Yeshuah*, end of Ch. 1, where the Chofetz Chaim exhorts the Jewish people to strengthen themselves in their perfor-

existed during the time of Adam before he sinned."[5]

In the Garden of Eden, God's presence was apparent. Man had no inclination to defy His will. Adam ate from the Tree of Knowledge, not out of defiance, but in an erroneous attempt to serve God better. However, by doing so he brought the evil inclination into man's being, where it could influence him internally.[6] Man was banished from the Garden into the natural world, where Hashem's presence was no longer obvious to perceive.[7] The spiritual struggle that ensued will end with Mashiach's arrival, because God's presence will then be apparent to all.

The Chofetz Chaim concedes that the familiar form of spiritual currency — perseverance in the face of difficulty — will become vastly devalued in the era of Mashiach, since obstacles will no longer exist. Nevertheless, he explains[8] that the Jewish people will not lose anything, for the great *kiddush Hashem* permeating the world will infintely increase the purity of our mitzvos.

Once Mashiach arrives, mitzvah observance will soar high above anything a person can attain now. Rav Dessler[9] elucidates how this will not only preserve, but decidedly enhance the eternal reward earned by performing a mitzvah, even without the element of self-sacrifice.

First, he explains that all motivations for fulfilling a mitzvah fall under one of two categories:

---

mance of mitzvos and study of Torah since when Mashiach arrives the *yetzer hara* will eventually leave us.

5. *Devarim* 30:6. See *Michtav MeEliyahu*, Vol. 3, p. 210, s.v. *terem*, which states that from the beginning of time until the end of days man is intended to rectify the sin of Adam. This rectification fell on the Jewish nation. When the Jewish people return [in the Messianic age] to the state that existed during the time of Adam before he sinned, then the whole world will have achieved its completed mission.

6. *Nefesh HaChaim, Shaar* 1, Ch. 6, *hagah*, s.v. *V'ha'inyan*, cited in *Michtav MeEliyahu*, Vol. 2, p. 138.

7. See *Sifsei Chaim, Pirkei Emunah U'Bechirah*, Vol. 2, p. 35, s.v. *HaRamchal*, citing the Ramchal in *Derech Hashem, Shaar* 1, Ch. 3, Column 6, which states that whereas before Adam sinned the *yetzer hara* existed external to man, after Adam sinned the deficiencies (potential for evil) existed within mankind. See also *Ohr Gedalyahu, Bereishis*, p. 21, s.v. *V'ha'beur*, citing the *Nefesh HaChaim*.

8. Cited in *Ohr Yechezkel, Elul*, p. 47.

9. *Michtav MeEliyahu*, Vol. 1, p. 16; *Strive for Truth*, Vol. 1, Part 1, p. 70.

(a) *Lishmah*, "for the sake of heaven," in which one's only intention is to serve Hashem and follow in His ways;

(b) *She'lo lishmah*, "not for the sake of heaven," in which one performs a mitzvah for his own reasons, even if the reasons are altruistic.[10]

Rav Dessler continues:[11]

> Only lishmah can fully prepare one's soul to enjoy the rarified delight of the World to Come. As the Gemara describes:[12] "The righteous sit...and enjoy the splendor of the Shechinah." This is a picture of righteous souls reveling in a sublime attachment to God, experiencing a great in-pouring of His glory. One who serves God lishmah will find that very holiness infusing his soul with redoubled vigor... His awareness will be heightened...a million-fold, until his consciousness expands to the uttermost limits possible... In short, the reward must be precisely equivalent to the quality of the deed.

Because every Jew will serve God *lishmah* in the times of Mashiach, every Jew's soul will be primed for this sublime reward in the World to Come. By performing the mitzvos to the utmost during the Messianic age, man will become elevated to a level at which his soul is capable of receiving the ultimate pleasure of the World to Come — not at the price of struggle and suffering, but rather, as the inevitable outgrowth of his pure, unobstructed attachment to God, through which he becomes a partner with Him in fulfilling the mandate of Creation.[13]

---

10. See *Rosh Hashanah* 28a, s.v *Lo lei'hanos nitnu*; *Beis Yosef, Orach Chaim, Siman* 586, *Os* 3. See also *Eglei Tal*, Introduction.
11. *Michtav MeEliyahu* loc. cit.; *Strive For Truth* loc. cit.
12. *Berachos* 17a.
13. See *Ahavas Chesed* II, Ch. 2, s.v. *Gam nuchal lomar*.

Take It With You

▸ *In the time of Mashiach, the battle with the yetzer hara will not require great effort, since God's presence will be apparent and the yetzer hara will exist outside of man.*

▸ *Holiness will be so pervasive in the world that our mitzvah observance will take on a vastly greater degree of purity and power.*

▸ *This will prime our souls to fully partake of the sublime spiritual pleasure the Talmud describes as the World to Come.*

ALONG THE ROAD

5 Tishrei

5 Teves

5 Nissan

5 Tammuz

*L*ouis and his wife Linda discovered the beauty of Orthodox Judaism late in life. They were already well-established in their "dream house," but as their dream changed, the house, located four miles from shul, became a test of their commitment. Undaunted, the couple passed the test week after week, walking the distance fueled by their desire for an authentic Shabbos atmosphere.

As their commitment grew, they decided to sell their home and move to a religious neighborhood. In their new home, the shul was across the street, visible from their living room window. They gained convenience, but did they lose the tremendous merit of their arduous weekly treks?

This question is at the essence of understanding how our spiritual achievements in the current world will influence the level of our spiritual standing in Messianic times. Right now, our merit comes from our struggles. After Mashiach, when there is no internal struggles, our merit will come from our exalted, all-pervasive relationship with God. However, as we will see, it is our struggles and exertions under the current circumstances that render us able to fully partake of the spiritual "feast" to come.

Will it be possible to wait until we see the menu at the feast, and then decide to earn our place at the table? The Maharal[1] replies in the negative, stating that spiritual growth in Messianic times will be reserved for "those who are already righteous." This is because once Mashiach comes, sincere change will no longer be feasible; people will be swayed by their desire to partake of the indescrib-

---

1. *Netzach Yisrael*, Ch. 46.

able good that God will dispense to the world, rather than by a pure desire to come close to Him.

Once Mashiach arrives, Rav Mattisyahu Salomon explains,[2] there will indeed be a vastly heightened ability to earn merit in the World to Come.[3] However, it will apply only to those whose lofty pursuit of spiritual excellence existed *before* Mashiach, when it entailed a daily struggle in a spiritually dark world.[4] Their past struggles will stand as a "launch pad" for their merit under a new world redeemed.

Citing Rav Elyah Lopian, Rav Salomon explains[5] that God bestows His reward in accordance with a person's initial struggle. In *Parashas Lech Lecha* Avraham is told by God:[6] "Count the stars if you are able to; so shall your offspring be." The Torah then informs us[7] that Avraham trusted in God, and "He [God] reckoned it to him as righteousness." This prompts Ramban[8] to wonder what in Avraham's response warranted the label "righteousness." He had exhibited his faith throughout many tests already; it would seem that his trust in God, by then, should have been regarded as unremarkable.

Nevertheless, says Rav Lopian, Avraham was given credit for the initial tests he had withstood. The fact that subsequently, his faith came without struggle, was only as a result of his surmounting those difficult initial tests. This analysis further explains how the merit for the World to Come will accrue to us after Mashiach comes and puts an end to our struggles. The triumphs we achieve now will remain in our account, providing the "seed money" for boundless, eternal dividends.

Like the couple in the opening story, we are called upon in these times to make the arduous trek, to sacrifice and struggle against the odds, all for the purpose of serving God. However, when the distance between us and God

---

2. *Matnas Chaim, Maamarim* 1, p. 223.
3. *Hilchos Melachim* 12:4.
4. *Machaneh Yisrael*, end of Ch. 25.
5. *Matnas Chaim, Maamarim* 1, p. 224, s.v. *V'shamati*.
6. *Bereishis* 15:5.
7. Ibid. v. 6.
8. Ad loc.

Take It With You

▸ *In the times of Mashiach, those who have been striving spiritually beforehand will continue to accrue merit for the World to Come.*

▸ *Spiritual growth after the coming of Mashiach will be motivated by the desire to partake of the good God is dispensing to the world.*

▸ *Even when there is no more struggle against the yetzer hara, God will apportion one's reward according to his efforts in the days when there was a struggle.*

becomes dramatically shorter, our previous struggles will still serve us well. Through them, our souls will be primed to engage God in a far more lofty way — as a close and constant presence, never far from our hearts.

> **5 Tishrei —**
> **5 Teves —**
> **5 Nissan —**
> **5 Tammuz —** In memory of Serach bat Eliezer
> In memory of Shemtov ben Benyahu

ALL GOOD

*T*here is a wealthy father who can give his children everything they need and desire. He is also eminently wise, and can guide them with complete clarity through every decision in life; he can also protect them against every danger. He can, but he does not. He allows them to make their own way, learning through trial and error, showing his love by picking them up when they fall and helping them behind the scenes.

6
Tishrei

6
Teves

6
Nissan

6
Tammuz

We know that God is *Av HaRachamim*, a compassionate Father, with everything we need for a life of total fulfillment at His disposal, and yet, choosing not to fully bestow it. We wonder why He doesn't reveal Himself, rebuild His home (our Holy Temple), end our confusion, and free us to enjoy all the goodness and blessing that are the very purpose of His Creation. Why does He seem to "stand back" and watch us fall into error, allowing pain and evil into a world that could be radiant with pure goodness? To begin to understand this, we must delve into the purpose of creation.

Ramchal[1] explains that God created the universe as an act of His love, so immense that the human mind cannot begin to fathom it. The world is meant to serve as a receptacle into which He can eventually pour His good. But God's love is so great that any good He bestows must be the greatest good possible. Anything less would not be Godly.

The greatest gift that God can bestow upon man is the

_____

1. *Daas Tevunos, Os* 18, cited in *Sifsei Chaim, Pirkei Emunah U'Bechirah*, Vol. 2, p. 56, s.v. *HaRamchal*; ibid., p. 436, s.v. *Yeish l'hadgish*.

ability to enjoy the optimal reward in the World to Come — to bask in the radiance of the *Shechinah*.[2] To enable man to earn his reward, God has given him the ability to choose between good and evil. As the *Zohar* states:[3] If there were no darkness, then light would not be discernible, and would produce no benefit...."

Because free choice is a necessary component of God's design for benefiting man, the possibility of choosing wrongly always exists in our world. If some aspects of power and physical pleasure were not invested with an allure that draws people away from God's will, there would be no real choice. Thus, inflicting pain, insults, damage, and loss often occur, due to the invariable short-term gain from doing wrong; it could be financial gain, pleasure, or a sense of power. These create further challenges.

For example, a man might cheat his partner in business, shaving off a small percentage of extra profit each month. "I actually do most of the work," the man rationalizes. "So I really am earning this money."

The man has chosen wrongly. Then, when his cheating is discovered, his partner must choose. Will there be revenge? Will there by an angry feud? Will there be a calm, resolute reaction? Will the wrongdoer restore the stolen money? The power of free choice infuses all these options with spiritual impact; the choices that are made determine the measure of eternal reward each party will enjoy.

God, like the father in the opening story, allows His children to choose their path, but the tools they need to succeed in their life's mission are part and parcel of the circumstances in which they have been placed. How they use those tools is a result of their own choices. By discerning God's will in the haze of darkness that comprises the

---

2. *Mesillas Yesharim*, Ch. 1, s.v. *V'hinei*. See *Ohr Gedalyahu, Bereishis*, p. 66, s.v. *B'Rashi*, citing the Introduction to *Avnei Milluim*, which states that Hashem wants to bestow kindness to His creations by rewarding them greatly when they perform mitzvos. Therefore, mankind accomplishes two goals when performing mitzvos: (a) They do God's will, and (2) they fulfill God's desire to reward His creations.
3. *Vayikra* 47b.

world in which we live, we earn a glorious, eternal light for ourselves in the World to Come.

6 Tishrei —

6 Teves —

6 Nissan —

6 Tammuz — לע״נ בינה מחלה בת יהודה ברוך ע״ה
Dedicated by her grandchildren and great-grandchildren

WHY NOT NOW?

DAY 7

7 Tishrei

7 Teves

7 Nissan

7 Tammuz

A *person can earn $200 an hour mind-ing the entrance gate of a lush, fragrant garden. He can earn the same amount guarding the gates of the city dump. If all other factors were equal, why would anyone be com-pelled to take the undesirable job rather than the appealing one?*

There seems no logical reason, all things being equal, why one would have to derive benefits in a painful way when a pleasurable way is equally available. Why, then, does Hashem cause us to earn our merit for the World to Come through trials and suffering when we could earn a reward so much richer by serving Him wholeheartedly, with pleasure and joy, as will be the case in Messianic times? Why does He refrain from bringing the ultimate good now?

The answer to this question can be derived from the following allegory:

> *Moshe was the mail-room clerk at a large pharma-ceutical company that had developed many lifesav-ing medications. One day, he received an invitation to the company's annual dinner, but it was not the usual, mass-produced invitation sent to the lower-echelon employees. Rather, it was an engraved invitation informing him that he would be seated at the dais with the CEO and the members of the Board of Directors.*
>
> > *Stunned and confused by the honor, he fully expected to be told that it was a mistake. How-ever, upon arriving at the dinner dressed in his*

modest suit, he found himself seated with the tuxedo-clad dignitaries. The evening's program began, and soon, the CEO was introducing the Employee of the Year, who would be asked to rise and receive a special award.

"This man has done more for our company — more for mankind — than any other single individual here," the CEO pronounced. "His wisdom is admired by all. His devotion, his long hours and priceless contributions to the medical world are unparalleled. I am proud to confer this award upon Moshe the Mailroom Clerk."

One can imagine the squirming embarrassment of the mail-room clerk when he is singled out for accomplishments he has never achieved and attributes he has never possessed, and then lauded above other worthy employees with undeserved honor. That, says the Ramchal,[1] is how the Jewish people would feel if they were allowed to bask in God's presence without earning that privilege. Such a reward, which the Kabbalists call *nahama d'kisufa,* or "bread of shame," would not be the ultimate reward; rather it would be an embarrassment.[2]

Therefore, God placed us in this world and pitted us against a *yetzer hara* so that we could earn our eternal reward by prevailing over it. By performing God's mitzvos to the best of our abilities during this pre-Messianic era of Divine concealment and difficult tests, we earn the opportunity to perform the mitzvos to perfection during Messianic times. Then, with no internal *yetzer hara* to obstruct our service and confuse our hearts,[3] we will no longer need struggle or suffering to earn our reward. Rather, our pure mitzvos will earn us the right to enjoy the ultimate

---

1. *Daas Tevunos, Os* 18, cited in *Sifsei Chaim, Pirkei Emunah U'Bechirah,* Vol. 2, p. 56, s.v. *HaRamchal.*
2. See *Matnas Chaim, Maamarim* 2, p. 131, which discusses why Hashem did not create man without the character trait of "shame," which would enable him to receive reward without effort and without feeling shame.
3. See *Succah* 52a, which states that the *yetzer hara* will be slaughtered during the days of Mashiach. See also *Bava Basra* 16a.

Take It With You

▸ *A person feels deep humiliation when he is singled out for a reward he has not come close to earning. This is called "nahama d'kisufa," the bread of shame.*

▸ *God pitted us against the yetzer hara so that we can earn our ultimate eternal reward.*

bliss — without the slightest shame — of basking in God's Presence in the World to Come.

7 Tishrei —
7 Teves —
7 Nissan —
7 Tammuz —

CHAPTER 2:
IN OUR GENERATION

DO IT ANYWAY

**8
Tishrei**

**8
Teves**

**8
Nissan**

**8
Tammuz**

*M*r. Brenner was a CEO who would occasionally visit members of his staff at home. He felt that these visits kept him apprised of his employees' lifestyles and gave him a better understanding of how to keep them happy and motivated in their jobs.

One Tuesday morning, Avi Steinberg, a junior member of the accounting department, received a memo that Mr. Brenner would be visiting his home one week from that date. Experiencing anxiety, he called his wife. "What should we do? How can we entertain a man like Mr. Brenner in our apartment?" Indeed, the struggling young couple lived with their four children in a small apartment furnished with hand-me-downs. No matter how hard they tried, it never looked neat and clean.

"Let's at least slap on a coat of paint in the living room and get a cover for the couch, and buy a really nice cake from the bakery and some good coffee to serve him," Avi suggested.

"Are you kidding? That's not going to do the trick," his wife countered. "We just don't have what we need to do this right."

"I'm sure he knows our situation," the husband replied. "We just have to do as much as we can to show him that his visit is important to us. He'll see that we went out of our way to prepare."

Like this young couple, the Jewish people do not have enough to impress God and make His Divine Presence feel welcome among us. The question is, do we take the approach of the wife in the above scenario — that we are so lacking as to make our efforts futile — or do we take the husband's approach, that we must do everything in our limited power to show that we truly welcome God's closeness to us.

The Chofetz Chaim addresses this question regarding our quest to hasten the *Geulah:*[1]

> *If you will ask what is appropriate for us to do to hasten Mashiach, I will answer and say that Hakadosh Baruch Hu does not want from us big things and things that are impossible to achieve…Rather, each person, according to his strength and ability, is required to prepare for the coming of Mashiach.*

When Hashem deals with man, He deals on man's level. This is the concept relayed in the Midrash's account[2] of Hashem's commandment to Moshe Rabbeinu to construct the Sanctuary in the Wilderness as a dwelling place for the Divine Presence.[3] On receiving this commandment:

> *Moshe began to tremble and said, "How can one make a house dedicated to the Name of Hashem?" Hashem responded, "I do not desire it according to My abilities and strength, rather in accordance with their abilities. Donations given for the building of the Mishkan[4] are to be given according to what their hearts desire to give."*

From this explanation, one may conclude that if we are commanded to "long for the *yeshuah*," we must possess the capability to actively prepare for and hasten its coming. This leaves each person with the obligation to reinforce whatever strengths and abilities he may have, as a verse in *Koheles* states:[5] "Whatever you are able to do with your might, do it."

---

1. *Zachor L'Miriam*, Ch. 18, s.v. V'haya im.
2. *Bamidbar Rabbah* 12:3.
3. *Shemos* 25:8.
4. Ibid. v. 2.
5. 9:10.

Take It With You

▸ *Presently, what we have to offer by way of welcome to the Shechinah seems inadequate.*

▸ *Nevertheless, God expects only that which is in our ability to offer.*

▸ *In doing our best under our own circumstances to welcome the Shechinah, we show God that we desire His closeness.*

RIGHT ON CUE

DAY 9

9
Tishrei

9
Teves

9
Nissan

9
Tammuz

A man from England visited the Chazon Ish. As the man prepared to leave, he asked what message he could relay to his fellow Jews back home. "The Torah states:[1] 'Noach was a righteous man, perfect in his generation,'" said the Chazon Ish. "Chazal deduced that a person is judged based on the level of his generation."[2]

But this message sparks further questions. What *is* the level of one's generation? When we view the troubles and confusion all around us, it is tempting to say, "I'm only human. I can't solve the world's problems." However, from a vast array of Torah sources, we learn that "only human" is a lofty status. *Mishlei*[3] reminds us that, "All of creation glorifies Hashem," and, as part of creation, each one of us has his or her own role to play in glorifying God's Name.

This is the meaning of the well-known Mishnah[4] that states that each person should think, *"Bishvili nivrah ha'olam* — The world was created for me."[5] Each newborn is like the lead actor walking onto the stage precisely on cue to play his part. If he misses his cue or stands in the wings crippled by stage fright, the play will not unfold as it should.[6] But unlike a play, in life there is no one to step

---

1. *Bereishis* 6:9.
2. *See Six Constant Mitzvos* (ArtScroll/Mesorah Publ, p. 57.
3. 16:4.
4. *Sanhedrin* 37a.
5. See *Ohr Gedalyahu, Bereishis,* p. 15. Rav Bunim from P'shischa taught that man must at all times have two pockets. In one he should keep a paper with the words *"Bishvili nivrah ha'olam,* The world was created for me" (*Sanhedrin* 37a), to realize his worth; and in the other he should keep a paper with the words *"V'anochi afar v'eifer,* I am but dust and ash" (*Bereishis* 18:27), to maintain his humility.
6. See *Nesivos Shalom,* Vol. 1, p. 31, s.v. *V'nichlal;* ibid., *Parashas Re'eh,* p. 75. See also *Vilna Gaon* commentary on *Yonah* 4:3, which states that

in to fill the void. Each individual's role is essential in completing God's creation.

> *Clara Hammer, who passed away on Nissan 10, 5770 (March 25, 2010), 30 days before her 100th birthday, was known as the "Chicken Lady of Jerusalem." She merited this title by providing chicken for Shabbos to hundreds of poor families in Israel.*
>
> *She began her campaign at the age of 71, when, standing in line at the butcher shop, she saw the butcher give a young girl a bag filled with fat and skin. When Clara got to the front of the line, she asked the butcher about the girl's unusual order, and found out that these discards formed the basis for the "chicken stew" for her large family. Having experienced starvation as a child, Clara's heart broke for the family's plight. "From now on," she said, "give the family a whole chicken and I'll pay for it!"*
>
> *At the latest count, Clara was assisting over 250 families and paying the butcher a monthly bill of over $10,000. The butcher has a separate computer file to keep track of Clara's purchases.[7]*

Clara was not a noted entrepreneur, a powerhouse of energy, or a millionaire. She started her chicken campaign when she was already a senior citizen, relying on nothing more than the response of her heart to the plight of another Jew. She asked, "What does Hashem want of me in this situation in which I have found myself?" and she acted on the answer.

That same motivation can steer each person toward meeting the challenge of doing what is necessary to hasten the *Geulah*. Everything a Jew does is important in the Heavenly scheme.

As the *Nefesh HaChaim* explains:[8]

---

it is possible for one to discern his *tafkid*, mission, in life. Generally, those sins that a person is drawn to the most are the area that he must correct in this life in order to fulfill his *tafkid*.

7. Aish.com, June 13, 2010/ 1 Tammuz, 5770.
8. Section 1, Ch. 4.

Take It With You

▸ To be "righteous in his generation" means to serve God to the best of one's ability in the situation in which he finds himself.

▸ Every one of a person's words, thoughts, and actions makes an impact on the spiritual world.

A Jew should never think to himself, "What difference can my insignificant actions make?" Rather, he should be conscious that no detail of his actions, words, and thoughts is ever meaningless, God forbid. On the contrary, how exalted are his actions, each one reaching up...to have its impact in the highest heights, in the worlds and the splendorous lights above!

The Arizal makes a powerful statement that reiterates the message of this day "The greatness of one's soul does not depend [solely] on one's actions. rather [it depends] on the time and generation in which he lives. Because one very small action in this generation is comparable to many great mitzvos in another generation.[9]"

---

9. *Shaar HaGilgulim* 62b.

---

9 Tishrei —
9 Teves — In Loving Memory of Rivkah bat Devorah a"h
By the Gotel Family
9 Nissan —
9 Tammuz —

ESPECIALLY NOW

DAY 10

*T*he elderly Mrs. Newmark sat in her wheel-chair, looking at familiar surroundings as if they were strange. "Where are we?" she asked for the hundredth time. "We're here, home, in New York," her daughter told her reassuringly.

"They'll be sending us away soon," her mother responded darkly.

This was the world she had known as a young woman during the Holocaust, and now, as her faculties diminished, it was the world that rose up to haunt her.

"No, Ma, don't worry. We're not going anywhere. This is America, the last stop until Mashiach comes."[1]

"Mashiach?" her mother laughed. "He hasn't come yet. Why should he come now?"

10 Tishrei

10 Teves

10 Nissan

1 Tammuz

On the surface, from those who have lived through the Jewish people's most traumatic upheavals, to those who have lived in times imbued with piety and unimaginable sacrifice for Torah, this elderly woman's assessment seems to make sense. If previous generations haven't brought Mashiach, how likely is it that the present generation will earn the merit to witness the Final Redemption?

Nevertheless, the Chofetz Chaim implores the Jewish people:[2]

---

1. Approximately 200 years ago, when the cornerstone for Rabbi Chaim Volozhin's illustrious yeshivah in Volozhin was laid, he called attention to the potential sanctuary for Torah across the ocean. "This haven for Jewry would be the last stop in their exile…The Torah is destined to wander further, to the wilds of America, before Mashiach Tzidkeinu arrives," he said… (*The World That Was: America*, by Rabbi A. Leib Scheinbaum [Shaar Press], Preface, p. vx).
2. *Tzipisa L'Yeshuah*, end of Ch. 2.

> *Heaven forbid, do not lose hope and faith due to the length of the exile, especially in our time... Praised is the one who does not lose hope in waiting for the Final Redemption and who gives heart to himself and his children to increase their study of Torah and performance of mitzvos...*

Nevertheless, it can be difficult to understand how the merit will exist to hasten the coming of Mashiach as each generation grows more superficial and less spiritually sensitive. *Chazal*[3] teach that, "If the earlier generations were like angels, we are but like mere humans; if they were like humans, we are like donkeys!" In that case, upon what foundation does continued hope for hastening the Redemption rest?

God has promised that the Jewish people will eventually be redeemed in the preordained time.[4] Thus, the progression of time itself brings us closer to Mashiach and continuously increases the inherent potential for redemption.[5]

Furthermore, we need not despair over the impact of the declining generations. The virtues of generations past[6] remain in our account like an inheritance from our forefathers. God has held onto each prayer for redemption that has issued from our ancestors' lips.[7] All the prayers, mitzvos, and good deeds of the past, added to our own, form an ever-expanding pool of merit for the Jewish people.[8]

In the words of the Chofetz Chaim,[9] we are "like a midget standing on the shoulders of a giant." The midget's position on the giant's shoulders gives him greater height than that of the giant himself. Likewise, the Chofetz

---

3. *Yerushalmi Shekalim* 5:1; *Shabbos* 112b; see also *Eruvin* 53a; *Yoma* 9b.
4. *Sanhedrin* 98a.
5. *Shem Olam, Shaar Hizchazkus,* Ch. 13.
6. *Sfas Emes* to *Devarim (year 5634)* cited in *Ohr Gedalyahu, Bein HaMetzarim,* p. 165, fn. 5.
7. See *Netzach Yisrael,* Ch. 31; *Moreh Nevuchim* III:10-12; *Tzavaas HaRivash,* Ch. 130.
8. *Chofetz Chaim al HaTorah, Devarim* 29:28; *Maasai L'Melech, Os* 2, p. 278.
9. *Machaneh Yisrael,* Ch. 25.

Chaim asserts, the merit of all the generations accumulates until it suffices to warrant the redemption. When that moment arrives, Mashiach will come immediately, even if the generation at that time is spiritually inferior.[10]

This answers Mrs. Newmark's question in the opening scenario. "Why would he come now?" *Especially* now, as the merits of the generations mount upon each other, we can be confident that this accumulation of merits serves to hasten the redemption.

Take It With You

▸ *As time progresses, we draw nearer to the designated end of days, thus increasing the potential for redemption.*

▸ *The merit and prayers of our ancestors still stand by us and our own merits and prayers are added to theirs.*

▸ *This proliferation of merits can hasten the arrival of Mashiach.*

---

10. *Chofetz Chaim al HaTorah, Devarim* 30:3.

10 Tishrei — In memory of Jan Eisenstein
לע״נ יוחנן זאב משה ז״ל
And as a z'chus for all those inspired
and for all of כלל ישראל
Norman & Linda Mintz
לע״נ מטל סאבל בת ר׳ פינחס ע״ה — **10 Teves**
10 Nissan —
10 Tammuz — לע״נ ר׳ אליהו שמשון ב״ר חיים צבי ז״ל

WE CAN DO IT

DAY 11

11 Tishrei

11 Teves

11 Nissan

11 Tammuz

Abarbanel[1] provides a description, easily recognized as today's world:[2]

The [Jewish] nation in exile is divided into two parts. The smaller remnant of Jews strengthen their observance of Judaism and follow God's Torah. The other part consists of the majority which, because of the hardships of the exile, has not followed the Jewish laws...[3]

Unfortunately, most of the Jews nowadays are very absorbed in the ways and lifestyles of the secular world. Regarding both parts, the verses state:[4] "...then you will take it to your heart among all the nations where Hashem, your God, has dispersed you. And you will return unto Hashem, your God..."

In such a society, from where will the redemption spring forth? Chofetz Chaim explains that both parts will play a role in hastening the Final Redemption.[5]

At the end of days...there will be a portion of Jews who fortify their spiritual strength with the performance of mitzvos and the study of Torah. They will not deviate from the letter of the law. They will hasten the Final Redemption.

---

1. Late 15th century Jewish statesman, philosopher, and Bible commentator.
2. *Abarbanel* on *Nitzavim*, p. 32, s.v. *Kasav haRam*.
3. Thirty-three percent of Jews don't believe in God, there is a 50 percent increase in Jews practicing another religion, 75 percent of adult Jews date non-Jews (from Aish.com, August 18, 2009).
4. *Devarim* 30:1-2.
5. *Tzipisa L'Yeshuah*, p. 5.

The nature of redemption itself, as expressed in the words of *Shir HaShirim*, offers more hope. A verse states:[6] "The voice of My beloved! Behold, it came suddenly to redeem me, as if leaping over mountains, skipping over hills." When the time comes for redemption, there are no obstacles.

The Midrash[7] explains that when Moshe told the Jewish people that they would be redeemed, they replied, "How can we be redeemed? We do not have good deeds... Egypt is full of our idols." Moshe responded, "Because Hashem desires to redeem you, He does not look as much at your bad deeds. To whom does Hashem look? To the righteous ones among you."

The redeeming power of a righteous minority comes through as well when Avraham interceded on Sodom's behalf:[8] "And Hashem said, 'If I find in Sodom fifty righteous people in the midst of the city, then I would spare the entire place on their account.'"

It is in this regard that the deterioration of society proves beneficial, by making our feeble efforts more valuable.[9] The fact that it is so much more difficult to achieve spiritual perfection lends that much more merit to our slightest virtues,[10] as "One thing in distress is better than a hundred in ease."[11]

Michtav MeEliyahu explains:[12]

> And that which it took the righteous ones of the prior generations many days and months to reach, it is possible for us to repair in one moment because our world is much lower[13]... Therefore, only a thin

---

6. *Shir HaShirim* 2:8.
7. *Yalkut Shimoni, Shir HaShirim,* Remez 986, s.v. *Kol dodi.*
8. *Bereishis* 18:26.
9. See R' Chaim Vital, *Shaar HaGilgulim*, Ch. 38: "A very small act in this generation is equal to many great mitzvos in others"; *Rambam, Hilchos Teshuvah* 3:2.
10. *Rambam* ibid.
11. *Avos D'Rabbi Nosson* 3:6; see *Shir HaShirim Rabbah* 8:10.
12. Vol. 4, p. 108.
13. See *Shevivei Lev* (back of *Lev Eliyahu*, Vol. 1), p. 326, s.v. *Shamati*, which states that one of Rav Yisrael Salanter's students heard from his rebbi, who said: "In these generations each person has greater Heavenly help than existed in the generation of the Tannaim, because

▸ *God will look toward the good deeds of those who remain righteous, while looking away from the deeds of others.*

▸ *The minority who follows the Torah's dictates has greater significance because of the difficulty it encounters.*

speck is asked of us...With an opening as small as the eye of a needle, one can merit great spiritual wealth.

_____

in a licentious generation, one who exerts effort with all his might in Torah and service of Hashem is more worthy to receive Heavenly help."

11 Tishrei —
11 Teves —
11 Nissan —
11 Tammuz —

IN OUR TIME

DAY 12

12 Tishrei

12 Teves

12 Nissan

12 Tammuz

*W*hen the Cohens' first daughter was born, they began putting away money each week toward her wedding. As time went on, additional children arrived, expenses mounted, and the wedding fund was depleted. Then, one day, their eldest daughter told her parents that she was ready to get married, and would like them to seek a suitable match. Suddenly, the wedding fund became top priority, with every spare dollar going straight into a special account that no one was allowed to touch.

There's a major difference between preparing for something that lies vaguely somewhere down the road, and preparing for something that is imminent. Our task, in these pre-Messianic times, is to inculcate ourselves with a firm belief that Mashiach's coming is literally upon us, so that this sense of imminence will guide our words and deeds.

"More than we want him [Mashiach] to come, he wants to come," the Chofetz Chaim[1] would often say. "However, he cannot come unless the Jewish people wait expectantly for him."

Fulfilling this mandate — *the* mandate of our times — is not an elusive task. There are clearly delineated, practical ways to hasten the Messianic redemption.

The Gemara[2] teaches the Jews were redeemed from Egypt due to five factors: the designated time had come, the pain they had endured, their crying out [in prayer],

1. *The Chofetz Chaim*, Rabbi Moses M. Yosher (ArtScroll/Mesorah Publ.), p. 451.
2. *Yerushalmi Taanis* 1:1; see *Devarim Rabbah, Parashah* 2:23; see also *Maharal, Netzach Yisrael*, Ch. 45, s.v. *U'b'Midrash*.

the merit of our Forefathers, and their sincere repentance. These are the same factors that will bring the Final Redemption.[3] This is alluded to in the Torah:[4]

> When you are in distress and all these things have befallen you, at the end of days, you will return unto Hashem, your God, and hearken to His voice. For Hashem, your God, is a merciful God. He will not abandon you nor destroy you, and He will not forget the covenant of your forefathers that He swore to them.

The Jewish people cannot measure God's calculations regarding the designated time for redemption, the pain endured throughout the ages, and the merit of our Forefathers. However, prayer and repentance are factors that rest solely in our hands. In addition, there are other means that are known to have the power to hasten the redemption.[5]

In the upcoming days, we will examine several ways in which each individual can actively help to hasten the Final Redemption in our time. Each of these strategies, when practiced properly, focuses our attention on God's dynamic presence in our lives and fosters *kavod Shamayim* — honor of Heaven — in the world.

The more one is able to truly feel God's presence, the more powerfully one feels what is lacking in our unredeemed world. Awareness leads to longing, and longing leads to action — energetic, persistent action to fill the void, to perceive Hashem's presence and hasten the speedy arrival of the Final Redemption.

STRATEGY 1: Longing for the Geulah
- *Metzapim L'Yeshuah* (Chapter 4)
- *Kiddush Hashem* in Everyday Life (Chapter 5)

STRATEGY 2: *Creating a People United* (Chapters 6-9)

---

3. See *Beis HaSho'eivah*, p. 102, s.v. *Amar hakoseiv*. See also *Chomas HaDaas*, Ch. 13, s.v. *U'beur ha'maamar*, where the Chofetz Chaim states that if the Jewish people repent fully, then that itself will immediately bring the Final Redemption.
4. *Devarim* 4:30-31.
5. *Chofetz Chaim al HaTorah, Devarim* 4:27-30, p. 228.

- The Problem — Hatred, Hurt, and Hostility (Chapter 6)
- Solution I: Living With *Emunah* and Bitachon (Chapter 7)
- Solution II: Internalize Gratitude (Chapter 7)
- Solution III: Ending Jealousy and Hatred (Chapter 8)
- Solution IV: *"V'ahavta L'rei'acha Kamocha"* (Chapter 9)

STRATEGY 3: Honor Shabbos Properly (Chapter 10)

STRATEGY 4: Pray for the *Geulah* (Chapter 10)

STRATEGY 5: The Power of *Tzedakah* (Chapter 10)

STRATEGY 6: Increase Torah Study (Chapter 11)

STRATEGY 7: *Teshuvah:* The Antidote to our Exile (Chapter 11)

These are not esoteric practices or impossible tasks. They are concepts from our Sages, defined by Jewish law and known by us to be achievable because God does not command the impossible. If we believe in our ability to hasten the redemption with these steps, and are thereby motivated to follow them sincerely, we will gradually, day-by-day, build our latent spiritual strength. Starting now, everyone of us can live each day in actual, patent anticipation of the Final Redemption.

Take It With You

▸ *Being metzapim l'yeshuah requires making an active effort to prepare for the coming of Mashiach.*

▸ *The same factors that brought redemption from Egypt will bring redemption to us.*

לעילוי נשמת הרב דוד בן הרב שמחה בונים זצ"ל — 12 Tishrei

12 Teves —

12 Nissan — Josef Friedman לע"נ יוסף מאיר בן משה ז"ל

Dedicated by the Friedman family

12 Tammuz —

HOW TO
START MOVING

DAY 13

13
Tishrei

13
Teves

13
Nissan

13
Tammuz

*Y*ou're all packed. You've got the tickets and the passport. The luggage sits by the door, ready to be loaded into the car. But you won't get anywhere, despite all your preparation, unless you step out the door.

Everyone finds change difficult, but that is what is needed if we are to truly redefine our approach to hastening the *Geulah*. Today's tried and true concepts have the time-tested power to catapult a person from paralysis to action.

No amount of preparation can transport us to a new place in life unless we get up and go. The following are several steps that have enabled people to achieve various goals, along their ascent up the spiritual ladder.

1. Identify a firm, achievable goal (i.e., saying "good morning" to each person on the way to school/work, remedying a specific sin, studying Torah five additional minutes each day).
2. Make a limited commitment of thirty days,[1] focusing on just one trait you hope to improve.
3. Hold yourself accountable — record your progress by keeping a daily journal tracking your results, motivations, and strategies for overcoming obstacles.

---

1. Rabbi Zelig Pliskin (*Growth Through Torah*, on *Devarim* 21:13, pp. 494-495) says that the *eishes yefas toar* must cry over her parents for a period of thirty days. The Ramban explains that thirty days is the amount of time necessary for her to remove her attachment to her idols from her mouth and heart. Rabbi Chaim Zaitchek comments that we learn from here that to actually change a trait, a thirty-day period of intense work is necessary. This is also the principle of the month of Elul, which is a time for us to focus on our behavior and traits in order to make a major improvement in ourselves (adapted from Hakhel Daily Bulletin, Elul 11, 5769).

4. Inform someone of your commitment, so that you will be held accountable.
5. Seek someone who can provide support if you feel yourself faltering.
6. Be proud of your accomplishments, noting every small success.
7. Do not overreach your goal. Even if it seems easier than you expected, stick to the plan.
8. If you find that you did not attain a particular goal, don't despair. Begin anew extending your effort until you get back on track.
9. Once you reach one goal, restart the process by focusing on another trait you wish to improve and/or change.

These are the steps one would take if one were in a situation that simply had to be improved or changed; a person who is suffering ill health due to being overweight will go to the trouble of keeping a journal and involving people and so on if it means a longer, healthier life. Someone who just wants to lose the weight for vanity's sake, however, would find the routine onerous. Likewise, for us, our willingness to make spiritual growth a serious, sustained effort depends on how keenly we feel its necessity and how motivated we are.

Obviously, our efforts will elevate us individually, but can that actually make an impact on the world — hastening the redemption? The Gemara[2] answers with an amazing statement, "… through a *single* person repenting, the whole world may be forgiven."[3]

We have mapped out several powerful and effective first steps along this magnificent path, which all Jews will travel together as the time of *Geulah* draws near. Now is the time to begin.

---

2. *Yoma* 86b.
3. See *Maharsha* ibid., s.v. *Shebishvil yachid*. See also *Rambam, Hil. Teshuvah* 3:4.

> 13 Tishrei —
> 13 Teves —
> 13 Nissan —
> 13 Tammuz —

CHAPTER 3:
A PRICELESS RELATIONSHIP

A PARTNERSHIP

*R*eb Mendel of Rimanov was walking with his chassidim when he noticed a boy sitting behind a tree and crying. The Rebbe asked, "Why are you crying?" The boy replied, "We're playing hide and seek, and it's my turn to hide, but no one is looking for me! No one's interested in finding me!"

The Rebbe turned to his chassidim and exclaimed, "Do you hear this child? 'No one is looking for me. No one's interested in finding me.' That is how Hashem feels in this long, bitter galus."[1]

Why is it not sufficient to be content to live our current spiritual life, which is complete with limitless opportunities to learn Torah and perform mitzvos, without pining for that which is missing? What is at the root of the mandate that a Jew hasten the *Geulah*? Life isn't perfect, but it's good. Why not focus on that goodness and spare ourselves the ache that comes from pining for something better? The reason is found in the unique relationship our forefather Avraham established with God, which makes us full-fledged partners in His design for the world.

How did this relationship come about? In *Parashas Lech Lecha*,[2] Avraham is concerned that his merit, earned by successfully navigating the many tests of his life, was depleted when God granted him victory against an alliance of powerful kings. God appears to Avraham and reassures him, "Do not be afraid, I will protect you. Your reward is very great."

---

1. *Listen to Your Messages*, Rabbi Yissocher Frand (ArtScroll/Mesorah Publ.), p. 137.
2. *Bereishis* 15:1.

Avraham then asks God, "What can You give me, seeing that I am childless?"[3] With these words, Avraham requests a covenant with God, through which he will father a child (i.e., a nation). God responds,[4] "Count the stars if you are able; so shall your offspring be," meaning that Avraham's request will be granted. Thereafter, God informs Avraham that his nation will sojourn in a foreign land (Egypt) and be enslaved for four hundred years.[5]

It seems odd to follow the glorious promise of nationhood with a prediction of national suffering and slavery. Rav Shimshon Dovid Pincus explains with a parable:[6]

Two partners establish a business and hire workers to sell their wares. The startup business barely turns a profit. The employees still receive their wages, but the owners forgo their own salaries in order to invest in their enterprise. Together, they ride out the storm, surviving on a meager subsistence, even though their employees enjoy the fruits of their labor.

With the words, "your reward is very great," God is offering Avraham "wages" for his good deeds. However, when Avraham responds that he wants more than "wages," that he desires a covenant to found a nation, he is asking to become a partner. God therefore informs Avraham of the "down side" of the partnership he is seeking, and that is the suffering that Avraham — along with God — will experience when his children are enslaved in Egypt. With the execution of this covenant, God and Avraham become partners in a pact, sharing in the "profits and losses."

Rav Pincus[7] elucidates that our pact with God, called Judaism, requires that we bear the pain of the *Shechinta b'galusa* — the exile of God's presence. A person who lives as a Jew only to collect "wages" from God for his mitzvos is like an employee, not a partner living with God under the terms of our covenant.

---

3. Ibid. v. 2.
4. Ibid. v. 4.
5. Ibid. v. 13.
6. *Galus U'Nechamah*, p. 113.
7. Ibid., pp. 113, 119.

Take It With You

- *Avraham forged a "partnership" between God and the Jewish people.*

- *Like business partners, the Jewish people and God share times of trouble and triumph.*

- *Since the Shechinah is displaced from Its home in the Beis HaMik- dash, God suffers.*

- *As God's partners, we share this sense of displace- ment.*

As long as the *Shechinah* remains "homeless," It cannot be content. Because we are partners in God's enterprise, His distress is our distress. Despite our relative prosperity and our religious freedom in many parts of the world, our hearts will remain unsettled until the Divine Presence is restored to its place, radiating holiness into the world from Its home in the Beis HaMikdash.

---

14 Tishrei —

14 Teves —

14 Nissan — לע״נ רפאל ליפא בן אליהו ז״ל

נלב״ע ד' תמוז תשס״ע

Dedicated by the Solomon family

14 Tammuz —

IN THE PRESENT

DAY 15

*C*haim awakened in the morning with another crippling migraine. He moaned pitifully as his wife rushed around tending to her morning routine. Wake the kids, make the beds, get breakfast ready… "Why does Chaim keep complaining? He knows it doesn't make it any better," she thought distractedly. "I have complete confidence that in another few hours the pain will be gone…There's nothing I can do about it right now." Meanwhile, Chaim lay in bed pleading silently for some help, some concern, an offer of a glass of water, or an aspirin.

15
Tishrei

15
Teves

15
Nissan

15
Tammuz

The relationship between God and the Jewish people is compared to that of a husband and wife. When the Jewish people received the Torah at Mount Sinai, *Chazal* comment[1] that Hashem came down to the mountain like a "bridegroom who goes out to greet His bride."[2]

In the role of "wife," however, the Jewish people are much like the overburdened wife in the opening scenario. We are dimly aware that our "Husband," God, is in terrible anguish over the exile. We have faith that some day the pain will be over. But His pain does not break our dis-

---

1. See *Rashi* to *Devarim* 33:2.
2. *Tanach* consistently refers to the relationship between Hashem and Bnei Yisrael as that of a husband and his bride. See *Rambam, Hilchos Teshuvah* 10:3, who states that *Shir HaShirim* expresses a passionate relationship between Hashem and His people. The central theme of *Shir HaShirim* depicts a wife (i.e., Bnei Yisrael) who disappoints her husband (i.e., Hashem). She yearns for her husband, and he, in turn, reunites with her. Even though Bnei Yisrael sin, Hashem gives us chance after chance to repent and return to Him. This can help explain what Rabbi Akiva said (*Yadaim* 3:5): "All the books of *Tanach* are holy, but *Shir HaShirim* is the holiest of holies."

tracted hearts, and therefore, we do not respond in an immediate, proactive way, to alleviate it.

A husband and wife do not marry primarily so that some day they will have *nachas* from their children, or so that in their old age they will have companionship. Their main goal is to live a life together in the present, with each spouse thinking of the other's needs and desires and promising to care deeply for the other regardless of the challenges that life holds.

Our covenant with God, epitomized by the principles of Judaism and by our eminent status as God's chosen nation,[3] requires that we live with God in the *present* day. Therefore, when God is in anguish over this long *galus*, we must endure along with Him and share His suffering that the *Shechinah* is in exile, just as a caring spouse would internalize her partner's torment and attempt to alleviate it in any possible way.

Only the arrival of the Final Redemption will completely alleviate God's anguish. Therefore, we must literally ache to relieve God's pain by yearning to bring the *Geulah*.

Geulah will come when Hashem redeems the Jewish people and, in the process, redeems the whole world.[4] Then we will celebrate the birth of the world that has been promised to us: a world brimming with peace; a world governed by truth, honesty and righteousness; a world where *tzaddikim* will flourish, where mitzvos and Torah learning will thrive and evil will disappear.[5] This is the vision of our

---

3. See *Emes L'Yaakov, Bereishis* 1:22; 9:25.
4. *Rambam, Hilchos Melachim* 11:1,4 lists the order of events: First "the *Melech HaMashiach* (the anointed king) will arise and renew the Davidic dynasty, restoring it to its initial sovereignty. He will rebuild the Temple and gather in the dispersed remnant of Israel. (However, see *Tos. Yom Tov, Maaser Sheni* 5:2, which states that the building of the Beis HaMikdash will precede the renewal of the Davidic dynasty. See also *Moadim U'Zemanim*, Vol. 5, p. 234, s.v. *Mi'yoma*.) Then…all the statutes will be reinstituted as in former times. Offerings will be brought and the Sabbatical and Jubilee years will be observed…as commanded in the Torah." All of this will result in the return of the Jewish people to full observance of Torah law.
5. The goal of the interconnecting aspects of the Final Redemption is for the Jewish people to fulfill its purpose and destiny — "to perfect the entire world, [motivating all the nations] to serve God together, as it is written (*Zephaniah* 3:9), 'For I shall then make the peoples pure

future, but being *metzapim l'yeshuah* commands us to strive with all our heart to realize this vision in the present, with every decision, every deed, and every prayer.

of speech so that they will all call upon the Name of God and serve Him with one purpose.' "

---

15 Tishrei — Fay Kasmer Broome לע"נ צפורה בת משה דוד ע"ה
Dedicated by Bernard H. Broome

15 Teves —

15 Nissan —

15 Tammuz —

Take It With You

▸ God's relationship with the Jewish people is compared to that of a husband and wife.

▸ Just as a spouse should feel acutely his/her partner's pain, the Jewish people should feel God's pain in the exile.

▸ This shared pain translates into doing everything possible, in word and deed, to bring the exile to an end and relieve God's suffering.

DAY 16

16
Tishrei

16
Teves

16
Nissan

16
Tammuz

With regard to the Third Holy Temple that will come into existence at the time of Mashiach,[1] the verse reveals:[2] "Many peoples will go and say, 'Come, let us go up to the mountain of Hashem, to the House of the God of Yaakov.'" The Gemara[3] wonders why specifically the God of Yaakov? Is the Holy Temple only the House of the God of Yaakov and not also the House of the God of Avraham and Yitzchak?

Rather, the verse teaches that the Holy Temple is not like the description found in the context of Avraham, where whom it is written *har*, "mountain,"[4] as it states:[5] "On the mountain Hashem is seen." Nor is it like the description found in the context of Yitzchak, where it is written *sadeh*, "field,"[6] as it states:[7] "Yitzchak went out to pray in the field." Rather, it is like the description found in the context of Yaakov, who called it *bayis*, "house," as it states:[8] "He named that place 'the House of God.'" What is the special significance of "house"?

Maharsha[9] explains that Avraham's "mountain" represents the First Temple — when the *Shechinah* watched over the Temple like a guard strategically stationed on

1. *Maharsha* on *Pesachim* 88a.
2. *Yeshayah* 2:3.
3. *Pesachim* 88a.
4. See *Eitz Yosef* on ibid., which states that although Avraham himself did not call it a "mountain," that description is identified with him.
5. *Bereishis* 22:14.
6. See *Ben Yehoyada* on *Pesachim* 88a, who explains that actually, Yitzchak was not praying then at the site of the Holy Temple. The verse, however, is interpreted to mean that during his prayer, Yitzchak stood in a field and directed his heart toward the site of the Temple.
7. Ibid. 24:63.
8. Ibid. 28:19.
9. *Pesachim* 88a.

top of a mountain. This protection was not permanent, for the First Temple was destroyed. Yitzchak's "field" signifies the Second Temple, which merited an even lesser degree of the Divine Presence. The "house" of Yaakov symbolizes the Third Temple, which will enjoy Divine protection that is permanent and complete.

A "house" also represents the place where one lives with close family members and which provides the environment in which the relationship between husband and wife develops. To Yaakov, the Temple Mount felt like home. His unique perception was that when the Temple (the House of God) will be built we will have the capacity to relate to God as a wife relates to her husband.[10] The essence of a loving relationship between husband and wife is solidified through each partner sharing in the other's joy in good times and feeling the other's pain in troubled times. It is this closeness and deep-rooted commitment that is missing from our relationship with God. *Shir HaShirim*, the Song of Songs of Solomon, is an exquisite expression of this loving bond — Israel's relationship to God as it is meant to be, dwelling in the palace together in perfect love and harmony.

During this long exile we have contented ourselves with the field of Yitzchak — a business relationship — a *quid pro quo* in which we pray and do mitzvos, and God supplies us with our daily needs. Our prayers are not the longing of an estranged wife, but rather, the pragmatic requests of a purchasing agent who requires certain material to make his business and his life run efficiently.

At worst, we don't even recognize that God is the Source of those gifts. At best, we tell God, "I want to do Your will, so please give me money, good health, and peace so I can do it." Sadly, our best is nowhere near what it can be. Like one who works the fields, our relationship with God is that of a business partnership. The farmer plants, tends, sows, and reaps, while God provides the sunshine, rain, nutrients, and the life-force that make things grow.

---

10. Heard from Rabbi Dovid Orlofsky, Chofetz Chaim Heritage Foundation Tishah B'Av Event — July 30, 2009.

▸ *Yitzchak
saw the
Temple
Mount as a
field where
one could
enter into a
productive,
"working
partner-
ship" with
God. This
represents
our rela-
tionship
today.*

▸ *Yaakov saw
the Temple
Mount as
a home,
where God
and Israel
would
dwell
together as
husband
and wife.*

▸ *The yearn-
ing for a
return to
this close
relationship
"at home"
with God is
at the heart
of awaiting
redemption.*

Achieving that loving closeness — a life of dwelling with our Beloved in His palace — is the true meaning of the Final Redemption. When we direct our yearning toward the total spiritual bliss of God's loving embrace, we prepare our souls, and the world, for *Geulah*.

> **16 Tishrei** — Refuah shelaimah for נחמה בת צירל שתחי׳
> **16 Teves** —
> **16 Nissan** —
> **16 Tammuz** —

HOMELESS

DAY 17

*B*oruch became a billionaire before he was 30. He had wealth beyond imagination, status, and power. Rather than living like a "king" enjoying the fruits of his labor, he created an international charitable organization focused on helping vulnerable individuals worldwide. The organization built roads, schools, and housing. It built supermarkets that were stocked with a wide variety of goods sold at a discount. It constructed hospitals and trained and paid doctors to care for the sick. It even enabled parents to marry off their children without accruing massive debt. The people regarded Boruch like a loving father.

17
Tishrei

17
Teves

17
Nissan

17
Tammuz

As the years passed, the older generation gradually aged. Their children were provided for but did not know the source of their sustenance. Although they continued to benefit from Boruch's benevolence, they were totally unaware that their relatively easy lifestyle was underwritten by Boruch's immeasurable kindness.

In time, Boruch's personal circumstances changed and he became destitute. This did not affect the foundation, as the original seed money had been invested in such a way that it generated enough income to sustain itself indefinitely. Embarrassed at the fluctuation in his personal fortune, Boruch retreated into himself and did not even avail himself of the services he had set in motion.

One day news leaked that Boruch was homeless. As word spread, the people recalled that all the good they had received was from Boruch. They decided that they must do whatever they could to provide

Boruch with comfortable quarters. Even this was an inadequate expression of the gratitude they felt for the individual who had been the catalyst for so many aspects of their wonderful life.

During the Holy Temple era the Divine Presence was so pervasive and apparent that anyone who bothered to open his eyes could perceive it.[1] On that fateful day 1,940 years ago and ever since, God too became "homeless" as His House — the Holy Temple — was demolished in ruins. Evidence of the manifestation of His homelessness is that in our world, where Divine concealment has replaced Divine revelation, we grope for proof of God's existence, like fish debating the existence of water. We are relegated to struggle to "believe" when "belief" was once simply plain to see. We struggle through prayer to experience a momentary inkling of the Divine Presence when once we basked in it. We are like amnesiacs who experience fleeting memories of a deeper, truer identity, but cannot quite grasp it.

It is easy to lament what *we* lost when the Divine Presence was removed from our midst. But more importantly we must grieve for what *God* "lost." God "suffers" while "waiting" in the wings, longing for the moment to once again reveal His presence and shower His creation with boundless blessing and goodness. His glory and splendor, intended to bathe the world in the light of His kindness, must dwell on the sidelines, dusting the world with only the tiniest fraction of their power.

How can we keep our loving Father waiting any longer? Even if we perceive all the facts on the ground telling us, "It's impossible for us to alleviate His pain," how can we sit idly by knowing that He is "in anguish"? When we recognize that the Final Redemption will end God's nearly 2,000 years of homelessness by bringing the Divine Presence back into the world, thereby ending all the national and

---

1. The second Beis HaMikdash manifested fewer of the miracles of the First Temple: it did not house the Holy Ark, the *Ner Maaravi* did not always burn throughout the night, and the Kohen Gadol was unable to interpret the *Urim V'Tumim*. Nonetheless, the Divine Presence still had a place It called "Home."

personal catastrophes that ensue in a world where God is not evident, how can we settle for life as usual?

Like the beneficiaries of Boruch's largesse in the opening scenario, we must feel our Father's pain in exile. We must long to sit at His table once more, basking in His wisdom and bounty. Thus motivated, we will have the wherewithal to do all we can for ourselves, and all we *must* do for Hashem.

Take It With You

▸ *God suffers in exile, for He has no home from which to dispense the full goodness and benefit He wishes to give His creation.*

▸ *Our concern for God's suffering is a powerful incentive, and the only truly relevant one, for working to hasten the Final Redemption.*

17 Tishrei —
17 Teves —
17 Nissan —
17 Tammuz —

STRATEGY 1: LONGING FOR THE GEULAH

Metzapim L'Yeshuah
(Ch. 4)

❧

Kiddush Hashem in Everyday Life
(Ch. 5)

CHAPTER 4:
METZAPIM L'YESHUAH

MUST I?

T he Thirteen Principles of Faith espoused by the Rambam[1] include such fundamentals as belief in God as the Creator and Supervisor of His creation; the Oneness and incorporeal nature of God; faith in the Torah and in the prophecy of Moshe, and other basic concepts, without which a Jew would not be bound to God, Torah, and mitzvos.

Belief in the imminent coming of Mashiach is the twelfth principle. Upon what basis does this belief fit within the framework of the others? Is it not possible to believe in God and serve Him wholeheartedly here and now, without focusing on an event that is to come in an unknown manner at an unknown time?

The Gemara[2] states that when one arrives at his Day of Judgment, he is asked, "*Tzipisa l'yeshuah*"[3] — Did you await salvation (i.e., the coming of Mashiach)?" *Smak*[4] reasons that we would not be asked whether we awaited salvation if we had not been commanded to do so.[5] He finds the source of this commandment woven into the first of the Ten Commandments, in the verse "*Anochi Hashem*

---

1. *Rambam, Commentary on Mishnayos, Sanhedrin,* Introduction to *Perek Cheilek.*
2. *Shabbos* 31a.
3. Chofetz Chaim in *Tzipisa L'Yeshuah,* beg. of Ch. 3, commented: "*Chazal* said, '*Tzipisa l'yeshua,*' and the root meaning of *tzipisa* is similar to one who stands on a high place and is on the lookout for what he is awaiting. This is how a Jew ought to wait for the immediate revelation of Mashiach."
4. *Sefer Mitzvos HaKatzar (Smak), Asin, Siman* 1.
5. Further evidence of the primacy of *tzipisa l'yeshuah* comes from the *Zohar* (introduction to *Bereishis* 4a), which makes this stark statement: "One who does not yearn for the Final Redemption in this world will not have a place in the World to Come."

Elokecha — I am Hashem, your God, Who has taken you out of the land of Egypt, out of the house of bondage."[6]

The mitzvah of *"Anochi Hashem Elokecha,"* often identified as the mitzvah of *emunah*, requires us to believe that God redeemed us from the Egyptian exile. The word *"Anochi"* — an expression of compassion — connects the past and future redemptions: The Midrash[7] states that *Anochi* is the word by which God identifies Himself in both of those promises.

God uses this word to answer Yaakov Avinu's objections to descending into the impurity of Egypt:[8] "I (*Anochi*) shall descend with you to Egypt, and I shall also surely bring you up..." *Anochi* also signifies the Final Redemption:[9] "Behold, I (*Anochi*) send you Eliyahu the prophet before the coming of the great and awesome day of Hashem."

Being *metzapim l'yeshuah* is not only mandatory, but especially essential now, because all the signs pointing to Mashiach's arrival have already been fulfilled.[10] We are like people coming to the end of a long journey, who are told, "Go over the bridge, pass two sets of traffic lights, and just keep going until you see the sign that says 'Entrance.' Then you're there."

Would a person travel the entire way and then, just when he must start looking for the "Entrance" sign, give up the effort? We have come so far, the Chofetz Chaim is telling us. Now, more than ever, we *must* indeed keep our eyes focused on the horizon, trying to catch a glimpse of the rapidly approaching Mashiach.

---

6. *Shemos* 20:2.
7. *Shemos Rabbah* 3:4.
8. *Bereishis* 46:3-4.
9. *Malachi* 3:23.
10. *Michtav MeEliyahu*, Vol. 1, p. 209; *Chofetz Chaim, Likutei Amarim*, Chapter 11, s.v. *Hinei hame'ayen.*

> **Take It With You**
>
> ▸ *The requirement of waiting for Mashiach is listed explicitly as one of the Rambam's Thirteen Principles of Faith.*
>
> ▸ *Even in a time of relative security and peace, we are still required to wait and long for the Messianic era.*
>
> ▸ *The Chofetz Chaim says that all the signs for Mashiach's arrival have occurred, making our active anticipation even more vital.*

---

18 Tishrei — לע״נ שיינדל בת ר׳ חיים ע״ה
Dedicated by her loving nieces and nephews,
the Jachter & Greenman families
18 Teves —
18 Nissan —
18 Tammuz —

DAY 19

AWAIT EVERY DAY

19
Tishrei

19
Teves

19
Nissan

19
Tammuz

The coming of Mashiach is the fulfillment of God's promise: "God will bring back your captivity and have mercy upon you. He will gather you [from among the nations]...Even if your dispersal will be at the ends of heaven, from there [God will gather you in].[1]

Therefore, we know that redemption will surely come. The Prophets[2] urge us to await the fulfillment of that promise and the Rambam[3] articulates this belief in Mashiach in the Thirteen Principles of Faith: "I believe with complete faith in the coming of Mashiach. Though he tarry, nonetheless I await him every day, that he will come."

The words "I await him" charge the Jewish people with an obligation beyond that of simple belief in the coming of Mashiach. In the Rambam's words, one is required not only to *believe*, but to *await*.

> *A mother expects that the schoolbus will arrive at the corner bus stop at noon, bringing her only child home from his first day at school. She is aware of this while making the beds, washing the breakfast dishes, or chatting on the phone. Ten minutes early, she is out at the bus stop. Her ears are piqued for the sound of the motor, her eyes focused on the approaching traffic. She checks her watch. At 12:05, she is already wondering, "What's taking so long?"*

"To await" means active anticipation of the imminent arrival of the redemption. The Rambam's words, "I await

---

1. *Devarim* 30:3-4.
2. *Chabakuk* 2:3, *Tzefaniah* 3:8, and *Yeshayah* 30:18. (See *Sanhedrin* 97b; also *Rashi* on *Yeshayah* 26:2 and *Tehillim* 130:6.)
3. *Rambam, Commentary on Mishnayos, Sanhedrin,* Introduction to *Perek Cheilek.*

him every day...,"[4] make it incumbent upon every Jew to maintain a constant vigil, feeling that at any moment, Mashiach *can* come.[5]

Nowadays, God's promise to redeem us just as He redeemed our ancestors from bondage and spiritual decay appears incongruous. We are not enslaved. We are not even near the state of upheaval that existed during World War I, when the Chofetz Chaim explained, "This war comprises the agonies and tribulations that must precede the advent of Mashiach..."

With the subsequent suffering of the Holocaust, many great Torah leaders, including Rav Yechezkel Levenstein,[6] the Steipler Gaon, Rav Yaakov Yisrael Kanievski,[7] Rav Eliyahu Lopian,[8] and Rabbi Shimon Schwab,[9] believed they had witnessed the final stages of pre-Messianic turmoil as they desperately longed for the ultimate redemption. The horrific times eventually passed, however, and the status quo of a pervasive though tenuous calm has settled in once again.

In times of peace and plenty, one may have a far more difficult time tapping into the heightened sense of longing that a Jew is required to feel. Nevertheless, as the Rambam states, the requirement to "await redemption" demands a passionate, personal longing.[10]

Rav Yonasan Eibeshutz articulates the essential void one should feel: [11]

> *A Jew must shed tears without pause when he recites the prayers for the rebuilding of Jerusalem and the*

---

4. See Zohar, Introduction to 4a: "Who among you awaits every day the light that will shine forth..." [i.e., awaiting the coming of Mashiach every day]. See also Zohar, *Midrash HaNeelam* I:140a: "...those who eagerly await the redemption each day, as it is said, 'A hoard of salvation' (*Yeshayah* 33:6), which refers to those who eagerly await salvation every day."
5. *Igros Moshe, Orach Chaim*, Vol. 5, *Siman* 8.
6. *Ohr Yechezkel, Emunah*, p. 313.
7. *Sefer Orchos Rabbeinu*, Vol. 1, p. 287.
8. *Lev Eliyahu, Parashas Va'eschanan*, p. 187.
9. *Selected Speeches*, Rav Shimon Schwab (CIS Publ., Abridged Edition), pp. 18-19.
10. See *Shulchan Aruch* 1:3.
11. *Cheilek* 1, *Drush* 1, s.v. *B'vircas Yerushalayim*.

Take It With You

▸ *We are commanded not only to believe in the coming of Mashiach, but to actively await him every day.*

▸ *In troubled times, the longing for Mashiach was fueled by the Jewish people's need to grasp onto hope for the future.*

▸ *In our more tranquil times, the mandate to await the redemption requires no less urgency and passion.*

Beis HaMikdash within it, because that is the purpose of the completion of man...If we do not have Jerusalem and the reign of David's dynasty, then... we do not have life in its fullest sense.

לע"נ יצחק אייזיק בן ר' יהודה אברהם ז"ל — 19 Tishrei

19 Teves —

19 Nissan —

19 Tammuz —

HOW TO WAIT

DAY 20

*A*nd so, in conclusion, I would like to thank you all for coming and supporting our yeshivah. May we merit raising sons whose devotion to Torah learning will hasten the coming of Mashiach speedily in our days," the speaker intoned. The audience mumbled "Amen" and gratefully went back to their grilled chicken with basil-infused wild rice.

As we learned previously, the fact that every public speech ends with a statement of longing for Mashiach does not signify that we, as a people, are fulfilling the mandate of *metzapim l'yeshuah*. Even the oft-repeated refrain in times of political or personal turmoil — "Oy, Mashiach just has to come!" — falls far short of the mark.

Nonetheless, the very yearning for redemption is one of the sources of merit that will hasten the redemption.[1] Therefore, it is vital to clarify and understand what is being asked of us. To analyze the current situation, we must go back in time and compare it to the first redemption of the Jewish people over 3,000 years ago.

Michtav MeEliyahu[2] explores the fact that many of the Jews enslaved in Egypt were hesitant whether to leave Egypt and to "...follow Me [Hashem] in the Wilderness, in an unsown land."[3] Because of their uncertainty, God told Moshe Rabbeinu to ask Pharaoh for only a limited, three-day respite for the purpose of bringing offerings.[4]

20
Tishrei

20
Teves

20
Nissan

20
Tammuz

---

1. *Yalkut Shimoni, Tehillim, Remez 736; Midrash Tehillim, Mizmor 40; Abudraham*, end of Yom Kippur Prayers; *Tzipisa L'Yeshuah*, Ch. 2. See *Sifsei Chaim, Moadim*, Vol. 3, p. 351, s.v. *Ha'tzipisa l'Mashiach*.
2. Vol. 4, p. 132, s.v. *Ad kamma*.
3. *Yirmiyah* 2:2.
4. *Shemos* 3:18.

The intent was not to deceive Pharaoh; rather, it was to ease the wary Jews into the idea of leaving Egypt.

What were their reservations? How could they have resisted the promise of freedom? The explanation is that 210 years into the exile the Jews in Egypt had no knowledge of any life except in Egypt. Their only concept of freedom was the freedom to be full-fledged Egyptian citizens, free from pain and persecution. In fact, in the entire story of their sojourn in and exodus from Egypt, the Torah does not record a single instance of the Jews asking to leave Egypt. The only barometer of the Jewish people's sentiments prior to the Exodus is in the Torah's words,[5] "The Jews groaned because of the work and they cried out." The verses describe a nation despondent and despairing — a people suffering the indignities of persecution.

In addition to those with a slave mentality who could not even dream of freedom, there were also corrupted Jews who had favored positions among the Egyptians and could not dream of giving up their wealth. These are the Jews who perished during the plague of darkness.[6]

Even after witnessing ten miraculous plagues and seeing God break the mighty Egyptian oppressors, most of the Jews enslaved in Egypt did not want to leave their familiar surroundings and attach themselves to this God of miracles and mystery. They simply wanted to be free "like everybody else."

With a leap forward in time, to the beginning of the 21st century, one can indeed see the paradigm of Egypt playing out again. The desire for redemption today is often stated as a desire to be free from the worries and troubles of our lives and times. Were the call to come today to leave behind all that is familiar in order to "follow Me in the Wilderness," there is no doubt that many Jews would need convincing.

Metzapim l'yeshuah requires us to begin prying ourselves loose from our mental and spiritual bondage by connecting more vibrantly with God, for as many renowned

---

5. Ibid. 2:23-25.
6. *Midrash Rabbah, Bo, Parashah* 14:3; *Mechilta Shemos* 13:18; *Midrash Aggadah, Bamidbar,* Ch. 26:12.

Rabbis[7] have written, all the signs of Mashiach's arrival have occurred. By nurturing an earnest longing for a new kind of world, permeated by God's obvious presence, we possess the power to help to bring that time closer.

Take It With You

▸ *Yearning for redemption is itself a merit for bringing it.*

▸ *This yearning must be more than a desire to be free of troubles and persecution.*

▸ *A Jew who awaits redemption must be prepared, as were the Jews who merited leaving Egypt, to "follow Me (Hashem)."*

---

7. *Michtav M'Eliyahu*, Vol. 1, pp. 207-209; *Chofetz Chaim, Likutei Amarim*, Ch. 11, s.v. *Hinei hame'ayen*.

20 Tishrei —
20 Teves —
20 Nissan —
20 Tammuz —

KEEP HOPING

DAY 21

21 Tishrei

21 Teves

21 Nissan

21 Tammuz

*K*eep walking, keep walking," the father urged his family. "We'll reach a safe place if we just keep going." It was an astounding escape plan for this family fleeing the Nazi invasion of Poland. They would keep walking east until they reached Asia. "Keep going, keep going," the parents urged their children. To stop, to quit — this would spell doom. To maintain their strength, they kept before themselves and their children a vivid vision of their ultimate goal — a safe harbor where they could wait out the war free of fear. They didn't stop until they reached the Himalayas; they survived.

The long journey from the present world to the times of Mashiach seems never-ending. Yet, like the family in the above story, the Jewish people keep going, traversing the rough terrain of history on a journey in which the estimated time of arrival is unknown. In the face of centuries of wandering, our persistent faith that there is an ultimate destination, and that we will reach it, is in itself a tremendous merit for the Jewish people.

Rabbi Shimon Schwab once commented that if he were asked what merit the Jewish people possess that makes them deserving of Mashiach, he would answer:[1]

> *Because of our emunah that Mashiach will come and our continued bitachon despite constant disappointments...Normally, a person who is disappointed over and over again would give up. Yet, my father and yours, and my mother and yours, and our*

---

1. Adapted from *Selected Speeches*, Rav Shimon Schwab (CIS Publ., Abridged Edition), pp. 27-28.

*grandparents and great-grandparents, year after year
at the Pesach Seder, all said "Next year in Jerusalem." Then came another year, and another Seder,
and Mashiach still did not come. Nevertheless, they
did not stop singing "Next year in Jerusalem"...And
if Mashiach does not materialize [the next year], we
still do not give up.*

*This requires emunah and bitachon. And if we ask
what our generation can say for itself as to why it war-
rants the coming of Mashiach, we reply that we merit
it for one reason: We didn't give up!*

The Chofetz Chaim similarly explains:[2] "With the
length of the exile, the merits of the Jewish people grow
and become greater from generation to generation from
the merits...of their waiting and hoping for the coming
of Mashiach for such a long time..."

One means by which to hasten and actualize the Messianic redemption is the very believing in, and anticipation of, the coming of Mashiach.[3] The Midrash[4] teaches
that the attribute of awaiting God's salvation characterizes
each pivotal event of Jewish history:

*Everything is connected with hopeful awaiting
(kivuy)...Who [Avraham and Sarah] waited in hope
to have a child? Who waited for Yosef HaTzaddik,
who went through horrific difficulties but eventually
became king [of Egypt]? Who waited for Moshe Rabbeinu to be drawn safely from the river?... "Wait for
salvation for it is close at hand!" Thus it says, "For My
salvation is near to come."[5]*

Another Midrash affirms God's guarantee to those who
hold onto their hope and faith in Him:[6]

*When the Jews enter their synagogues and houses
of Torah study, they say to the Holy One, Blessed is*

---

2. *Tzipisa L'Yeshuah*, Ch. 2.
3. *Yalkut Shimoni, Tehillim, Remez* 736; *Midrash Tehillim, Mizmor* 40;
Abudraham, end of Yom Kippur Prayers.
4. *Shemos Rabbah* 30:24; see *Bereishis Rabbah* 98:14.
5. *Yeshayah* 56:1; see *Bereishis Rabbah* 88:7.
6. *Midrash Tehillim* 31:1.

Take It With You

▸ **The merits of the Jewish people become greater in the merit of their continual waiting and hoping for the redemption.**

▸ **Our continual belief in and anticipation of Mashiach's coming is, in itself, a powerful merit for hastening the redemption.**

He, "Redeem us!" He responds to them: "Are there righteous people among you? Are there God-fearing people among you?" They reply: "...as we go from generation to generation it grows darker for us..." The Holy One, Blessed is He, then says to them: "Trust in My Name and I shall stand by you...for I shall save whoever trusts in My Name."

NOTHING IS BEYOND GOD

DAY 22

*I*f one were to be told that rain flies upward rather than descending, or that the moon shines at noon and the sun at night, one would say, "Impossible." The reason for the disbelief would be because it has never happened. If one has never seen nor heard of such a phenomenon actually occurring, it seems beyond the realm of possibility.

In our lives and in our history, Mashiach has not come. We have never witnessed redemption on the scale of that which we are promised in the End of Days. Therefore, human nature surrounds the idea of Mashiach with a cloud of uncertainty. It hasn't happened yet; how can we know that it will happen at all? That tinge of uncertainty *in our heart* is a major obstacle in one's ability to fulfill the mandate of *metzapim l'yeshuah*.

The means to break through that obstacle is to realize that the very nature of this redemption is to come in a way and at a time that is unexpected. When that time comes, regardless of how unlikely redemption appears to be, it will arrive. The prophet Chabakuk says:[1] "For there is another vision, regarding the appointed time, and it speaks of the End, and it does not lie. Though it tarries, wait for it. For it will surely come; it will not delay."

In one's thinking about God and His works, the concept of "impossible" does not exist. The Torah illustrates this with God's promise of a son to the Matriarch Sarah. The Torah records her response:[2] "And Sarah laughed at herself, saying, 'After I have withered shall I again have deli-

22
Tishrei

22
Teves

22
Nissan

22
Tammuz

---

1. 2:3.
2. *Bereishis* 18:12.

▸ *Since no
one has
ever expe-
rienced
redemption
on the scale
of the Mes-
sianic age,
it can be
difficult to
believe it
can
happen.*

▸ *No matter
what state
the world is
in, redemp-
tion can
happen at
any time,
because
nothing
is beyond
God's abili-
ties.*

▸ *Events in
recent his-
tory bear
out the
prophe-
cies of the
world on
the verge of
redemption,
providing
us with a
foundation
for our
hopes.*

cate skin? And my husband is old.'" The Midrash[3] explains that Sarah thought that it would not be possible for her to have children at her age. God answers her doubts in His response to Avraham:[4] "Is anything beyond God? At the appropriate time I will return to you at this time next year, and Sarah will have a son."

The Chofetz Chaim[5] explains that, since "the deeds of the Forefathers are a precedent for us," God's response to Sarah's doubts instructs us regarding our belief in the redemption. Like Sarah, who wondered whether it was possible to have a son after all the years of barrenness, we too may wonder, after the interminable length of the exile, if it is possible that the Final Redemption will actually arrive. In answer, the Torah responds, "Is anything beyond God?" The Chofetz Chaim observes that God did not say, "Is *this* thing beyond God?" Instead He said, "Is *anything* beyond God?" This teaches us that *nothing* is beyond God — including bringing the Final Redemption.

Therefore, we have a basis upon which to believe that the scene that now appears uncertain will suddenly burst into full, glorious color. God has provided signs upon which to base our belief. One can already see the many prophesied signs of redemption that have emerged dur-ing the past century. The Chofetz Chaim writes: [6]

> *Certainly, in our days when we see that all that the Sages wrote in the Mishnah in Sotah[7] and also all the signs [of the end of days] that are enumerated in Perek Cheilek[8] ... all have come to pass, then, certainly we must await [and hope for] the coming of Mashiach.*

3. *Tanchuma, Shoftim* 18.
4. *Bereishis* 18:14.
5. *Chofetz Chaim al HaTorah, Bereishis* 18:12.
6. *Likutei Halachos*, end of *Maseches Sotah*.
7. 49a.
8. *Sanhedrin* 98a.

KNOWING WHY
TO YEARN

DAY 23

*I*n June 1967, when the Israeli Defense Forces were victorious in the Six Day War, the para-troopers who captured the Old City of Jerusalem were among the first to visit the Western Wall. Many of the soldiers, overcome with great emotion, stood weeping at the Wall. One non-religious soldier stood far back and was weeping, too. "Why are you crying?" asked his friend. "I am crying because I don't know why I should be crying."[1]

**23
Tishrei**

**23
Teves**

**23
Nissan**

**23
Tammuz**

Given the mandate of *metzapim l'yeshuah,* we are aware that we should be feeling something — something intense and vivid as we long to feel God's presence filling the world. Nevertheless, like the soldier in the true story above, our tears come from a source apart from the yearning itself, and that is the pain of knowing that we suffer from a partial spiritual paralysis; we do not truly *feel* that which we should be feeling.

Fulfilling the obligation to anticipate the imminent coming of Mashiach, and to actively and persistently strive for the end of our exile, clearly depends on cultivating the necessary personal feelings, and *sensing* the intrinsic splendor of living in a redeemed world. Yet, feelings cannot be legislated. How, then, can we fulfill such an obligation?

The void created by *hester panim* — a diminution of God's Presence, Glory, and Providence in the world — throws a thick cloak of darkness over the *Shechinah,* making it difficult to feel His presence while standing before God in prayer. We cannot see the *Shechinah* and can only, with great spiritual effort, attain a fleeting sense of what

---

1. Aish.com, June 22, 2002, "The Temple: Do We Feel the Loss?" by Rabbi Shraga Simmons.

▶ *Our lack
of direct
experience
makes it
difficult to
sincerely
long for the
Shechinah's
presence
to manifest
Itself.*

▶ *Our inabil-
ity to feel
this long-
ing should
cause us
pain.*

▶ *As Jews
we have an
obligation
to feel the
pain of the
Shechinah's
exile.*

the *Shechinah* does and how God manifests Himself in our world. All of this is a mystery. Nevertheless, it is our duty as Jews to feel the pain of the *Shechinah's* exile, for this is the root of *metzapim l'yeshuah.*

A person cannot truly miss what he has never known. The people of the 18th century did not miss the electric light bulb or air conditioning. Nighttime darkness and summertime heat were accepted components of the world in which they lived, and no one could have conceived of a world that was any different. Similarly, without having experienced the glory of living in the *Shechinah's* close proximity, a person can hardly be expected to miss it and to pine for it.

No one alive today has ever experienced the awesome glory of the Kohen's service in the Beis HaMikdash on Yom Kippur. There are no ears that have heard the Divine Name emerge from the Kohen's lips, and no eyes that have seen the mass of Jewish people drop to the ground and prostrate themselves, roaring in unison, "Blessed is His glorious Name for ever and ever."[2] No one knows in his heart what it means to have God's presence clearly before us, and therefore, no one can actually feel what it is that we are longing for.

For this reason, we all require assistance in reaching a level of longing for redemption that will enable us to truthfully answer, "Yes!" when we are someday asked, "*Tzipisa l'yeshuah?*" In reality, the concepts that lead to true, eager preparation for the coming of Mashiach are the same concepts that bring a person to his or her optimum spiritual growth. In the coming days, we will explore these concepts in a methodical, accessible way, enabling every reader to take concrete steps, doable in his own, everyday life, to help push open the door into a new era of redemption, clarity, and perfection.

---

2. *Yoma* 35b.

THE SOURCE OF TEARS

DAY 24

A *small child suffers a life-threatening illness. A fine young woman languishes for years, waiting for her spouse. A couple waits and wonders when they will have a child. A breadwinner faces the abyss of a failed business or a lost job. An entire family of young children mourns their mother.*

In our world, unfortunately, tears flow. Grief and sadness are part and parcel of the human experience. All those tears, from all the generations since the destruction of the second Beis HaMikdash, flow together into one rushing river. Throughout the centuries, tears of sickness, war, persecution, and poverty, have fed the river like an intricate web of tributaries, sweeping us along in one direction — toward the Ultimate Redemption.

The Midrash[1] relates that Rabban Gamliel had a neighbor whose child had passed away. Each night the mother would cry bitter tears. Awakened by her weeping, the Torah sage would weep as well, but his tears would be in mourning for the Beis HaMikdash. Why did he cry for the *Churban,* rather than for the bereft mother?

Rav Gifter[2] explains that Rabban Gamliel keenly perceived, in the woman's cries, the absence of the Beis HaMikdash and the protective presence of the *Shechinah.* His response pierced directly into the heart of the matter, for all tragedies that we experience emanate from the destruction of the Beis HaMikdash, and the consequent diminution of God's Presence, Glory, and Providence.

This point has been borne out throughout history. The

24
Tishrei

24
Teves

24
Nissan

24
Tammuz

---

1. *Pesikta Eichah Rabbah* 25 on *Eichah* 1:2.
2. *Tehillim Treasury,* Rabbi Avrohom Chaim Feuer (ArtScroll/ Mesorah Publ.), p. 39.

expulsion of Jews from England in 1290, and from France in 1306, and from Spain in 1492 all happened on Tishah B'Av. That was the day the First Temple was destroyed by the Babylonians, led by Nebuchadnezzar. One hundred thousand Jews were slaughtered and millions more exiled. The Second Temple also was destroyed on Tishah B'Av, by the Romans, led by Titus. Some two million Jews died, and another one million were exiled. What was quite arguably the true genesis of what would culminate in Germany's "Final Solution," the First World War, also broke out on the eve of Tishah B'Av, when Germany declared war on Russia. German resentment from the war set the stage for the Holocaust.[3]... On July 31, 1941 (on the evening of 8th of Av) Hermann Goering signed the document implementing the "final solution of the Jewish problem."[4]

Shlomo HaMelech teaches:[5] "It is better to go to a house of mourning than to go to a house of feasting (for that is the end of man) and the living should take it to heart." The simple meaning of this statement is that this brush with mortality motivates the visitor to examine his priorities.[6] However, there is a deeper, core lesson in the prayer one says upon departing from the mourner. "May God comfort you among the rest of the mourners of Zion and Jerusalem."

In effect, one tells the mourner that his sadness is shared by the entire Jewish people. All Jews have lost the comfort and security of living in the presence of our Beloved One.

---

3. During the time of Moshe, Jews in the Wilderness accepted the slanderous report of the ten Spies, and the decree was issued forbidding them from entering the Land of Israel. About 65 years after the destruction of the Second Temple, there was a city named Beitar where tens of thousands of Jews lived; they were led by Bar Kochba, a man whom all of Israel and its Sages thought was the Mashiach. The city fell to the Romans and all its inhabitants were killed. It was a catastrophe akin to the Temple's destruction. The Bar Kochba revolt was crushed by the Roman emperor Hadrian. The city of Beitar — the Jews' last stand against the Romans — was captured and liquidated. Over 100,000 Jews were slaughtered. See *Rambam, Hilchos Taanis* 5:3.
4. Aish.com, August 17, 2005, "The Final Solution on Tishah B'Av," by Yaakor Astor.
5. *Koheles* 7:2.
6. See *Ibn Ezra* ad loc.

From that loss, all other losses unfold. One who understands the deeper meaning of this prayer will indeed feel spurred to reorder his priorities, not only because life is so short, but more so because he will be motivated to do whatever is necessary to hasten the day when the *Shechinah's* full presence is restored, the day when all sorrows will end.

Take It With You

▸ *The tears one sheds over his own or another's personal suffering can also be channeled into mourning over the exile of the Shechinah.*

▸ *We need to recognize that Hashem's exile is the loss from which all losses unfold. This awareness enables us to experience more keenly the necessity for redemption.*

24 Tishrei —
24 Teves — לע"נ יענטא רחל בת
מוה"ר חיים משולם פייביש לענגער ז"ל
Dedicated by her family
24 Nissan —
24 Tammuz —

CONNECTING TO THE SOURCE

DAY 25

25
Tishrei

25
Teves

25
Nissan

25
Tammuz

*A*aron had been coming to shul since his father first brought him at age 5. He had grown up playing in the shul, running between the rows of seats, hiding in the coat closet, and snacking with his friends on the front stairs. It had become like an extension of his house. Now, at age 19, Aaron still feels at home whenever he is in shul. He doesn't regard the shul as an exalted place.

David had never been to shul before in his life. The first time he entered, he was already 19, following uncertainly behind a rabbi he had met in the Old City of Jerusalem. As he walked through the front door, heard the sound of the men's voices and watched them swaying passionately, wrapped in their flowing tallesim, he thought, "This must be what it's like in Heaven."

For David in the above story — and those who prayed wholeheartedly in the shul he had entered — a mystery of Jewish life became solvable. What does it feel like to be near the *Shechinah*? We may not have access to the full experience provided only by the presence of the Beis HaMikdash; however, we each have the opportunity each and every day to have a glimpse.

Although we have never experienced the miracles, the *kedushah,* and the presence of the *Shechinah* that existed in the Beis HaMikdash, we can connect to the idea of this intense holiness through the experience of praying in shul. Though the presence of the *Shechinah* may not be obvious, It does indeed dwell within our shuls. For this reason, a shul is called a *mikdash me'at*,[1] a small Beis HaMikdash. *Chazal*[2] tell us that our prayers substitute for the *korbanos*, the sacrificial offerings. So holy are our shuls that according to *Chazal*,[3] they will be transported intact to Yerushalayim when Mashiach arrives.

The *Mishnah Berurah*[4] explains that since a shul is called *mikdash me'at*, the exhortation "and My Sanctuary shall you revere"[5] applies to every shul, each of which has the halachic status of *kedushah*.[6] The building itself must be approached with the recognition of its exalted status.

By safeguarding the holiness of the shul and the environment within it, we accomplish two vital spiritual goals. First of all, we educate our own hearts and souls in the knowledge of what it feels like to be in the *Shechinah's* presence, thereby giving ourselves the understanding we need to sincerely yearn for Its glorious return with the rebuilding of the Beis HaMikdash. Second, we show Hashem that we truly treasure the opportunity to encounter the holy *Shechinah*,[7] making the strongest case possible for bringing It back again into our midst.

Although the shul holds the exalted status we have

---

1. The Gemara (*Berachos* 6a) teaches that the *Shechinah* resides in places of holiness, such as in a shul when ten men pray together. *Rabbeinu Yonah* on *Berachos* 4a (pages of the *Rif*), s.v. *Eimasai*, and *Lechem Mishneh* to *Hilchos Tefillah* 8:1, explain that a prayer offered in a shul will certainly be heard regardless of whether it is offered by a single individual or with a *minyan*. This is in contrast to the prayer of one who prays at home or elsewhere, who cannot be sure that his prayer will be heard, unless he prays at the same time as a *minyan*.

2. See *Mishnah Berurah* 151:1, which cites the verse in *Yechezkel* 11:16: "And I will be for them a *mikdash me'at* (small sanctuary) in the lands where they arrived."

3. *Megillah* 29a.

4. 151:1.

5. *Vayikra* 19:30.

6. See *Chayei Adam, Klal* 17, *se'if* 6; *Pri Megadim, Mishbetzos Zahav* 151:1; *Sdei Chemed, Klalim, Maareches Beis, Siman* 43; *She'eilos U'Teshuvos Maharsham*, Vol. 1, *Siman* 10; and *She'eilos U'Teshuvos Yabia Omer, Orach Chaim* 7, *Siman* 24, for a discussion as to whether the *kedushah* is Biblical or Rabbinic.

7. See *Sifsei Chaim, Moadim*, Vol. 3, p. 394.

Take It With You

▸ *In the absence of the Beis HaMikdash, our shuls provide a place of kedushah where the Shechinah — albeit in a far lesser intensity — is present.*

▸ *Preserving the sanctity of the shul by according the building and the prayer services due respect offers us an opportunity to sense the Shechinah's presence.*

▸ *By demonstrating a desire to feel the Shechinah, we show God our eagerness to bring Him fully into our midst.*

described, it is by no means the only place where one can be aware of and feel God's presence. Connecting with the Divine Presence is always achievable to us, for there is no time or place devoid of God's presence. As we will examine in the next chapter, every situation is an opportunity to rouse oneself into awareness of yearning for His presence and to enable God's Name to be sanctified and honored throughout the world.

25 Tishrei —
לע"נ האשה פרומע מושע בת ר' זלמן משה ע"ה — 25 Teves
25 Nissan —
25 Tammuz —

CHAPTER 5:
KIDDUSH HASHEM IN EVERYDAY LIFE

BECAUSE OF YOUR WORD

DAY 26

26
Tishrei

26
Teves

26
Nissan

26
Tammuz

*I*magine you have everything you need and desire — a loving family; fine, upstanding children; a warm, supportive community; ample financial resources; a full, vibrant spiritual life; and good health. What would you feel that you have to gain with the coming of Mashiach? If you tried your utmost to feel the longing of metzapim l'yeshuah, upon what would that longing be based?

If the purpose of redemption is to enable us to enjoy a utopian life, the above question would be difficult to answer. On the surface nothing is missing from this scenario. Despite the fact that all good things will be bestowed in abundance and all delicacies will be as accessible as dust, that is not the purpose of redemption. Rather, it is for God to reveal His presence and establish His rule over the world.

From the beginning of the Jewish people's journey through history until the prophesied end of days, this specific goal — *kiddush Hashem*, the sanctification of God's Name — has been the primary purpose for which we have been sustained throughout the ages.[1] That is the message in the episode of the Spies, the scouts sent to assess the situation in Eretz Yisrael. Because of their fearful, faithless report,[2] the Jewish nation was threatened with complete annihilation.[3] In response, Moshe Rabbeinu pleaded on their behalf, saying:[4]

---

1. See *Daas Tevunos*, pp. 51, 178; *Shaarei Teshuvah, Shaar* 3; *Michtav MeEliyahu*, Vol. 1, p. 22, s.v. *Ach anu*; ibid., p. 313, s.v. *Hashem Yisbarach*; Vol. 3, p. 250, s.v. *Tachlis*.
2. *Bamidbar* 13:27-29.
3. Ibid. 14:11-12.
4. Ibid. vs., 14-16.

Then Egypt...will hear, and they will say about the inhabitants of this land... "You killed this people like a single man!" Then the nations that heard of Your fame will say, "Because Hashem lacked the ability to bring this people to the land that He had sworn to give them, He slaughtered them in the Wilderness." And Hashem responded,[5] "'I have forgiven because of your word."

Rashi[6] notes that the major thrust of Moshe Rabbeinu's prayer to God was that God's Name would be desecrated if the Jewish people were to be wiped out. God had manifested His presence among Israel so publicly that none of the nations would believe that Israel was to blame for its own downfall. Instead, the Egyptians and others would gloat that the "mighty" God was too weak to combat the Canaanites and their gods. This would defeat the purpose of creation, which is to bring glory to God.[7] Moshe Rabbeinu contended that God should forgive the Jewish people to protect His own honor, and God agreed "because of your word." It is for that reason that God added to His response, "But as I live — and the glory of Hashem shall fill the entire world..."[8]

The Netziv explains:[9] "Before the Spies sinned, the world was to have achieved its true purpose simply through the Jewish people's entering and inhabiting Eretz Yisrael." The Jews living according to the Torah and cleaving to God in their holy land would have been enough to sanctify God's Name throughout the world,[10] as foretold in the verse, "Then all the peoples of the earth will see that the Name of Hashem is proclaimed over you [the Jewish nation] and they will revere you."[11]

The Jewish people's purpose would have been fulfilled in peace, and there would have been no need for exile. Instead, God spread His Name by scattering His people

---

5. Ibid. v. 20.
6. Ad loc. s.v. *kidvarecha*.
7. See *Yeshayah* 43:7.
8. *Bamidbar* 14:21.
9. *Haamek Davar* on *Bamidbar* 14:20.
10. See *Ohr Gedalyahu, Shemos*, p. 82, s.v. *V'haArizal hiksheh*.
11. *Devarim* 28:10.

Take It With You

- *Redemption is necessary for God to reveal His presence.*

- *Because the Jewish people sinned, God spread His name by scattering them throughout the world.*

- *Metzapim l'yeshuah includes refining our behavior through the filter of kiddush Hashem.*

throughout the world.[12]

Rav Friedlander[13] explains that *metzapim l'yeshuah* is not only a belief in the future — that God will redeem us speedily in our time. It also defines our service of Hashem each and every day. *Metzapim l'yeshuah* is more than believing in and hoping for the coming of Mashiach; it is the refining of our words and actions through the filter of *kiddush Hashem*,[14] striving to eliminate anything that prolongs the suffering of the Jewish people's beloved "Husband."[15] Thus, the significance of being *metzapim l'yeshuah* is that God's Name be sanctified and honored throughout the world.[16]

One of the most powerful steps one can take right now, as the Messianic era moves closer, is to speed up this slow process by reaching a level of longing for the redemption, and by taking every opportunity that presents itself to help reveal and sanctify God's glorious Name throughout our communities, our cities and countries, and our entire world.[17]

---

12. See *Ohr Gedalyahu, Bereishis*, p. 23, s.v. *Ha'Ohr Ha'Chaim*; *Michtav MeEliyahu*, Vol. 2, p. 255, s.v. *V'kasvu ha'mekubalim*.
13. *Sifsei Chaim, Pirkei Emunah U'Bechirah*, Vol. 2, p. 218. s.v *K'fi*.
14. God will achieve His underlying purpose for creation — bestowing the ultimate kindness on mankind — only when His presence is no longer hidden. In our time, *kiddush Hashem* — sanctifying God by revealing His greatness to the world — is the means to achieve that purpose. God wants us to sanctify His Name not because He wants his power and glory to be known, but because He can give His creation the benefit of His boundless goodness only when mankind finally comes to recognize and serve Him.
15. *Sifsei Chaim, Moadim*, Vol. 3, p. 353, s.v *lamadnu*.
16. *Sichos Mussar* (Rav Chaim Shmulevitz), *Shaarei Chaim, Maamar 27*, p. 113 [5733 Maamar 12]. See *Rambam, Hilchos Melachim* 12:5, which states that this will result in the opening of the door to His bountiful blessing.
17. See *Ohr Gedalyahu* loc. cit.

> **26 Tishrei —**
> **26 Teves —**
> **26 Nissan —**
> **26 Tammuz —** In memory of ה"ע יצחק בת יענטקא מורדתי אמי
> P.K. & JoD Koenigsberg and family

IN LIFE AND DEATH

DAY 27

*I*mmediately prior to his murder by the Nazis, Rav Elchonon Wasserman addressed his fellow prisoners:

"Apparently, they consider us tzaddikim in Heaven, for we were chosen to atone for Klal Yisrael with our lives. If so, we must repent completely here and now...We must realize that our sacrifices will be more pleasing if accompanied by repentance, and we shall thereby save the lives of our brothers and sisters in America."[1]

The term *kiddush Hashem*[2] most often brings to mind the courage of one put to death because he is a Jew.[3] It finds powerful expression in the requirement to be prepared to die[4] rather than be forced to violate one of the commandments; this pertains primarily to the three cardinal sins of murder, idolatry, and forbidden relations.[5]

27 Tishrei

27 Teves

27 Nissan

27 Tammuz

---

1. *Reb Elchonon*, Yonoson Rosenblum (ArtScroll/Mesorah Publ.), p. 410. Rav Elchonon also cautioned the prisoners that no impure thought should enter their minds, God forbid, which would render their sacrifice (similar to a sacrificial offering) unfit, as they were now fulfilling the greatest mitzvah.

2. The obligation to sanctify God's Name is recorded in *Sefer HaMitzvos, Mitzvas Asei* 9; *Hilchos Yesodei HaTorah* 5:1. Regarding *chillul Hashem*, see *Sefer HaMitzvos, Mitzvas Lo Saaseh* 63. See also *Rambam, Hilchos Yesodei HaTorah* 5:4 and 10.

3. See *Michtav MeEliyahu*, Vol. 1, p. 11, s.v. *Mah niflah*, which discusses what enables a simple Jew to have the courage to die for being a Jew.

4. See *She'eilos U'Teshuvos HaRashba*, Vol. 5, *Siman* 55, and *Sefer Chareidim* 9:16, which state that one who is prepared, when reciting "with all your soul," to fulfill this dictum is considered as if he had given his life for being a Jew and has sanctified Hashem's Name. See also *Yesod V'Shoresh HaAvodah, Shaar* 1, Ch. 11; *Tzidkas HaTzaddik*, *Os* 158.

5. See *Ramban* to *Vayikra* 18:21, s.v. *V'hinei hizkir*, which states that

But today, when *baruch Hashem* most Jews live in freedom and peace, our challenge is not so much in giving up our lives, but rather, in the way we live. The following words, written by Rav Avraham Pam, define the task of today's generation:[6]

> *Over a half-century ago, six million Jews gave up their lives to sanctify Hashem's Name. Today, there are many hundreds of thousands of Jews who carry the names of these kedoshim. While the kedoshim gave up their lives for kiddush Hashem, our task is to live a life of kiddush Hashem. By acting courteously and honestly, by speaking in a kind and pleasant way, a person will promote kiddush Hashem in his personal interactions. This will help bring the fulfillment of the beautiful prophecy of Yeshayah,[7] who foresaw the day when "All those who see them will recognize that they are the seed that Hashem has blessed."*

A verse in *Tehillim*[8] provides an insight into one's duty to sanctify God's Name in both life and death. It speaks of Jewish life as "A song whose foundation is in the holy mountains." Rav Pam,[9] citing the *Midrash Shocher Tov*,[10] comments that Judaism is based on two great mountains: *Har HaMoriah*, where *Akeidas Yitzchak* took place, and *Har Sinai*, where God gave the Torah to the Jewish people. *Har HaMoriah* taught Jews how to sanctify God's Name by sacrificing their lives for Him. *Har Sinai* taught Jews how to live a life of *kiddush Hashem* by following the Torah.

However, the concept of *kiddush Hashem* is not only

----

there are certain sins that, by their very nature, constitute *chillul Hashem*. See *Vayikra* 19:12; *Toras Kohanim, Kedoshim, Parashah* 2; *Rashi* to *Taanis* 23a, s.v. *Nimtza Shem Shamayiin mischaleil*. See also *Vayikra* 19:2, 21:6,8; 22:2; *Malachi* 1:11-12; 2:11); other examples of *chillul Hashem* are mentioning God's Name in vain (*Shaarei Teshuvah of Rabbeinu Yonah* 3:61); cheating in business (*Toras Kohanim, Kedoshim* 8); and lying (*Sefer HaYirah of Rabbeinu Yonah,* 177).
6. *Atarah L'Melech*, pp. 99-104; *Rav Pam on Chumash*, Rabbi Sholom Smith (ArtScroll/Mesorah Publ.), p. 138.
7. 61:9.
8. 87:1.
9. *Atarah L'Melech* loc. cit.
10. *Mizmor* 87:3.

to be understood within the realm of performing mitzvos. An act can be a *kiddush Hashem* without being a specific Torah commandment, and likewise, an act can be a *chillul Hashem* — a desecration of God's Name — Heaven forbid, without being a specific sin. The defining factor is whether a certain act creates a positive or negative impact on the glory of God and the esteem with which His Torah is regarded by others, Jew and non-Jew alike.[11] Through our actions, others assess Judaism's role in shaping the conduct and character of man.

The Rambam delineates the prescription for successful *kiddush Hashem*:[12] treating people well, dealing honestly in business, and maintaining a positive attitude. As the Gemara teaches,[13] one who treats others with kindness and honesty will cause people to say, "Fortunate are the parents and teachers who raised such a person." Conversely, there is no greater degradation for a Jew than to act in a way that will make people say the opposite.

Over sixty-five years ago, millions lost their lives solely because they were Jews. Today, in place of the bitter pill of giving up one's life, God offers us the sweet elixir of serving Him with honesty, patience, and kindness. *Metzapim l'yeshuah* mandates that we grab the offer.

Take It With You

▸ *Giving up one's life so as not to commit a cardinal sin, or because one is a Jew, is a powerful expression of kiddush Hashem.*

▸ *Today, most people are called upon to sanctify God's Name by conducting their lives in a way that brings glory to His Name.*

---

11. See *Bava Kamma* 113a, *Yoma* 86a. See also *Rashi* to *Vayikra* 25:48; *Choshen Mishpat* 348:1; *Mesillas Yesharim*, Ch. 11, s.v. *Anfei chillul Hashem*.
12. *Hilchos Yesodei HaTorah* 5:11.
13. *Yoma* 86a.

27 **Tishrei** — לזכות מרים אורה בת מאטיל
27 **Teves** — In memory of
Lester and Annabel Abberbock a"h
Dedicated by Ellen Abberbock
27 **Nissan** —
27 **Tammuz** —

GOD'S AMBASSADORS

DAY 28

28 Tishrei

28 Teves

28 Nissan

28 Tammuz

Greta, a cashier in a local supermarket, thinks the Jewish people are really something special. She has frequently seen them dig a small item out of the recesses of the shopping cart and plop it down on the conveyor belt with an apologetic, "Here, I almost forgot this."

Nancy, a hard-working customer service representative in a local discount store, occasionally feels a sense of foreboding when she sees a Jewish customer waiting for her assistance. "Sometimes it seems they're out to get more than they should," she tells her boss.

Although the majority of Torah law governs our interactions with fellow Jews, when *kiddush Hashem* and *chillul Hashem* are at stake, the sensitivities of non-Jews are vitally important to consider.[1] A Jew cannot fulfill his obligation to make God beloved by the people of the world unless he pays careful heed to how he treats *every* individual.

One of the first examplars of this was Avraham Avinu. After saving his nephew Lot and the captives of Sodom, Avraham Avinu returned the spoils that he had recovered to their original owners.[2] In doing so, he is credited with sanctifying God's Name.[3]

One of the most-frequented areas of interaction between Jewish and gentile life is in the world of business.[4] It is in these many daily interactions that one has the opportunity to literally make or break God's Name,

---

1. See *Devarim* 9:28; see also *Shemos* 32:12.
2. *Bereishis* 14:22-24.
3. *Tanna D'Vei Eliyahu*, Ch. 23; see *Sefer Chassidim*, Os 14.
4. See *Pele Yo'eitz, Erech Chillul Hashem.*

making the Jewish creed and lifestyle synonymous with honesty, or *chas v'shalom* the opposite.

> *Rabbi Shimon ben Shetach received a donkey that had been purchased from a non-Jew as a gift from his students. After taking possession, Rabbi Shimon's students noticed that a pearl had become lodged in the animal's neck. They joyfully informed their teacher that he would now have enough resources to spend all of his time in study.*
>
> *Rabbi Shimon, however, knew that the law that the pearl need not be returned was intended to protect Jews against mistreatment in business dealings with gentiles.[5] Rabbi Shimon knew that he had not been victimized and therefore, he determined that the pearl must be returned to the seller. "Do you think Rabbi Shimon ben Shetach is a barbarian?" he asked. "I would rather hear 'Blessed is the God of the Jews' than have any profit in this world."[6]*

At an address at the Agudath Israel of America's 87th National Convention,[7] Rabbi Mattisyahu Salomon, citing the *Smag*,[8] explained the prophet Yeshayah's prophecy that the Jews who will usher in the arrival of Mashiach will be those who "do not engage in dishonest behavior, do not speak falsely, and whose mouths contain no language of misleading."

These traits are prerequisites, said Rav Salomon, because Mashiach's arrival is to bring unprecedented *kiddush Hashem* into the world, awakening the other nations

---

5. *Yerushalmi Bava Metzia* 2:5. See also *Tosafos, Bava Metzia* 87b, s.v. *Ela; Bava Kamma* 113a; *Rambam's Commentary to the Mishnah, Keilim* 12:7.
6. *Devarim Rabbah* 3:3.
7. November 26, 2009.
8. *Mitzvas Lo Saaseh* 2, *Mitzvas Asei* 74, which state that all those who steal from gentiles are guilty of *chillul Hashem* for they cause the gentiles to say, "The Jews do not uphold the Torah," and they cause them to say, "See how God chose for His portion a people of thieves and frauds." See also *Smag, Lo Saaseh* 152; *Hagahos Maimoniyos, Hilchos Gezeilah V'Aveidah* 1[a]; *Meshech Chochmah* to *Shemos* 21:14; *Maharsha, Kesubos* 67a, s.v. *I'ba'eis eima lichvodo hu de'avid; Sefer Chareidim*, Ch. 29, *Os* 101; and *Rambam, Commentary to the Mishnah, Keilim* 12:7.

Take It With You

▸ *Every Jew is a representative of Torah and Judaism to the world.*

▸ *Acts of integrity have a positive impact; conversely, business indiscretions impact negatively on the Name of God.*

▸ *Those who will usher in the arrival of Mashiach will be the ones who conduct themselves honestly.*

to the truth of God and His Torah. Were he to come at a time when Jews are regarded as dishonest, the world's reaction would be "What? He has come for those swindlers!"

"Hashem will only bring Mashiach," Rabbi Salomon exclaimed, "when it will be a *kiddush Hashem*!"

All Jews are ambassadors of God and His Torah. Whoever we are and wherever we may be, others will draw conclusions through our actions. Our small indiscretions can leave an indelible stain on the Name of God Himself.[9] And by the same token, our small acts of integrity can illuminate the world.

---

9. See *Yoma* 86a; *Mesillas Yesharim*, Ch. 11.

28 Tishrei —
28 Teves —
28 Nissan —
28 Tammuz —

MITZVOS DONE RIGHT

DAY 29

*X*enix, a visitor from another planet, inexplicably finds himself in the office of a diamond merchant in Manhattan's Diamond District. *He watches the merchant weighing and examining tiny colorless rocks, which look much like the gravel on the surface of his planet. He sees the merchant wrap the rocks in paper and lock them securely in a vault. Xenix has no idea what purpose these little rocks serve, but from his observations, he perceives their great value to the merchant.*

29
Tishrei

29
Teves

29
Nissan

29
Tammuz

Like Xenix in the merchant's office, a gentile who observes a Jew performing a mitzvah may have no inkling as to its value. Why does the Jew refuse to eat something, when stuck in an airport, because there is nothing with an acceptable *hashgachah?* Why do Jewish men and especially women dress far more modestly than is today's norm?

The actual spiritual value of any mitzvah is not even given to the Jewish people to understand fully.[1] For the gentile, it would appear to be all the more mystifying. How, then, can a Jew's observance of Torah and mitzvos constitute a *kiddush Hashem?*[2] Does the rest of the world see God's glory in our seemingly inexplicable lifestyle, or do they see an interesting oddity?

According to the Chofetz Chaim,[3] to transmit the mes-

---

1. *Avos* (2:1) states, "Be careful to perform a minor mitzvah in the same manner as a major one, for you do not know the reward for each mitzvah." See *Derech Hashem, Chelek* 1, Ch. 4:7, for an explanation.
2. *Rambam, Hilchos Yesodei HaTorah* 5:10.
3. Cited in *Tzidkasam Omedes La'ad,* p. 271. See *Midrash Tanchuma, Parashas Vayigash, Siman* 6, s.v. *Yelamdeinu rabbeinu.* See also

sage of *kiddush Hashem,* our observance of the mitzvos must convey that they possess priceless value in our eyes. Like the merchant's careful handling of his diamonds, our reverent, joyful handling of our service to Hashem can convey to those lacking in understanding of what we are doing that this is a treasure.

As Jews, we know that even though God created a physical world, it was not meant to be merely dirt and stone, vegetation, animals and humanity, living and dying and returning to the earth. The physical world was to be imbued with the spirit of Godliness, but how could holiness be channeled into life on Planet Earth? It would be like trying to teach a stone to appreciate music.

God gave us the Torah and mitzvos as the means to infuse His light into the material world. When Jews follow the Torah's teachings with sincerity, consistency, and sacrifice, the rest of the world will come to perceive the priceless value of our Divine mitzvos. Therefore, Jews who conduct themselves in this manner are praiseworthy in the eyes of others.

> *A rabbi was driving on the New York State Thruway when his car broke down. He called for a tow truck. As he rode to the repair shop, the friendly driver mentioned that he was fascinated by "the rabbi's people."*
>
> *"Can I ask you a question?" the driver said. "What happens on Friday afternoon when the sun starts to set? Whenever I come to service a car at that time of day, they hand me the car keys and say, 'Do whatever you can. I'm leaving.' What's so important?" The rabbi explained that when Shabbos begins, Jews cease all weekday activity.*
>
> *"But what happens," the driver asked, "if it's an expensive car?"*
>
> *"If Shabbos is coming," the Rabbi replied, "it doesn't matter how expensive the car is."*
>
> *"That's incredible," the driver responded. "You people really stand up for what you believe in!"*

Kochvei Ohr, end of *Siman* 2.

It isn't the deep explanation of the Torah that awakens the rest of the world to its value. Rather, it is the astounding vision of a nation living by the Torah's laws — a diverse, vibrant, thriving people united by the same galvanizing force that forged us into a nation when we stood together at Mount Sinai. And this is the means whereby we can hasten Mashiach's arrival, rouse ourselves into yearning for God's Presence, and enable His Name to be sanctified and honored throughout the world.

Take It With You

▸ *Performing mitzvos and keeping the Torah serve as an opportunity to create kiddush Hashem.*

▸ *A person loses an opportunity by not giving mitzvos their proper value.*

▸ *When others see how precious a mitzvah is to a Jew, they perceive on some level that this is indeed the manifestation of God's will in the world.*

29 Tishrei —
29 Teves —
29 Nissan —
29 Tammuz —

NO SECRETS

DAY 30

30
Tishrei

1
Shevat

30
Nissan

1
Av

Since the purpose of *kiddush Hashem* is to reveal God's Name among the people of the world, does it matter what a Jew does when he is alone? If there is no one present to get a negative impression of God and the Jewish people, what harm is done?

One way to arrive at an understanding of why private actions have an impact on *kiddush Hashem*[1] is to examine what is actually meant by holiness and sanctity. The command, "*V'nikdashti — I shall be sanctified* among the Children of Israel"[2] — describes the Jewish mission of revealing the Divine and distinctly separate nature of the Creator and the wisdom of His laws before the eyes of the world. The Hebrew word *kedushah*, generally translated as "holiness" or "sanctity," literally means "separate."[3]

God is called *Hakadosh Baruch Hu — the Holy* [Separate] *Blessed One*. This connotes that He is entirely removed from all physical existence and its inherent limitations.[4] We sanctify God's Name not merely by adhering to God's commandments, but by separating ourselves from the downward pull of our physical natures and elevating ourselves in pursuit of spiritual ideals and spiritual goals.[5] To the degree that we succeed, we bring about a *kiddush Hashem* — a sanctification of God's Name. By continually cultivating our own *kedushah*, we augment and emulate God's *kedushah* in the world.[6]

---

1. See *Michtav MeEliyahu*, Vol. 1, p. 22.
2. *Vayikra* 22:32.
3. *Rashi, Vayikra* 19:2, s.v. *Kedoshim tiheyu.*
4. See *Michtav MeEliyahu*, Vol. 4, p. 146, s.v. *Amru.*
5. *Nesivos Olam, Nesiv HaPerishus*, Ch. 1, as explained in *Mi'maamakim* on *Bereishis*, p. 213. See also *Michtav MeEliyahu*, Vol. 4, p. 147, s.v. *V'nidrash mei'itanu.*
6. Ibid. Vol. 2, p. 255, s.v. *V'kasvu ha'mekubalim;* ibid. Vol. 4, p. 147,

But the physical nature of our world constantly tugs at our hearts, distracting us from the subtler, yet deeper longings of our souls. By excessively giving in to these urges — for power, money, glamour, honor, sensory gratification, and so forth — we add paint-strokes to a man-made picture of a world that is just-for-the-moment, and lacking in design and purpose. This is *chillul Hashem*, related to the Hebrew word *challal*, which implies emptiness.[7]

The pursuit of *kiddush Hashem*, in fact, begins with oneself.[8] A person cannot be full of guile and arrogance in his private dealings and believe that he can create *kiddush Hashem* by "making a good impression" on the world. If a person does not ingrain *kiddush Hashem* deep within his personality, the void is like an empty well from which nothing can be drawn.

Rav Dessler[9] confirms that of three levels of *kiddush Hashem*, the first and foremost is for a person to seek sanctity within himself. Once he achieves that level, he can strive to make a *kiddush Hashem* in public among ten Jews or more.[10] The last step is to perfect *kiddush Hashem* among non-Jewish people.[11]

This is a personal journey, one that each person takes at his own pace, beginning at his own starting line. Yet, if

---

s.v. *V'nidrash mei'itanu*, where Rav Dessler includes this in the mitz-vah of "*V'halachta bid'rachav.*"

7. See *She'eilos U'Teshuvos Noda BiYehudah, Orach Chaim, Siman 35*, s.v. *V'adayon*, which states that the sin itself, even if no one else knows about it, is a *chillul Hashem*. See also *Rambam, Hilchos Yesodei HaTorah* 5:10; *Sefer Yereim, Mitzvah* 6; *Michtav MeEliyahu,* Vol. 4, p. 88; *Chasam Sofer, Parashas Emor,* s.v. *V'lo sechalelu.* However, see *Tos. Yom Tov, Avos* 4:4.

8. *Michtav MeEliyahu,* Vol. 3, p. 117, s.v. *Kol maaseh; Leket Sichos Mussar,* pp. 265, 269.

9. *Michtav MeEliyahu* loc. cit.; also cited in *Matnas Chaim* on *Yomim Nora'im,* p. 165, s.v. *kvar.*

10. See *Rambam, Hilchos Yesodei HaTorah* 5:2. Whereas private transgression affects only an individual sinner's relationship with God and the sway of Torah in his life, public transgression has the added dimension of diminishing God's honor in the eyes of others. The negative consequences increase geometrically. See also *Kochvei Ohr,* end of *Siman* 2; *Chochmah U'Mussar,* Vol. 2, p. 302; *Chofetz Chaim, Pesichah* 6.

11. *Michtav MeEliyahu,* Vol. 3, p. 118, s.v. *Baal ha'madreigah;* see *Sotah* 10b.

Take It With You

► *Even though the recognition of God's "glory" is the central issue in kiddush Hashem, acts done in private can constitute either a kiddush Hashem or a chillul Hashem.*

► *Making a kiddush Hashem is a journey initiated with one's seeking sanctity within himself. It then proceeds to interaction among other Jews, and then to interaction among gentiles.*

each Jew in the world today would take it upon himself to embark on this journey, the ultimate destination — *Geulah*, a world in which God's Name is sanctified among all people — would surely come rapidly into view.

WITHOUT APPLAUSE

DAY 31

*I*n the middle of a busy Sunday afternoon, Shayna threw one more load of laundry into the washing machine, dressed her baby in his snowsuit, strapped him into his car seat, and drove to a small, brick school building two miles away. There, she pulled into a line of cars idling adjacent to the sidewalk and waited.

Five minutes later, a group of children emerged from the building. Shayna spotted Baruch, the child she had come to pick up. A sweet young woman held him by the hand and was patiently guiding him to Shayna's car. Baruch wasn't Shayna's son — he was one among a few dozen special children who took part in a Sunday program to give their families a bit of respite. No one but Shayna's husband knew that she was one of a handful of volunteer drivers who helped make the program possible.

In the scenario above, Shayna knows she will never get recognition for her weekly sacrifice of time. Her friends will never have the chance to laud her for her selflessness. Even in her own mind, her commitment is a small one; it takes one half hour, once a week, to pick up Baruch and bring him home. She is not motivated by the desire to be a hero of *chesed* or a role model to the community. What motivates her is the opportunity to help a fellow Jew. It is pure *ahavas Yisrael*, and a pure *kiddush Hashem*.

Deeds one performs without fanfare or public notice comprise a strong level of *kiddush Hashem*. Even though it may seem that the glorification of God's Name would be greater if the act were publicly acknowledged, *Michtav MeEliyahu*[1] explains that a private act is guaranteed to

1. Vol. 3, p. 117, s.v. *Kol maaseh*, and p. 118, s.v. *Mipnei mah*. See

1 Cheshvan

2 Shevat

1 Iyar

2 Av

Take It With You

▸ *Kiddush Hashem done in private is guaranteed to be purely for God's sake, with no ulterior motive of honor or other gain.*

▸ *Even a small private act of kiddush Hashem has inordinate value.*

be pure of any potential ulterior motives such as a desire for honor, fear of rejection, or the expectation of receiving a return favor in the future. For this reason, *kiddush Hashem* done in private, when a person is alone with God, is a most powerful act.

Illustrating this point, there is an episode recorded in the Gemara[2] in which Rabbi Yose asks Rabbi Chanina ben Tradyon to enumerate his merits. Despite his exalted stature in learning and teaching Torah, Rabbi Chanina names only one deed: One time, his own money had become intermingled with money that had been set aside for the poor people's Purim feast. Because he could not differentiate between his own money and the charity funds, he gave everything to the poor. The merit of this act done in private, he knew, was unadulterated.

When no one is watching, and yet a person acts meritoriously, he proves that he knows that Someone is indeed watching. He confirms God's presence in his life, and thereby augments God's presence in the world, validating his desire to yearn for *Geulah*.

Mi'maamakim on *Bereishis*, p. 213.
2. *Avodah Zarah* 18a.

1 Cheshvan —
2 Shevat —
1 Iyar — לזכות עקיבא אליעזר בן דוד
Dedicated by Jonathan & Ilene Wilson
2 Av —

THE VALUE OF ULTERIOR MOTIVES

DAY 32

Chazal teach that *"maaseh avos siman le'banim"*[1] — the actions of our Patriarchs are a model for the children. Yaakov Avinu,[2] a paradigm of truth, was shown "a ladder stationed on the ground with its head (the top rung) reaching the heavens" as a symbol of his life's task, to demonstrate that one cannot successfully ascend the spiritual ladder in one stride.[3]

We all want to sense the spiritual world, to drink from the pure wellspring of spiritual life. However, at times it is difficult. In our service of Hashem, a person must complete the tasks required by each level of growth; it is not possible to always reach the top rung in one huge leap.

> On the long winter Friday nights, when Rav Dessler was 9 years old, he joined his revered father and his uncle in the pre-dawn hours and they would learn Torah together, until the morning service. Rav Dessler's mother rose too, and occupied herself by learning Midrash, Ramban, and the weekly parashah and commentaries. Rav Dessler recalled the joy he felt when his mother descended the stairs — "it was like a Yom Tov" — for she would bring steaming hot cups of coffee and delicious cakes for everyone.[4]

Even at the age of 9, Rav Dessler was motivated to rise in the early hours of the cold winter nights to learn. It wasn't the coffee or cakes that motivated him, and yet, those

---

1. See *Ramban, Lech Lecha* 12:6.
2. *Michtav MeEliyahu*, Vol. 1, p. 25.
3. It is for this reason that Yaakov Avinu, upon awakening, immediately began to pray to Hashem.
4. *Rav Dessler,* Yonoson Rosenblum (ArtScroll/Mesorah Publ.), p. 9.

special treats provided a bit of extra encouragement that helped him overcome the difficulty of doing that which he really wanted to do.

A pure mitzvah is difficult to achieve. Nevertheless, one should not simply abandon the effort in despair of reaching perfection. *Chazal*[5] teach that a person should always occupy himself with Torah and mitzvos even if they are done "*shelo lishmah* — for ulterior motives," because from that beginning, a person can come to do the mitzvos "*lishmah* — for their own sake."

Rav Chaim Volozhin clarifies the valuable role played by ulterior motives:[6]

> Learning Torah "shelo lishmah" is an important key to the stage at which one comes to learn lishmah. In fact, without this [preparatory stage] one is incapable of combating the evil inclination.

Initially, the sparks of *lishmah* are weak, without enough heat to sustain the consistent, passionate performance of the mitzvah. *Shelo lishmah* therefore acts like the kindling, providing the fuel to keep the flame burning and growing until *lishmah* is powerful enough to assume the role on its own. This occurs bit by bit, with each small spiritual advance one's soul achieves.

Nevertheless, ulterior motives do not always launch a person into the realm of higher motives. Rav Simchah Zissel Ziv[7] explained that only when one's underlying intention is pure from the beginning does *shelo lishmah* lead to *lishmah*. When one's primary goal is to achieve a pure mode of service of Hashem, *shelo lishmah* can be used successfully to ease one's struggle against the *yetzer hara* and thus lead eventually to the stage of *lishmah*. If one's basic desire is for the *shelo lishmah* for its own sake, then one's actions will not lead to *lishmah*. "In the spiritual life," says Rabbi Ziv, "one arrives only at the destination one intended in the first place."

Thus, even in our times, when God's presence in the

---

5. *Pesachim* 50b.
6. *Ruach Chaim* on *Pirkei Avos*. See *Michtav MeEliyahu*, Vol. 3, p. 115.
7. Cited in *Michtav MeEliyahu*, Vol. 3, p. 115. See ibid., p. 334.

world seems hopelessly submerged in a sea of materialism and physicality, we have the ability to succeed in serving God with near perfection. We can begin to sanctify the physical world around us, using its beauty and pleasure to take us where our souls truly long to go. With the proper destination firmly implanted in our hearts, God will ensure that we find our way.

Take It With You

▸ *A mitzvah performed with ulterior motives is valuable in leading a person to eventually do the mitzvah with pure motives.*

▸ *The pure motives can emerge only if that is the person's intent in the first place.*

▸ *Even in a materialistic world we (the Jewish people) can succeed in serving God properly.*

---

2 Cheshvan — In honor of our mother and bubby,
Rosalyn Snitow
by her children and grandchildren
3 Shevat — לע"נ העלמה שרה לאה ע"ה בת הרב יוסף שליט"א
2 Iyar —
3 Av —

THE WORLD OF ACTIVITY

DAY 33

3 Cheshvan

4 Shevat

3 Iyar

4 Av

*R*abbi Eliyahu Eliezer Dessler would encourage the boys whom he tutored privately during his days as a rabbi in London to actively pursue kiddush Hashem. He counseled Aryeh Carmel to walk to his lessons along a road where there was always a long line of beggars and to drop a coin into each cup. And he told Mordechai Miller to always go to the top deck of London's double-decker buses. Perhaps the fare collector would not arrive before it was time to alight, and then the obviously religious boy could hand his fare to another passenger and in a loud voice request of that person to pay the fare owed.[1]

Hidden within each aspect of the mundane world, there is a spark of holiness.[2] This must be so, for each part of creation is a work of God. Nevertheless, the spark is not readily noticeable. One does not experience a continual state of awe and reverence upon seeing the grass, trees, buildings, insects, animals, and objects that fill the landscape.

When a Jew, acting according to the dictates of the Torah, interacts with any element of the mundane world, he has an opportunity to unveil the spark of *kedushah* embedded within it. As Rav Tzadok HaKohen[3] phrases it, he "retrieves the sparks" of holiness that are scattered

---

1. *Rav Dessler,* Yonoson Rosenblum (ArtScroll/Mesorah Publ.), p. 154.
2. *Ohr Gedalyahu, Shemos,* p. 83, s.v. *U'b'vias Yisro.*
3. *Pri Tzaddik, Parashas Parah, Os* 3. See *Be'er Mayim Chaim, Bereishis* 32; *Pesachim* 87b, Maharsha ibid, s.v. *Lo higlah; Michtav MeEliyahu,* Vol. 2, p. 255, s.v. *V'kasvu ha'mekubalim.*

throughout the material world.

When a person interacts with the world in accordance with the Torah's teachings, he performs an act that rises to the level of learning the Torah's teachings. As the Baal Shem Tov stated, if someone who studies the Mishnah[4] about "one who exchanges a cow for a donkey" is considered to be engaged in God's Torah, then the same certainly is true for the person who actually makes this exchange in the marketplace, carefully carrying out his transaction according to the Torah's laws.

> *"Torah im derech Eretz,"*[5] *Rav Samson Raphael Hirsch's phrase referring to the application of Torah to all areas of worldly activity, describes this path toward kiddush Hashem. Seeking to make a kiddush Hashem in one's daily involvement in the outside world elevates everything in one's life, revealing its inherent spark of kedushah and turning it into a glimpse of God's glory.*
>
> *A student was about to leave Yeshivas Dvar Yerushalayim to take a position in a large auditing company in Boston. He asked his rebbi how to maintain his spiritual sensitivity and avoid being swallowed up by the secular outlook of the workplace.*
>
> *The rebbi advised, "Each time you begin a new project that will occupy you for a few months, closet yourself in your office for a short while... Sit down and ask yourself: How can I make this a kiddush Hashem?...This will help you not only spiritually, but financially as well, because you will make sure to do an efficient and thorough job. Keeping this thought in mind will transform your work into a vehicle for increasing Hashem's honor and you will grow from it."*[6]

The opportunity exists to sanctify God's Name even in our everyday lives in our everyday world. The Slonimer Rebbe explains that when a Jew performs God's will, aside

---

4. *Bava Kamma* 100a.
5. *Avos* 2:2; 3:17.
6. Adapted from *Hamodia* Magazine, February 4, 2009, 10 Shevat 5769.

from the actual fulfillment of the mitzvah, he is also accomplishing a *kiddush Hashem*.[7] The quality of our deeds is defined by their intent; thus, even the simple day at the office can become a source of spiritual bounty, overflowing with opportunities for *kiddush Hashem*.

Mesillas Yesharim[8] states the fundamental concept that the world was created for mankind to use in the service of God. Each Jew therefore has the right, and the obligation, to utilize this world and its bounty, not to satisfy his own cravings, but to serve God and to pursue holiness. In this way, we reveal the holiness in our otherwise mundane material world. With the Torah as our guide, we are equipped to ascend to each new level, and the world ascends with us as preparation for *Geulah*, a world in which God's Name is sanctified among all people.

▸ *Everything in creation harbors sparks of kedushah, for everything is a creation of God.*

▸ *When a person interacts with any part of creation according to the Torah's directives, he reveals the kedushah within that entity.*

▸ *A Jew who performs God's will accomplishes making a kiddush Hashem*

---

7. *Shaarei Teshuvah, Shaar* 3, p. 148; *Chovos HaLevavos, Shaar* 3, Ch. 5 (p. 244 in *Lev Tov*). See *Daas Chochmah U'Mussar*, Vol. 1, p. 225. Similarly, when he flouts God's will by refraining from a mitzvah or committing a transgression, then he creates a *chillul Hashem*.
8. Ch. 1.

---

3 Cheshvan —
4 Shevat —
3 Iyar —
4 Av — In memory of Rabbi Eliyahu Dov Glucksman
Dedicated by his daughter, Tzila Pass

STRATEGY 2: CREATING A PEOPLE UNITED

The Problem — *Hatred, Hurt, and Hostility* (Ch. 6)

❦

The Solutions — Solution I: *Living With Emunah and Bitachon* (Ch. 7)

Solution II: *Internalize Gratitude* (Ch. 7)

Solution III: *Ending Jealousy and Hatred* (Ch. 8)

Solution IV: *"V'Ahavta l'rei'acha kamocha"* (Ch. 9)

CHAPTER 6:
THE PROBLEM —
HATRED, HURT,
AND HOSTILITY

OUR LOSS

DAY 34

Note: This chapter is not intended to criticize any member of the Jewish people nor to point out deficiencies; rather, it is a heartfelt attempt to help overcome an unfortunate reality. The need for unity and ahavas Yisrael must be addressed so that we can truly hasten the Final Redemption, for the sake of every individual and for the Jewish nation.

4 Cheshvan

5 Shevat

4 Iyar

5 Av

*F*or many years, Yeshivah Middos Tovos prided itself on turning out graduates who were honest, helpful, and kind-hearted. The boys developed these traits through their sincere Torah learning and the example of their rosh yeshivah, Rabbi Goodman.

Gradually, however, the students became less receptive. Each new class was slightly more selfish and abrasive than the class that had preceded it. The harder the yeshivah tried to revitalize the spirit of its earlier years, the more the students scoffed. Finally, Rabbi Goodman decided to close the doors of the institution.

If, ten years later, a group of parents were to approach Rabbi Goodman and ask him to reopen his school, his first step would be to ascertain who their sons were. If they were no different from the classes enrolled a decade earlier, he would undoubtedly decline to reopen.

That reasoning helps to explain the Chofetz Chaim's teaching[1] that "If Hashem destroyed the Beis HaMikdash because of *sinas chinam* (baseless hatred) [and *lashon hara*, evil gossip], He won't permit it to be rebuilt if we have not cured ourselves of these spiritual maladies."

---

1. *Shemiras HaLashon* 2:7; see *Sefer Chofetz Chaim*, Intro.

God insists that His children, despite their diversity, regard each other as loving brothers. This is the condition for Him to manifest His clear presence among us. When we hate, slander, and hurt one another, He withdraws His presence. For this reason, say *Chazal*,[2] the second Beis HaMikdash was allowed to fall to our enemies.

The first Beis HaMikdash, however, was destroyed for reasons that appear far more serious than fractious interpersonal relationships. The generation living during the first destruction, the Gemara[3] explains, was engaged in cardinal sins: idol worship, immorality, and murder. In contrast, the Jews of the second Beis HaMikdash excelled in Torah, mitzvos, and charitable deeds. Nevertheless, their *sinas chinam* was enough to bring destruction down upon them. Thus we learn that *sinas chinam* is equated to the three cardinal sins.

If the two types of sins are comparable, a further question emerges. Why is the exile from the second Beis HaMikdash so lengthy — more than 27 times longer[4] so far — than the 70-year exile suffered after the first destruction?[5]

The Chofetz Chaim[6] explains that this enduring *galus* is not simply a punishment for the sins of those who lived during the second Beis HaMikdash. As in the opening scenario, the yeshivah remains closed, not because of the misdeeds of the students who were in the fateful final class ten years earlier, but because the new group of boys behaves no better.

It is simple logic that if *lashon hara* and *sinas chinam* brought down the second Beis HaMikdash, there can be no rebuilding until those sins no longer prevail. Sadly, after nearly 2,000 years, we have yet to complete this vital self-improvement project.

Obviously, there are complex forces at work when we cannot master a *middah* that is essential to our destiny. To

---

2. *Yoma* 9b.
3. Ibid.
4. The year 5770 is 1,940 years after the destruction of the second Beis HaMikdash.
5. *Netzach Yisrael*, Ch. 4.
6. *Sefer Shemiras HaLashon* 2:7.

▸ *The current
galus is the
outcome
of sinas
chinam.*

▸ *The galus
will not end
until sinas
chinam is
eradicated.*

▸ *Sinas
chinam
and lashon
hara are
symptoms
of
underlying
spiritual
ailments.*

▸ *Metzapim
l' yeshuah
requires
actively
working to
cure these
ailments.*

treat this spiritual malady, we must look beyond its symptoms and uproot its causes. In the coming days, we will place these negative forces under a powerful microscope and attempt to find the source of their stubborn tenacity: What is *sinas chinam* and why is it so harmful? Why is *lashon hara* so destructive? What are the root causes of these behaviors and how can we address the causes in a complete and lasting way?

Clearly, our goal is to disarm these "weapons of mass destruction," enabling the Jewish people to revel in the holiness and increased spirituality that the Final Redemption promises.

4 Cheshvan —
5 Shevat —
4 Iyar —
5 Av — לע״נ שמעון בן ראובן הכהן ז״ל
לע״נ ראובן בן אהרון הכהן ז״ל
Dedicated by the Levy & Greenfarb families

SINAS CHINAM DEFINED

DAY 35

I hate him," says the child about his classmate.
"Why do you hate him?" the child's mother asks.
"I just do," is his only answer.
"You can't hate someone for no reason," the mother responds. "There must be a reason."

5 Cheshvan

6 Shevat

5 Iyar

6 Av

If this mother is correct, then the term *sinas chinam*, baseless hatred, leaves us confused. Baseless hatred would seem to be the rare phenomenon of an unhealthy mind, not a trait plaguing sixty-five generations[1] of Jews.

To understand the term better, the first place to look is at the definition. *Sinas chinam* is not necessarily a passionate enmity. Rashi[2] defines it as disdain toward those who have committed an act for which it is not halachically justifiable to hate them.[3] According to the Gemara,[4] even a person who intentionally refrains from speaking to an acquaintance for three days is called a "*sonei*" — one who hates.

It takes only a small misunderstanding to plant the seeds of resentment. If a person resolves his grievance with the other party, nor expunges the negative feelings from within himself, then the seeds will quietly take root and grow. The Torah therefore warns:[5] "You shall not hate your brother in your heart; you shall reprove your fellow,

---

1. Based on generations of thirty years.
2. *Shabbos* 32b, s.v. *Sinas*.
3. See *Pesachim* 113b; see *Chofetz Chaim, Hilchos Lashon Hara, Klal* 4 and 8:5-6 for situations when it is permitted to bear ill feelings toward another person.
4. *Sanhedrin* 27b.
5. *Vayikra* 19:17.

and do not bear a sin because of him."[6] These words escalate simmering resentment from an unhealthy emotional state into a full-fledged Torah prohibition. *Sefer HaMitzvos*[7] and *Sefer HaChinuch*[8] count this prohibition as one of the Torah's 613 mitzvos. With some notable exceptions,[9] most commentators limit this prohibition against hating to the arena of the heart.

Surprisingly, the Torah does not regard a string of hateful insults, nor even a punch in the nose, as a transgression of the commandment "do not hate."[10] The Gemara[11] argues that when a person strikes or curses his fellow Jew, his transgression is defined by his act, such as hitting,[12] insulting,[13] cursing,[14] bearing a grudge,[15] or taking revenge,[16] rather than by the hatred motivating his act.

In the secular legal system, one cannot be prosecuted solely for his inner feelings, but only for his express actions. Yet the Torah seems to teach that there is a special toxicity to unexpressed hatred.[17] The Rambam[18] explains that when a person expresses negative feelings to his adversary, there is a potential for reconciliation. Hiding one's hatred leaves no possibility to improve the relationship

---

6. See *Pesachim* 113b regarding the permission, or even the mitzvah, to hate a sinner. See also *Rambam, Hilchos Rotze'ach* 13:14; *Kehillos Yaakov* to *Makkos* [old], *Siman* 19.
7. *Mitzvas Lo Saaseh* 302. See *Rambam, Hilchos Dei'os* 6:5.
8. *Mitzvah* 238.
9. *Raavad, Toras Kohanim; Ramban, Vayikra* 19:17; see *Rashi, Arachin* 16b, s.v. *Yachol lo yakenu*.
10. See *Magen Avraham, Orach Chaim* 156:2; *Mishnah Berurah* 156:4.
11. *Arachin* 16b, according to *Rambam, Hilchos Dei'os* 6:5 and *Sefer HaMitzvos, Lo Saaseh* 302. See also *Sefer HaChinuch, Mitzvah* 238.
12. *Rambam, Hilchos Sanhedrin* 66:12.
13. Ibid., *Hilchos Dei'os* 6:8.
14. Ibid., *Hilchos Sanhedrin* 26:1-2.
15. *Vayikra* 19:17.
16. Ibid.
17. However, see *Kesef Mishneh* to *Rambam, Hilchos Dei'os* 6:5, who says that the *Rambam's* focus is on hitting or yelling when not out of hatred. But certainly hating someone to the point of lashing out at him is worse than the explicitly prohibited act of hating him internally, without expression.
18. *Sefer HaMitzvos, Lo Saaseh* 302. See also *Chofetz Chaim, Pesichah, Lavin* 7, with *Be'er Mayim Chaim*.

and foster unity.[19]

Besides the damage hatred causes on its own, many other transgressions sprout from its toxic soil. That is why Rabbeinu Yonah[20] advises ridding oneself of hatred as a vital part of *teshuvah*. Without attacking this root cause, says Rashi,[21] a person will inevitably speak *lashon hara* about the subject of his hatred.[22]

Baseless hatred is the tiny splinter of negative feeling that gets under our skin and makes another person an irritation to us. Getting rid of these sharp shards of strife and smoothing out the edges of our relationships with our fellow Jews is a paramount objective for making our world ready for redemption. As the clock moves forward, minute by minute, day by day, and the struggles and anguish of the exile continue unabated, it becomes all the more urgent to dig in and complete this essential task that has eluded us for nearly 2,000 years.

Take It With You

▸ *The Torah prohibits us from hating a fellow Jew in our hearts, i.e., secretly.*

▸ *The Torah defines hatred as a feeling, rather than an act such as striking or cursing someone.*

▸ *Harboring secret hatred is especially harmful because doing so eliminates the possibility of reconciliation.*

▸ *Ridding ourselves of feelings of baseless hatred is the prime objective to make the world ready for redemption.*

---

19. See *Kehillos Yaakov, Chelek* 10, *Siman* 54; *Bircas Peretz, Parashas Kedoshim*, for further discussion.
20. *Shaarei Teshuvah, Shaar* 3, *Os* 39.
21. *Devarim* 22:14.
22. See *Matnas Chelko* on *Shaarei Teshuvah*, p. 230.

5 Cheshvan —
6 Shevat —
5 Iyar —
6 Av —

A SONG

DAY 36

6
Cheshvan

7
Shevat

6
Iyar

7
Av

Anyone who studies history knows that the era of the second Beis HaMikdash was a time of great Torah learning. It was the time of the yeshivah in Yavneh and the early Tannaim: Hillel,[1] Shammai,[2] and Rabban Yochanan ben Zakkai.[3] Nevertheless, there was *sinas chinam*, and that was enough to bring destruction. Even amid such greatness, God saw fit to remove His presence and allow His "home" to be destroyed.

Rav Schwab[4] explains that, in the chaotic period of Roman oppression, the Jews were violently divided as to how to respond. The chief division was between the religious Jews: those who followed the guidance of the Sages, and the *Biryonim*, those who favored an uncompromising militaristic approach. Therefore, the strife that resulted in the destruction of the Holy Temple was not only between the religious and the irreligious, but also, there were divisions within the religious ranks. [5]

---

1. Hillel was a noted Jewish religious leader, one of the most important figures in Jewish history. He is associated with the development of the Mishnah and the Talmud.
2. Shammai also was a scholar of the 1st century, and an important figure in Judaism's core work of Rabbinic literature, the Mishnah. Shammai was the most eminent contemporary and the halachic opponent of Hillel.
3. Rabban Yochanan ben Zakkai, one of the Tannaim, was an important sage in the era of the Second Temple, and a primary contributor to the core text of Judaism, the Mishnah.
4. Adapted from *Selected Speeches*, Rav Shimon Schwab (CIS Publ., Abridged Edition), pp. 22-23.
5. See *Meishiv Davar* 1:44, s.v. *V'hinei hamaarech*, where the Netziv explains that the hatred existed between those who had differing viewpoints as to how to serve God: A person who followed more stringent observances would see another person following a halachic leniency, and brand the practitioner a heretic. The Netziv laments that such hatred existed in his own time (the late 19th

Differing paths in doing God's will are not an enigma. Yaakov Avinu gave each of his sons, the progenitors of the twelve tribes, a different blessing,[6] reflecting each son's own character and potential.[7] When the tribes left Egypt, the Torah details the individuality of each one, encamped under its own flag,[8] each of them with one common path and one common goal, following in the path of Hashem under the canopy of the Clouds of Glory on the way to the Promised Land.[9]

The Torah is called a "song"[10] because of its diversity and complexity — similar to all the instruments of an orchestra and all the voices in a choir joining in harmony. These different components are the key to its splendid beauty.[11]

The Talmud[12] itself illustrates that righteous people can differ, most notably through the renowned disputes between Hillel and Shammai. These disputes also instruct us on *how* to differ: When each side hears and respects the other, and both are on a quest for truth,[13] then differences add depth and texture to the picture without diminishing unity by the smallest measure.[14]

Take It With You

▸ *In the Second Temple era there were notable disputes between prominent Torah scholars. We can learn how to differ from them.*

▸ *Differences can exist without engendering hatred.*

▸ *When each side is on a quest for truth and hears and respects the other, differing viewpoints serve a proactive role, and indeed add to the overall depth and texture of the picture.*

---

century) as well, and was extremely difficult to uproot. See also *Selected Speeches* loc. cit.

6. *Bereishis* 49:1 ff.

7. See *Michtav MeEliyahu*, Vol. 1, p. 22, s.v. *Ach anu*; p. 313, *Hashem Yisbarach*.

8. *Bamidbar*, Ch. 2.

9. See *Ohr Gedalyahu, Bereishis*, p.136, s.v. *Mizmor*.

10. *Devarim* 31:19, "So now, write this song for yourselves, and teach it to the Children of Israel."

11. *Aruch HaShulchan*, Intro. to *Choshen Mishpat*, s.v. *V'chol machlokes.*

12. *Yevamos* 14b.

13. *Avos* 5:17; Rav Bartenura on ibid.

14. *Ohr Gedalyahu, Bereishis*, p. 136, s.v. *Af she'kol.*

DAY 37

7
Cheshvan

8
Shevat

7
Iyar

8
Av

THE PRICE OF
SINAS CHINAM

*F*or years, Chaim's doctor had been telling him to stay away from sugar. There was a family history of diabetes. He was over-weight, and if he were honest, he would admit that he always felt slightly ill after indulging in a big wedge of chocolate cake.

Despite the warnings, Chaim continued taking "sliver" upon "sliver" of his favorite cakes. Then came the day of reckoning: His doctor told him that he had diabetes. He shouldn't have been surprised, but he was. "Somehow," he said, "I never really believed sugar could hurt me."

Like Chaim, the Jewish people have been receiving highly credible warnings about the damage being caused by our own negative trait — *sinas chinam.*

And like Chaim, we act as if we have trouble believing that it is really doing any long-term harm.

If we want to avoid the most drastic outcome of our *sinas chinam* — delaying the Final Redemption until it must come, in its time, with an onslaught of travail[1] — then the time to act is now. Now is when we can pay heed to all that our Sages and rabbis have been telling us:

- *Sinas chinam* is not a one-shot transgression. It is a constant and ever-expanding transgression that continues to compound itself as long as hatred remains in a person's heart.

- A physical infection that is allowed to fester over a long period of time becomes increasingly difficult to cure. In the same way, the longer *sinas chinam*

---

1. See *Kreisi U'Pleisi*, Intro.

remains within a person, the greater is the effort required to "treat" the malady.

- As mentioned earlier, *sinas chinam* causes a person to commit other sins,[2] such as: divisiveness, *lashon hara*, *rechilus*, *onaas devarim*, embarrassing others, and *motzi shem ra*.
- The *Sifri*[3] says that a person who transgresses "do not hate" will eventually transgress "do not kill." As the Torah states:[4] "And a man will rise up against his brother and lie in wait for him and kill him." This is exactly what happened to Hevel, who was killed because of his brother Kayin's *sinas chinam*.[5]
- Chofetz Chaim[6] cites the Gemara[7] that recounts the troubles right here in the physical world that may beset a person who bears *sinas chinam*: "There will be fighting in his house, his wife will miscarry, and his sons and daughters will die young."

One reason that hatred leads to so much spiritual and physical difficulty is that it gives a person no rest. His grievance prods his heart, relentlessly demanding a response. *Mesillas Yesharim*[8] explains that "hatred is very hard to control because the person who hates greatly feels the pain of the wrong he believes was inflicted on him."

Inevitably, says the *Orchos Tzaddikim*,[9] the feeling leads the person to continually speak about his hatred. Many of us know someone who seems obsessed with a grievance. He is angry at his child's teacher or his brother-in-law or his boss or someone else by whom he believes he has been wronged. It seems that every conversation leads to that topic, and opens the floodgates to *lashon hara*. It almost appears as if the person actually enjoys reliving his suffering over and over again.

All of these points describe a spiritual malady that no

---

2. *Shaarei Teshuvah, Shaar* 3, Os 39.
3. *Sifri, Devarim* 19:11.
4. *Devarim* 19:11.
5. See *Bereishis*, Ch. 4.
6. *Ahavas Yisrael*, Ch. 1, s.v. *V'hinei chutz mizeh*.
7. *Shabbos* 32b.
8. Ch. 11.
9. *Shaar HaSinah*.

▸ *Sinas chinam is a continual state of sin that persists until the hatred is gone from one's heart.*

▸ *It gives rise to countless other sins, such as lashon hara, rechilus, divisiveness, and slander.*

▸ *The longer it remains within a person, the more difficult it is to eradicate.*

▸ *Awarness of the harm wrought by sinas chinam should motivate us to push it away.*

clear-thinking person would invite into his life. Knowing the harm *sinas chinam* does as we indulge in another small piece and then another, we can find the motivation to push it away and begin to restore ourselves to emotional and spiritual health.

7 Cheshvan —
8 Shevat —
7 Iyar —
8 Av —

ONAAS DEVARIM — SPEECH AS A SWORD

DAY 38

8 Cheshvan

9 Shevat

8 Iyar

9 Av

For many troubled Jews facing illness, marital problems, childlessness, and other difficult challenges, the home of HaRav Aharon Leib Shteinman is the address for comfort, advice, and blessings. In July, 2009, Rav Shteinman decided to take a strong preventive measure against the growing tide of woes. He wrote a letter to parents and teachers, urging them to avoid speaking onaas devarim — harmful words[1] — to their children and students, and to thereby protect themselves from tribulation:

"I wondered, what is going on?" wrote Rav Shteinman. "I tell people who need a *yeshuah* to try to remember whether they have hurt the people closest to them — I'm referring to teachers, parents, and friends. A father sometimes thinks that he can slap his son, or insult his wife. He thinks it's permitted because after all, they're his…

"Teachers also think that they have the child's benefit in mind when they criticize him…and even humiliate him. Everything is done in the name of well-meaning *mussar* and rebuke, which he is responsible to do. But that's not the case."

The following are sections of Rav Shteinman's letter,[2] which carry an important message for all educators:

---

1. See *Mesillas Yesharim*, Ch. 11, s.v. *Honaas devarim*, which states that it includes shaming one's neighbor by words in private, shaming him in public, and doing something to him that causes him to be ashamed in public.
2. *Positive Word Power, Michtav Oz.*

It is known in our holy Torah that there are laws between man and God as well as between man and his fellow man…The Rosh at the beginning of Peah[3] explains that Hakadosh Baruch Hu especially desires mitzvos that bring goodwill among mankind more than mitzvos that are between man and God.

Discussing the impetus for the letter, Rav Shteinman explained the difference between earlier and later generations:

In the past, teachers would educate the student properly and correct him if they saw he wasn't behaving as he should. Today, a teacher must control classes of upwards of forty children, and when a child makes noise or disturbs, he strictly admonishes the student even to the point of humiliating him. He doesn't do it to educate the child but to keep order in the class, and to vent his ire on the troublesome student.

The problem is that we're hurting our children and our students, the people who are the closest to us, even if we do it in all innocence.

People find justification for themselves, such as when a teacher or rabbi says he has to humiliate someone to ensure discipline. But it's not that way…A rabbi or teacher must get his point across, but in a way that doesn't embarrass the student.

Generally, the one who feels he is being humiliated will pay him back double. What the teacher said is certainly in the category of onaas devarim. One must be very careful with this. Parents also shouldn't embarrass their children.

Rav Shteinman then addresses the reason for the overflowing number of tragedies that have hit the religious community:

When one causes suffering to others, he is punished in this world too.[4] Every person must pay attention to what he does and what he says so as not to hurt

---

3. *Os* 3.
4. See *Tzidkas HaTzaddik, Os* 175.

his fellow man. *The truth is that the punishment is much worse in the World to Come, but most people are not aroused by what they can't see directly, so I am speaking about something that everyone understands well.*

Rav Shteinman concludes:

One who is careful not to hurt other people, all the blessings mentioned in the Torah will be granted to him and he will enjoy a pleasurable life in This World and the Next.

Take It With You

▸ *Rav Shteinman connects personal tribulations to onaas devarim — hurting or humiliating with words.*

▸ *Rav Shteinman cautions parents and teachers to the terrible harm done to their children, and ultimately to themselves, by engaging in onaas devarim.*

▸ *Rav Shteinman writes that there is no justification for onaas devarim, humiliating another individual.*

▸ *One who is careful not to hurt others will be granted all the blessings of the Torah.*

8 Cheshvan — In Honor of Rabbi and Mrs. Moshe Mintz
Dedicated by Shaya and Mindi Mintz
9 Shevat —
8 Iyar —
9 Av —

LASHON HARA: THE
LANGUAGE OF GALUS

9
Cheshvan

10
Shevat

9
Iyar

10
Av

*S*canning the list in his hand, the Chofetz Chaim addressed his customer.

"I see you've ordered all of my books except for *Sefer Chofetz Chaim*," he told the customer, a businessman from Warsaw. "Why leave that one out?"

"Well, I really do want that *sefer*," the man replied. "But, I'm in business. I meet many people every day, and it's impossible that I won't speak or hear *lashon hara*."

"I see," the Chofetz Chaim sympathized. "In fact, I thought about that problem myself, and even went to speak with Rav Yisrael Salanter about it. He told me, 'It's worthwhile for someone to read your *sefer* on *lashon hara* even if the only result will be a sigh when he completes it.'"

Lashon hara and *galus* are intertwined entities. The snake's *lashon hara*[1] launched the exile from the Garden of Eden. Generations later, during the Jewish people's most difficult period of exile in Egypt, the role of *lashon hara* again became clear. In *Parashas Shemos*,[2] Moshe Rabbeinu intercedes in a fight between two Jews, Dasan and Aviram. "Why would you strike your fellow Jew?" Moshe asks the wicked one. He replies, "Who appointed you as a dignitary, a ruler, and a judge over us? Do you propose to murder me, as you murdered the Egyptian?" Moshe realizes, "The matter is known." [3]

---

1. *Bereishis Rabbah* 19:4.
2. *Shemos* 2:13.
3. Ibid. v. 14.

156 / YEARNING WITH FIRE

The obvious meaning is that Moshe now realizes that his slaying of the Egyptian is general knowledge, and he may be called to answer for it. However, Rashi understands a deeper message. If Dasan and Aviram knew about the murder, then others must be spreading the tale. There must be *lashon hara* among the Jews, and therefore, "the matter is known" — Moshe understood why the Jews deserved such a bitter exile. Where there is *lashon hara*, there is *galus*.

For those who have internalized the destructiveness of *lashon hara*, there is no problem keeping away from it. They avoid it like a deadly virus.

> During the 1948 Israeli War of Independence, Rav Eliyahu Lopian was holed up in a crowded bomb shelter. A few of the people inside the shelter were speaking lashon hara, when suddenly Rav Elyah got up, opened the door, and stepped outside. "But there are rockets raining overhead," the people shouted, "You're putting yourself in great danger!" Rabbi Lopian calmly turned to them and said, "By sitting amid gossip, I am in even greater danger."[4]

How does one come to such vivid clarity on the stubborn habit of *lashon hara*? How does one put such a realistic sense of its danger into one's heart, that if forced to choose between falling bombs or *lashon hara*, one would see *lashon hara* as the greater danger? [5]

Apparently, knowledge is not enough. One can assume that every member of the Orthodox Jewish world knows that *lashon hara* prevents the Redemption. From early elementary school, Jewish children learn that *lashon hara* involves thirty-one Torah transgressions,[6] and that it sullies the holy work of a person's mouth, preventing his Torah

---

4. Aish.com, "Jewish Unity," Nov. 3, 2002.
5. See *Shemiras HaLashon*, Ch. 9 and (cited in) *Maarachos HaTeshuvah* (back of *Lev Eliyahu*, Vol. 3), Number 13, s.v *V'ha'Gra*, which quotes what the Vilna Gaon wrote in a letter: "Everything will come to justice, nothing will be lost, not even a 'slight word,' a sin with speech is more than everything…and *lashon hara* is equivalent to everything."
6. *Sefer Chofetz Chaim, Pesichah*. See ibid., which states that speaking or listening to *lashon hara* includes *chillul Hashem*.

▸ *Many
people
believe
lashon
hara is
impossible
to over-
come.*

▸ *One who
has a vivid,
internalized
sense of
lashon
hara's
damage has
no trouble
staying
clear of it.*

▸ *Intellectual
knowledge
alone
seems to
lack the
power to
initiate
a real
change.*

learning and *tefillah* from being accepted in Heaven.[7] In short, it brings misery into one's life.

So why are we not running away from it as Rav Elyah Lopian ran from the bomb shelter? One simple reason is that our knowledge about *lashon hara* has yet to enter our hearts. Most of us are like the businessman in the opening scenario, who cannot imagine a normal lifestyle without *lashon hara*. Nevertheless, as we look around us today, at a world limping through more than 708,000 days of exile, we know that now (today) is the time to do things differently.

---

7. Ibid.

> **9 Cheshvan** — In memory of our beloved mother
> and nana, Rita Aronson a"h
> לע"נ שיינדל רבקה בת זאב אלטר ע"ה
> Dedicated by the Rubinstein family of Sharon, MA
> **10 Shevat** —
> **9 Iyar** —
> **10 Av** —

THE ROOT OF
LASHON HARA

DAY 40

10 Cheshvan

11 Shevat

10 Iyar

11 Av

*M*y next-door neighbor has a beautiful, direct-from-the-factory new car. I can't afford a car like that. Therefore, I hate my neighbor. Everything he does bugs me, and I feel compelled to criticize him whenever his name comes up in conversation.

If one were to follow the train of thought above from its inception ("My neighbor has a new car") to its ending ("I feel compelled to criticize my neighbor"), it would seem to make no sense. Why would a person's longing for an object bring him to hatred and *lashon hara* against someone who happens to own that object?

By analyzing this senseless sequence of thoughts, we can begin to understand why *lashon hara* is so hard to control, and so pervasive that the Gemara[1] names *avak lashon hara* (the "dust" of *lashon hara)* as one of "three sins from which a person is not saved every day."

A person is usually attracted to sin by some benefit that makes the indiscretion seem worthwhile, at least for that moment. *Lashon hara,* on the other hand, offers no personal benefits.[2] It has no sensual appeal, and confers neither financial gain nor honor upon the person who indulges in it. Given these facts, speaking *lashon hara* appears to be an almost ludicrous pursuit.

However, if we take one step backward along the chain of cause and effect, we arrive at the powerful motiva-

---

1. *Bava Basra* 164b.
2. *Koheles* 10:11; *Arachin* 15b.

tion behind *lashon hara*: hatred. As cited earlier, Rashi[3] declares that a man who hates another will eventually commit slander. Rav Mattisyahu Salomon[4] adds that one might not even be aware of his resentment. Nevertheless, Rashi warns that "by transgressing the prohibition of 'hating his brother,' one will come to transgress the sin of *lashon hara*."

That still leaves a question: what causes the hatred? If we take one further step backward along the cause-and-effect chain, we find the answer. In the words of Rav Chaim Vital:[5] "Jealousy causes one to come to hatred."[6]

To be jealous, to envy what others have, is expressly prohibited in the Tenth Commandment, "You shall not covet."[7] This human tendency is prohibited in such a prominent, unequivocal way, perhaps because of the strife that follows in its wake.

Jealousy arouses vengeance[8] because the jealous person allows himself to illogically believe that the other person's gain is to blame for his deprivation.[9] That is the reason, explains Rav Salomon,[10] that jealousy is different from other material or sensual desires. A jealous person is

---

3. *Devarim* 22:14.
4. *Matnas Chaim, Maamarim*, Vol. 1, p. 230.
5. *Shaarei Kedushah*, Part 2, *Shaar* 4.
6. See *Ahavas Yisrael*, Ch. 3, where the Chofetz Chaim suggests that envy is one of the causes that lead to *sinas chinam*.
7. *Shemos* 20:14. See also *Devarim* 5:18, "And you shall not covet your fellow's wife, you shall not desire your fellow's house, his field, his slave, his maidservant, his ox, his donkey, or anything that belongs to your fellow." *Ramban* ibid. explains that this prohibition to covet forbids one to take action, such as seeking to coax or pressure the owner of the house to sell it. See also *Shulchan Aruch, Choshen Mishpat* 359:9,10; *Rambam, Hilchos Gezeilah* 1:9,10; *Chinuch, Mitzvah* 416; *She'eilos U'Teshuvos B'Tzeil HaChochmah*, Vol. 3, *Siman* 43, *Os* 10; *Sdei Chemed*, end of *Klal* 130; and *Aruch HaShulchan, Choshen Mishpat* 359:8. See *Tosafos, Sanhedrin* 25b, s.v. *Mai'kara savar*.
8. *Bamidbar* 25:11.
9. *Ramban* on *Shemos* 20:2 explains that the word "jealousy" is found by Hashem only in reference to the Jews serving idols and not in regard to any other sin. That is because in addition to the sin that exists when serving idols, the act itself is considered a "rebellion" against God. See *Pachad Yitzchak, Shavuos, Maamar* 14:2, p. 87.
10. *Matnas Chaim, Maamarim*, Vol. 1, p. 231.

not simply longing for the object of his desires. Rather, he wants vengeance against the one who does possess that object. This sentiment can be seen in its most elemental form among young children who fight over a toy; the winner loses interest in the toy soon after taking possession.

The hatred that arises from jealousy, says the *Orchos Tzaddikim*,[11] is so corrosive that, "It is appropriate for one to even agonize greatly to distance himself from it."

The *Gra*[12] warns that "It is the way of the evil inclination to burden a person with jealousy when he sees people of his status that have it good in this world. This brings about his separating himself from Torah and mitzvos… One should not listen to the evil inclination."

Despite jealousy's long reign over the human heart, there are ways to weaken and, ultimately, uproot it from within us. In doing so, we deprive hatred of its fuel, which in turn destroys the impetus for *lashon hara*. At that point, the path is paved for *Geulah*.

Take It With You

▸ *Unlike other sins, lashon hara does not provide any benefit, or any gain in status or money.*

▸ *Jealousy motivates hatred, which in turn motivates lashon hara.*

▸ *In overcoming the jealousy in one's nature, one is doing something powerful to hasten the Geulah.*

---

11. *Shaar HaSinah*, s.v. *Yeish raah*.
12. *Even Sheleimah*, Ch. 3, Os 5.

---

10 Cheshvan —
11 Shevat —
10 Iyar — לע"נ פישל אלי' בן חיים ז"ל
Dedicated by the Singer & Nussbaum families
11 Av — In honor of the Bar Mitzvah of
Daniel Eliezer Rubenstein
May you continue to go in the Derech HaTorah.
With love from your proud parents

CHAPTER 7:

SOLUTION I:
LIVING WITH EMUNAH AND BITACHON

❧

SOLUTION II:
INTERNALIZE GRATITUDE

STEP BY STEP

DAY 41

11
Cheshvan

12
Shevat

11
Iyar

12
Av

Nearly 2,000 years have passed and we, the Jewish people, still find ourselves in exile, longing for the Ultimate Redemption. Each incident of personal interactions gone awry — each instance of hostility, feud, communal strife, or division — indicates that the time is ripe to examine the possible solutions and to strive to remedy the situation. One thing is certain, we all — each and every one us — have the ability to repair our interpersonal relationships, thereby removing the final roadblock to the *Geulah*.

Although many people believe that we must build mountains of merit to warrant the *Geulah*, Rav Mattisyahu Salomon[1] assures us that this is not the case. We can hasten the *Geulah* by dismantling the barrier erected by *sinas chinam*.

By internalizing the message of the daily lessons and concretizing our new awareness through action, we can come one step closer to accomplishing this goal.

Each of the upcoming days in Chapters 7-9 offers a deeper understanding of the negative interpersonal forces at work beneath the surface. This will enable us to bring an end to hatred, hurtful speech, and negative behaviors, thereby setting the stage for the unity and brotherly love God longs to see among His children.

To facilitate implementation of the strategies, have highlighted practical suggestions in the "You Can Do It" section.

> *A master who asks his servant to fetch an item*
> *from the attic will not be angry when the servant*
> *does not leap from the bottom rung of the ladder*

---

1. *Matnas Chaim, Moadim.*

straight to the top. He understands that his servant can ascend the ladder only one step at a time.

Rav Chaim Volozhin[2] explains that Hashem is not disheartened by our slow progress in climbing the ladder to *achdus;* neither should we lose patience with ourselves. Every small step that we successfully take toward our goal is not just a pause upon a new, higher level; it is a springboard that energizes our continuing climb to *Geulah.*

The Torah states:[3] "And these words that I have commanded you today shall lie on your heart." The Rabbi of Kotzk explains the particular choice of words in the *pasuk* as follows:[4]

Intellectual knowledge is similar to water that accumulates behind a wall. Eventually, the water will soften the wall and a crack will emerge, allowing all the water to surge through.

Even if the "Solutions" about *achdus* lie only on the surface of the heart, it is worthwhile to study them, because at any moment, a minuscule crack will materialize, and through it, all the accumulated wisdom will flow into the heart, primed for use.

Having laid the foundation, the following daily lessons offer a deeper understanding of the forces at work beneath the surface, and suggest practical solutions to help end hatred, hurtful speech, and harmful behaviors.

SOLUTION I: Living With Emunah and Bitachon
- Know What's Yours (Day 42)
- Tasting Faith (Day 43)
- Arriving at *Bitachon* (Day 44)
- *Gam Zu L'Tovah* (Day 45)
- Making *Emunah* Work (Day 46)

SOLUTION II: Internalize Gratitude
- Unwrap Your Gifts (Day 47)
- Live in Real Time (Day 48)
- Grasp Your Jewish Identity (Day 49)

---

2. *Ruach Chaim, Avos* 3:1.
3. *Devarim* 6:6.
4. Cited in *Living Each Day — Tishrei-Cheshvan,* Rabbi Abraham J. Twerski, M.D. (ArtScroll/Mesorah Publ.), p. 63.

▸ *There is
every indi-
cation that
the time is
ripe for us
to make
every effort
to hasten
the redemp-
tion.*

▸ *We can
hasten the
Geulah by
dismantling
the barrier
erected by
sinas
chinam.*

▸ *Every step
we take
toward
achdus is
a spring-
board to
Geulah.*

SOLUTION III: Ending Jealousy and Hatred

- Speech Therapy (Day 50)
- Talk It Out (Day 51)
- Love to Give (Day 52)
- Remedial Giving (Day 53)
- Do Something (Day 54)
- A Good Eye (Day 55)
- Judge Others Favorably (Day 56)
- Judicial Ethics (Day 57)
- Expand the Inner Circle (Day 58)
- Behind Closed Doors (Day 59)
- Getting Over It (Days 60)
- Getting Over It, Part II (Days 61)
- Get Ready to "Let It Go" (Day 62)
- Walk in God's Ways (Day 63)

SOLUTION IV: "V'Ahavta l'rei'acha kamocha"

- Your Reality (Day 64)
- Game Change (Day 65)
- One for All (Day 66)
- Gather Together (Day 67)
- For a Sacred Purpose (Day 68)

Each of these solutions offers a means to traverse the vast ocean that prevents us from being a people united. The message we glean from each day will place us on the proper path to brotherly love among Hashem's children, thereby hastening the redemption.

> 11 Cheshvan —
> 12 Shevat —
> 11 Iyar —
> 12 Av —

KNOW WHAT'S YOURS

DAY 42

*A*n elephant watches a bird in envy. "I wish I had wings so I could fly," the elephant thinks. Suddenly, wings sprout from his shoulders. He flaps them wildly, waiting to take off, but they cannot lift his five-ton body off the ground. Now his wings are just a deformity, use- lessly hanging by his side and interfering with his normal elephant functions.

12
Cheshvan

13
Shevat

12
Iyar

13
Av

Rav Daniel of Kelm[1] uses a similar allegory as a powerful antidote to the poison of jealousy. The active ingredient in this antidote is *emunah*. If one can understand how ridic- ulous and useless wings would be on an elephant, one can understand as well how unbefitting his neighbor's house or his friend's children or his uncle's job would be for him.

Just as God gives each creature the "equipment" he needs to fulfill its purpose in the world, He equips each person to perfection, as well. If God did not equip a per- son with a certain asset or trait, then that trait cannot help that person arrive at *his* predestined goal. Accordingly, he is better off without it. Were he to pursue and eventually grasp that asset, he would steer himself away from his life's purpose.[2]

The Rosh[3] prescribes a strong dose of *emunah* for any- one suffering from jealousy, assuring sufferers that their malady is curable.[4] The cure, however, does not seem to

---

1. Cited in *Matnas Chaim, Maamarin*, Vol. 1, pp. 232-233.
2. See *Alei Shur*, Vol. 1, p. 38.
3. *Orchos Chaim L'HaRosh, Siman* 113. See *Mesillas Yesharim*, Ch. 11.
4. See *Shemiras HaLashon, Shaar HaTevunah*, Ch. 11, where the

match the illness. How does a stronger relationship with God solve a flaw in one's relationship with his fellow man? The answer lies in a deeper understanding of the nature of the baseless hatred that precipitated the destruction of the second Beis HaMikdash. [5]

Although the Gemara[6] states that the second Beis HaMikdash was destroyed because of *sinas chinam,* the *Tosefta*[7] adds that "the people loved money." For Rav Elyah Lopian,[8] this added element reveals a "base" for the baseless hatred. If "people loved money," then their hatred had its roots in jealousy of another person's money. Hatred based on something so lacking in legitimacy is indeed baseless.[9]

However, such jealousy exists. In fact, it seems

Chofetz Chaim concludes that the root cause of stealing is the lack of *emunah.* If one truly believed that Hashem provides a person's sustenance then he would not resort to stealing.

5. In addition to the better known reason for the *churban* — *sinas chinam,* baseless hatred — the Gemara in *Yoma* 9b states that the insistence on every legal right is also what brought about the destruction of the Beis HaMikdash. Jerusalem was destroyed because the litigants limited their *din* to the letter of the law of the Torah, and did not go beyond it. *Tosafos* to *Bava Metzia* 30b, s.v. *Ha v'ha,* reconciles this apparent contradiction by attributing the *churban* to both, i.e., two disparate causes.

Pnei Yehoshua to *Bava Metzia* 30b, s.v. *V'yeish l'dakdeik* explains that baseless hatred is defined as hatred for insufficient cause. One Jew has a claim or complaint against another and is unwilling to compromise in the spirit of going *lifnim mi'shuras hadin,* beyond the letter of the law; he insists on the letter of the law as he perceives it. Such an approach often leads to hatred of the party who refuses to go above and beyond. This hatred results from his insistence on invoking his legal rights, both real and perceived. It is called *sinas chinam* because the hate is halachically unjustified — the other party is not required to go *lifnim mi'shuras hadin.* Hence, there were not two separate causes of the *churban,* rather there was one (invoking all legalisms in a court battle) that led to another (*sinas chinam*). Indeed, the legalism caused quarrels and unjustified hatred. These are the two related factors that led to the *churban.*

6. *Yoma* 9a.

7. *Menachos* 13:22; *Matnas Chaim,* Vol. 1, p. 233.

8. *Lev Eliyahu,* Vol. 3, *Parashas Eikev,* s.v. *V'chein amru.*

9. See *Mesillas Yesharim,* Ch. 11, s.v. *V'amnam:* "Envy is nothing but foolishness, for the one who envies gains nothing for himself and deprives the one he envies of nothing. He only loses."

to be an immutable part of human nature.[10] The Ibn Ezra[11] takes note of jealousy's pervasiveness, and wonders how God could prohibit it in the Tenth Commandment "You shall not covet."[12] He resolves the dilemma with a profound psychological insight:

> A peasant sees the beautiful daughter of a neighboring family, and wants her for his wife. The next day, the king's daughter stops in the village on the way to her summer home. Although she is strikingly beautiful, the peasant does not entertain a thought of marrying her. He knows she is beyond his reach.

The Ibn Ezra's point is that a sensible person does not brood over something totally out of his reach. A person who is jealous has not internalized the concept that all those objects of his envy are inaccessible to him. God gave them to the other person because they are the right tools for that other person's life. They are no more relevant to his life than the princess is relevant to the peasant's life.[13]

This idea is the lynchpin of *emunah*, the key to a true and total belief in God. Thus, the Tenth Commandment is an achievable commandment.[14] Rav Mattisyahu Salomon[15] suggests a two-pronged approach for fulfilling this commandment: building one's distaste for jealousy and hatred by studying the words of *Chazal*, and building one's *emunah* and *bitachon*.[16] In this way, ridding oneself of jeal-

---

10. See *Sanhedrin* 105b, which states that all people experience jealousy except a parent for his children and a rebbi for his students. Regarding great people who may have had jealousy, see *Sanhedrin* 19a. See also *Yoma* 71b (Kohen Gadol and Shemaya and Avtalyon), *Berachos* 28a (R' Gamliel and R' Elazar ben Azariah), *Shabbos* 10a,b (Shevatim, the sons of Yaakov Avinu and Yosef).
11. *Shemos* 20:14.
12. Ibid.
13. See *Mesillas Yesharim*, Ch. 11, s.v. *Ha'kinah*: "If they recognized that everything proceeds from God in accordance with His wondrous judgment and unfathomable wisdom, they would have no reason whatsoever to anguish over their neighbor's good."
14. See previous note.
15. *Matnas Chaim, Maamarim*, Vol. 1, p. 233.
16. See also *Sefer HaChinuch*, Mitzvah 241; *Chofetz Chaim*

ousy produces a beautiful, enduring renovation of one's entire spiritual life.

> ▶ *God gives each person what he needs to fulfill his purpose.*
>
> ▶ *Other people's assets do not serve a positive purpose in one's life.*
>
> ▶ *Truly believing that God supervises the world and endows a person with what he needs is the basis of emunah.*
>
> ▶ *Jealousy cannot coexist with true emunah.*

The "You Can Do It" actions inserted below and in the following days have been chosen for ease of accomplishment. Small actions have the power to enable people to make big changes. Rav Yisrael Salanter (Ohr Yisrael, Letter 6; see also Ali Shur, Vol. 2, pp. 189-191) explains that the best way to fight against the yetzer hara is with actions that are within reach. If you feel an exercise is difficult, break it down into a smaller task or move on to the next one.

YOU CAN DO IT

Identify those traits that define you, i.e., love of learning, quick or deep understanding, kindness, sense of humor, perseverance, emunah, non-judgmental. Write down how they have had a positive impact on your life and the lives of others.

---

al HaTorah, Parashas Mishpatim; Shem Olam, Shaar Shemiras HaShabbos, Ch. 3 (all cited in Matnas Chelko on Mesillas Yesharim, pp. 138-139).

---

12 Cheshvan —
13 Shevat —
12 Iyar — לע״נ שרח דינה ע״ה בת שלום דוד יבלח״ט
In memory of Serach Dena Friedman
Dedicated by her loving family, Philadelphia, PA
13 Av —

TASTING FAITH

DAY 43

*C*lose your eyes for a moment and imagine a tree. Every detail — the fruit growing on the tree, the branches, the children playing under it — is an expression of you. Because you are the sole creator of that tree, it's all united by a single common thread — you.

Open your eyes and what happens to the tree? It's gone. The tree exists only as long as you will it to be. Not only are you its creator, you are its sustainer as well. Without you, there is no tree.

This visualization, in a simplified manner, describes God's role as Creator and Supervisor of the world. When a person resolves to fortify his *emunah*, the realization that God is the Source of each and every moment of life is what he is seeking to clarify and confirm in his heart.

As the Rambam states:[1]

The foundation of all foundations and the pillar of wisdom is to know that there is a Primary Being Who brought into being all existence. All the beings of the heavens, the earth, and what is between them came into existence only from the truth of His being.[2]

In addition to belief in God as the sole Creator, *emunah* requires belief in *hashgachah pratis*[3] — that Hashem supervises His creation moment to moment, and that

13
Cheshvan

14
Shevat

13
Iyar

14
Av

---

1. *Hilchos Yesodei HaTorah* 1:1.
2. See *Nefesh HaChaim, Shaar* 3, Chs. 1 and 2, which state that Hashem is called *Makom*, "Place," because He is the Source of all existence and grants life to all that is in the world.
3. See *Praying With Fire 2*, Day 16, "Emunah Defined," p. 76, regarding *hashgachah pratis*.

nothing happens by chance, but only because He wills it.[4]

As Rabbi Yechezkel Levenstein explains:[5] "Just as Hashem *alone* created the world, He *alone* runs the world. And since *emunah* and *hashgachah* are one, whoever does not believe this does not believe in *hashgachah* and he is not considered to be a believer in God."

For the believing Jew, *emunah* would seem to be a minimal challenge. After all, our days, our weeks, our years, and our lives are structured around the mandates of God's Torah. However, much of the *emunah* we experience in our day-to-day lives resides in our minds. We have an intellectual understanding that God is behind the scenes. This type of faith — *emunah sichlis* — lacks the galvanizing force of the deeper, more visceral belief, called *emunah chushis*.

The Alter of Kelm explains the difference between the two types of belief with a parable:

> A person has never tasted bread. His friend describes exactly what bread is like, including its taste, texture, and ability to satiate the appetite. The person accepts the information, but it is not as if he has actually tasted bread, for if someone argues convincingly that bread is totally different than initially described to him, he might believe that second opinion instead. On the other hand, someone who himself has tasted bread even once will not be swayed by any argument to the contrary.

Similarly, one whose belief in God is based on actual experience has a rock-solid faith that will not be called into question, even if that person is presented with apparently powerful counter-arguments.[6] One of the foremost experiences that imprinted *emunah* upon the Jewish peo-

---

4. *Orchos Chaim L'HaRosh, Piskah* 25, cited in *Ohr Yechezkel, Emunah*, p. 99; *Nesivos Shalom*, Vol. 1, p. 44, s.v. *U'miklal*. Also see *Ramban, Bereishis* 18:19; *Rabbeinu Bachya* ibid.; *Rambam, Moreh Nevuchim* 3:17-18; *Sforno, Vayikra* 13:47; *Michtav MeEliyahu*, Vol. 5, pp. 308-310, and Vol. 2, p. 76.
5. *Ohr Yechezkel, Emunah*, p. 105.
6. See *Halichos Shlomo* on *Tefillah*, "*Shema Yisrael* — *Yesod HaEmunah*," p. 367.

ple's national consciousness was the splitting of the Sea of Reeds, a revelation so great that even those on a lesser spiritual level reached tremendous levels of knowledge of God, resulting in an unshakable faith.

In building our personal *emunah chushis*, however, we need not depend on witnessing Biblical miracles. Experiences that create a rock-solid faith are available to everyone, every day, in a myriad of ways. Whether it is a challenge — financial loss, traffic jam, toothache, toddler tantrum, insult — or a gift, such as business success, recovery from illness, a family *simchah* — it is all God's doing.

Daily life is, in reality, the opportunity to establish *emunah chushis*. The key is to internalize that every occurrence comes from Heaven.[7]

YOU CAN DO IT

Think of a specific happy experience that occurred in the recent past. Verbally thank Hashem for bringing this about.

Take It With You

▸ *Emunah is the belief that God created the world and continues to run every facet of it.*

▸ *Emunah sichlis is an intellectual understanding. Emunah chushis is a deeper belief that results from direct experience.*

▸ *On a personal level, one can develop emunah chushis by taking the time to recognize God's hand in the matters of everyday life.*

---

7. See *Alei Shur,* Vol. 1, p. 102.

13 Cheshvan —
14 Shevat —
13 Iyar —
14 Av —

ARRIVING AT BITACHON

DAY 44

14
Cheshvan

15
Shevat

14
Iyar

15
Av

*L*evi knows that his rabbi is a righteous man. He founded the shul thirty years ago and is beloved by his community. He is a revered Torah scholar whose advice is sought by people throughout the region. If someone would ask Levi, "Do you have faith in your rabbi?" he would answer with a heartfelt, "Of course!"

Nevertheless, when Levi's father passed away and a vicious inheritance battle erupted between him and his brother, Levi could not quite bring himself to entrust the matter to his rabbi. "What if he sees things my brother's way?" he asked himself. "It could cost me a fortune. After all, he's a rabbi, not a businessman." Levi turned to his lawyer instead.

One could say that Levi had *emunah* in his rabbi, but not *bitachon*. What is the difference? *Emunah* is faith: one believes that God exists and runs the world. *Bitachon* is trust: one's belief is so strong and solid that he trusts his fortunes to God, knowing that His work is perfect. Of course, whether or not one has *bitachon*, God runs the world. The question is, does a person live his life with that knowledge forefront in his mind?

The foundation of *bitachon* is an *emunah* so deep that it becomes instinctive. The Ramban[1] and *Orchos Tzaddikim*[2] explain that *bitachon* cannot exist without *emunah*. A person will not trust God to sustain his life unless he has complete faith in His presence and power.

The Chazon Ish[3] sees *emunah* and *bitachon* as two sides of the same entity. The difference is that *emunah*

---

1. *Kisvei Ramban, Sefer Emunah U'Bitachon,* Ch. 1.
2. *HaShaar HaTeshi'i, Shaar HaSimchah, s.v. Ach haderech.*
3. *Emunah U'Bitachon,* Ch. 2.

— faith — is the awareness, while *bitachon* — trust — is putting that awareness into action.

As the Chazon Ish explains:[4]

> When a calamity befalls a person, it is natural to be afraid…It is critical in such circumstances to make a special effort to reinforce the truth that…everything that happens is from God… and one's faith can remove the fear and give one the courage to believe in the possibility of salvation…This awareness is called bitachon.
>
> …Consequently, the person with bitachon has a different understanding of how to be rescued from danger than someone without bitachon. He will carefully examine his deeds and direct his heart to repentance, prayer, and charity to remove the terrible decree.[5]

Bitachon does not mean there is no need to make a reasonable effort. It means that one views his efforts only as channels through which God can send salvation. Furthermore, even though one trusts that God will do good, one must also pray for this to occur. A person with *bitachon* trusts that God sends what is best for him, even if it does not conform to his hopes. In such a person's heart, there is no place for jealousy or hatred, for he knows that in every matter, God's will prevails — for the good.

YOU CAN DO IT

Contemplate a negative event that recently happened. Reflect on how this is the will of Hashem.

---

4. Ibid.
5. End of Ch. 21; *Beis HaLevi, Parashas Mikeitz; Akeidas Yitzchak, Shaar* 26. See also *Lev Eliyahu*, Vol. 3, *Parashas Va'eschanan*, p. 204, s.v. *V'al hakol,* which states: "Even if one is a *baal emunah* and a great *baal bitachon*, it is still necessary for him to pray."

> **14 Cheshvan —**
> **15 Shevat —**
> **14 Iyar —**
> **15 Av —** Dedicated in honor of our parents Jack & Cynthia Hackner and Tuvie & Gertie Tobias
> By their children, Jaron & Shelly Tobias,
> Johannesburg, South Africa

Take It With You

▸ *Bitachon is trust in God, which is expressed by one's decisions and attitudes in life.*

▸ *Bitachon is rooted in a strong, almost instinctive level of emunah.*

▸ *A person with bitachon has no place for jealousy or hatred, for he realizes that everything that happens to him comes directly from God.*

GAM ZU L'TOVAH

15
Cheshvan

16
Shevat

15
Iyar

16
Av

*R*ochel lost the position she had held at an accounting firm for seven years. Although her husband, Yaakov, runs a successful small business, Rochel's salary pays the tuitions and camp fees for their five children, and covers many other extra expenses.

"I'm sure we'll see soon that this is gam zu l'tovah (this, too, is for the good)," Yaakov reassured her.

Months later Rochel had still not found a job comparable to her old one. The tuitions were long overdue, camp registration forms sat untouched in a pile, and Pesach was on its way.

She thought about her old boss, who had safe-guarded his firm's profits by letting her go. "I'll bet he's not worried about making Pesach," she thought, her heart brimming with resentment.

The difficulty with *bitachon* — trust in God's management of the world and one's personal affairs — is that a person must make an effort to believe there is benefit in that which hurts or disappoints him. Nevertheless, that is what God demands of us. The *Orchos Tzaddikim* teaches:[1]

One should accept with love all of God's decrees, and he should not place his trust in man. If he would have been meritorious he would have received it [that which he is envious of] from God even without man's assistance. And if he is impoverished and mired in difficulties… he should think that God is doing this for his benefit, and he should accept all of it with love…

And one who accepts upon himself to acknowl-

---

1. *Shaar HaSinah,* s.v. *Yeish raah.*

edge everything God does with love, and to say regarding everything that happens to him "Gam zu l'tovah,"[2] he will be saved from feelings of hatred and jealousy.

When a person cannot see the *"tovah"* of a particular situation in his life, upon what can he base his *bitachon?* Does he have to deny the reality of his own distress? Upon what can he base his assertion, realistically, that what has happened reflects God's goodness?

The basis for his belief is God's identity as total good. Rav Chaim Shmulevitz[3] explains that by applying the words *"gam zu l'tovah"* to events that appear, at the moment, to be troubling, the person declares that everything that happens belongs within God's script of goodness for His world. And although man does not have the ability to perceive this script from its beginning to the end, if he knows the nature of the Author, he knows that all that happens in the script is good.

For jealousy and hatred to enter a person's heart, there has to be a breach in this wall of *bitachon.*[4] The nature of that breach is a false belief that other people have the power to alter one's destiny.[5] In other words, "Someone is to blame for this." In the opening story, that belief manifests itself in Rochel's contemplation of her boss' financial situation in comparison to her own.

Often, a person holds onto this false premise as a means of self-defense. He tells himself that "If I don't put the blame where it belongs and let other people know what's been done to me, everyone will think they can walk right over me." The truth, however, lies in exactly the opposite direction. A person who accepts that his difficulties are

---

2. One of the great Tannaim, who was a teacher of Rabbi Akiva, is known as Nachum Ish Gamzu. He was called by this name because his response to any difficulty was *"Gam zu l'tovah* — This too is for the good."
3. *Sichos Mussar, Shaarei Chaim, Maamar* 13, p. 53, *"Gam zu l'tovah"* [5732 Maamar 9].
4. *Shaarei Kedushah* (Rav Chaim Vital), Vol. 2, *Shaar* 4; *Pele Yo'eitz, Erech Chemdah; Zohar, Parashas Acharei Mos*, p. 78b; *Smak* 19.
5. *Pele Yo'eitz, Erech Nekimah U'Netirah.*

▸ *The main focus of someone who lives with emunah and bitachon is that every-thing that happens comes from God.*

▸ *By firming one's belief that God is all good, a person can learn to trust that everything that hap-pens to him is also for the good.*

▸ *Master-ing the response of "gam zu l'tovah — This, too, is for the good" eliminates jealousy, hatred, and the need to blame from a person's heart.*

from God frees himself to move forward, energized by a positive view of the world that leads inevitably to good, for himself and for the Jewish people.[6]

YOU CAN DO IT

Think of an event that at the time it occurred you found to be a challenge, but which turned out to be for your good. When you are facing a difficult situation remind yourself of the incident and how you eventually realized it had turned out for the good.

---

6. *Chovos HaLevavos, Shaar HaBitachon*, Ch. 4.

לע"נ אליהו בן אבא הלוי ז"ל — 15 Cheshvan
ולזכות הענא בת נחמה שתחי׳
Dedicated by their children
16 Shevat — In loving memory of my great-grandfather
לעילוי נשמת אברהם משה בן רב ישראל צבי ז"ל
and my grandfather לעילוי נשמת שעפסל בן רב שאול ז"ל
and in honor of my grandmother פייגא בת מלכה שתחי׳
15 Iyar —
16 Av —

MAKING EMUNAH WORK

R euven was terrified of the dentist. But he had a toothache and his appointment was in one hour. His wife coached him with strategies to stay calm. With newfound courage, Reuven arrived at the dentist's office, sat down on the chair, and broke into a cold sweat. Observing his grey skin and blue lips, the dental assistant asked, "Are you going to faint?"

16
Cheshvan

17
Shevat

16
Iyar

17
Av

Sadly, a person's resolve does not always translate into an improved reaction when he is once more faced with a challenge. This is certainly true of *emunah* and *bitachon*. People can work on their shortcomings and think all the right thoughts but then, when the challenge presents itself, they slip into the "default mode" of envy and anger.

The Chofetz Chaim[1] analyzed typical challenges to one's *emunah* and formulated a set of beliefs to counteract these challenges. If one calls these beliefs into play whenever envy surfaces, he will reset his "default mode" to one of accepting God's will.

- **Problem:** *The Golden Boy:* He has a thriving business, a palatial home, and a family that sparkles with refinement. Seeing him makes you feel like a lackluster drone.
- **Resolution:** Each morning, we acknowledge that our needs are fulfilled as we recite the blessing in *Birchos HaShachar:* "She'asah li kol tzorki — Who has provided me my every need." Nothing is missing from your life![2]

---

1. *Ahavas Yisrael,* Ch. 3.
2. *Alei Shur,* Vol. 1, p. 36, s.v. *Hein, Hakadosh Baruch Hu.*

Therefore, the Chofetz Chaim[3] explains, additional wealth may not be a blessing. If you are someone to whom God can entrust wealth, knowing that you will dispose of it according to His will, then God will give you wealth. If you are not, the wealth you receive will only detract from your reward in the Next World. If God is withholding wealth in this world, it is for your eternal benefit, for as *Chazal* state:[4] "One hour of pleasure in the Next World is better than the entire life of this world."

- **Problem:** *"Unfair" Competition:* Your restaurant, the first kosher House of Pancakes, took off like a rocket, and now Shimon has opened a competing pancake house — *in a better location!* Your "rocket" is losing altitude, but what does Shimon care? Everything *he* touches turns to gold.

- **Resolution:** *Chazal*[5] state that one person cannot affect the wealth God allots for another, "by even a hairsbreadth." One person's business cannot diminish the wealth preordained for another person. You are receiving your full allotment.[6]

- **Problem:** *The Guest of Honor:* You're at a yeshivah dinner and your neighbor ascends to the podium to receive yet another honor. He sits on every board of every *tzedakah,* and all over town, there are buildings named for his late parents. You wish you could tell it as it is — he's not such a great guy!

- **Resolution:** The Chofetz Chaim[7] writes that the envious person should realize that "God honors those who honor Him."[8] By refraining from speaking negatively about the honoree, he himself will be spared from embarrassment, because God returns one's deeds, measure for measure.[9]

---

3. *Ahavas Yisrael,* Ch. 3.
4. *Pirkei Avos* 4:22.
5. *Yoma* 38b.
6. See *Mesillas Yesharim,* Ch. 11, s.v. *V'amnam; Sefer HaChinuch, Mitzvah* 241.
7. *Ahavas Yisrael,* Ch. 3.
8. *I Shmuel* 2:30
9. *Shabbos* 105b. See *Mesillas Yesharim,* Ch. 19, s.v. *V'amru od.*

- **Problem:** *Mr. Popularity:* He knows everyone. He helps everyone. Everyone loves him. You like him too, but inexplicably, you'd just like to see him knocked down a peg or two.
- **Resolution:** Recognize that God blessed him with a pleasant personality and he uses it for good. Then realize that God has likewise blessed you with qualities that you can utilize to do good.

The common thread in these solutions is the acceptance of God's administration of the world. This entails a deep conviction that God apportions blessings and challenges with perfect judgment. A person who masters this belief leaves behind a life of blood-boiling frustration and opens the door to a world of tranquility.

YOU CAN DO IT

Choose one scenario listed above that is relevant to you. Implement the resolution. Focus on any change in your feelings.

Take It With You

▸ *Even when a person resolves to improve his emunah, he may falter when real-life challenges arise.*

▸ *By preparing to deal with life's challenges, one can improve his ability to respond with emunah.*

▸ *Accepting that all that happens is God's will is the common thread in strategies to maintain emunah.*

DAY 47

UNWRAP THE GIFTS

17
Cheshvan

18
Shevat

17
Iyar

18
Av

*F*rom the first Erev Shabbos of their married life, Shalom brought home a lavish bouquet of flowers each week for his wife, Tovah. After the first few weeks, Tovah ceased to marvel at the expense and effort that the bouquets represented.

Several months into their marriage, Shalom was caught in a traffic jam on his way home one Friday afternoon. He had no time to wait at the florist's shop for a lush bouquet to be assembled and arranged, so he picked up an inexpensive bouquet from a street vendor. This time, Tovah noticed the flowers. She smiled graciously, but her disappointment was written on her face.

We sometimes act like Tovah, and her reaction highlights our response to our loving, ever-giving God. We notice what is missing so much more quickly than we notice what we receive; the more consistent and reliable our gifts become, the less we notice them. Thus, at times, we feel deprived when in fact we are blessed. Our sense of deprivation leads us to envy those who have what we seem to lack. Yet, if our hearts were filled with gratitude for all we receive, jealousy would be crowded out,[1] like a weed that can't find a place to take root in a healthy, lush lawn.

Gratitude is a relative term. For a person to feel grateful, he must feel that he is receiving something beyond that which is owed to him. In the story above, Tovah felt enti-

---

1. *Alei Shur*, Vol. 1, p. 37, s.v. *Hamakir*.

tled to her lush bouquet of flowers each week. Therefore, she stopped feeling grateful and instead, subconsciously added the flowers to her list of entitlements.

In thinking about jealousy, therefore, we have a burning question to answer. To what is a human being entitled? What is the basic "benefits package" due to him upon being born into this world? The answer to that question is that nothing is an entitlement — *everything* is an incalculably precious gift.

As the *Chovos HaLevavos* states:[2]

> If a person's actions would equal the amount of sand on the seashore, they would not equal even one benefit received from God in this world... And the reward that one receives for doing mitzvos is [also] from the benevolence of Hashem.

When a person examines the workings of nature, the scheme of history, the providential events of his own life, and the mysterious intricacies of his own body, God's gifts reveal themselves to be nothing short of astounding. The Gemara awakens us to this sense of amazement by comparing the normal operation of the world to the splitting of the Reed Sea. This comparison applies to earning a livelihood[3] and to finding a spouse.[4]

Even the process of eliminating waste from our bodies is, according to the Gemara,[5] a precious gift from God. The Vilna Gaon marvels that the act of swallowing calls into play five different, inter-related functions that must each do its part in the right order, in the right way, if a person is to survive.

Despite the grandeur of God's gifts, people do not realize the magnitude of what they have been given. No one swallows and says "What a miracle!" unless he has suffered from some swallowing disorder. Therefore, most of God's gifts lay neglected in the recesses of our consciousness. If that is so, how can they fill up our hearts with gratitude and crowd out feelings of depriva-

---

2. *Shaar HaBitachon*, Ch. 4.
3. *Pesachim* 118a.
4. *Sotah* 2a.
5. See *Pesachim* loc. cit.

tion and jealousy?

Tomorrow we will explore the tools that the Torah has provided to help us savor the bounty God bestows upon us constantly.

YOU CAN DO IT

Take a few minutes and visualize what your life would be like if you did not have use of your right hand. How would you give a hug? How could you carry a heavy package? How could you scratch an itch on your left elbow? Think of your own scenarios.

Now wholeheartedly thank Hashem for giving you your right hand.

---

17 Cheshvan —
18 Shevat —
17 Iyar — L'zchus the V'Ani Tefillah Foundation and continued Hatzlachah in all their endeavors.
Dedicated by Ittamar Janowski
18 Av —

LIVE IN REAL TIME

DAY 48

*L*ittle Yaakov could smell the distinct, sweet fragrance of the peaches the second he walked into the kitchen. There they were, ripening on the counter. He poked one, feeling the fuzzy skin and the slightly yielding flesh underneath. Perfect!

"Baruch atah Hashem, Elokeinu Melech Ha-Olam, borei pri ha'eitz" (Blessed are you, Hashem, our God, King of Universe, Who created the fruit of the tree), he recited. His teeth sank into the soft fruit, releasing a cascade of juice that delighted his taste buds and trickled down his chin. To think — this sweet, soft, fragrant fruit sprouted on a piece of wood!

18 Cheshvan

19 Shevat

18 Iyar

19 Av

Eating can be a truly spiritual experience.[1] However, anyone who has ever reached the bottom of a longed-for bowl of ice cream, only to wonder where it has all gone, can attest that even the most delicious treats can be eaten on automatic pilot.

Worse yet, one's relationships with others can lapse into mindlessness. Feelings — between spouses, between parents and children, or among friends — are often blunted by the thousands of distractions occupying people's minds.

Worst of all, our relationship with God can become rote and almost mindless. A person can recite a blessing and perform a mitzvah, or march through all nineteen blessings of *Shemoneh Esrei,* all the while thinking about something else.

In this way, the incalculable instances of God's good-

---

1. *Tzidkas HaTzaddik, Os 7.*

ness that fill our lives can pass unnoticed. Even the method the Torah gives us to revitalize our awareness — reciting a blessing — can be done without much consciousness. Therefore, if we content ourselves with such emptiness, we fail to grasp the spiritual life-line God has provided us to save us from drowning in the mundane circumstances of our lives.

A blessing is meant to subtly direct our attention to the presence of God in our lives, dropping measure after measure of appreciation into our hearts.[2] If a person were to receive a cake from his neighbor, he would thank the giver profusely. He would be touched by the giver's thoughtfulness and kindness. Yet our continual gifts from God somehow lose their power to stir such joy. Therefore, Rambam states:[3] "Our Sages established many blessings of praise, thanks, and requests in order that we remember our Creator constantly."

The result, says the Sefer HaChinuch,[4] is that, "Through this focus and the awakening of our soul, we praise Him as the Source of all benevolence."

However, the words will have an impact on us only if we focus on their meaning. Once awakened to the Source of the benefit[5] or of the mitzvah that we are about to perform, we can open our minds and senses to its grandeur.

What spiritual worlds are we affecting as we lift our *lulav* in the air?[6] What is this taste and texture that God has created for our enjoyment? What beauty is there in the song being sung around the Shabbos table? How great is the God we are praising in *Shemoneh Esrei*, and how very much do we need His closeness? When we engage our religious lives and everyday lives with true

---

2. The *Rashba (She'eilos U'Teshuvos HaRashba*, Vol. 5, *Siman* 51) explains that the word that starts each blessing, "*baruch*," is derived from the word "*bereichah*," meaning a pool or spring of flowing water. A person reciting a blessing is therefore acknowledging that he is about to partake of a benefit that flows from God's limitless stream of both physical and spiritual sustenance.
3. *Hilchos Berachos* 1:3.
4. *Mitzvah* 430.
5. See *Matnas Chaim, Maamarim*, Vol. 1, p. 160.
6. *Succah* 37b.

mindfulness, gratitude and delight can be our constant companions.

YOU CAN DO IT

Before you make a berachah, focus on how God in His goodness made our food appealing.

Take It With You

▸ *Any experience will lose its impact through mindless engagement.*

▸ *Reciting a blessing awakens us to God's benevolence.*

▸ *By focusing on the words of a blessing — connecting to God as the Source of good, and truly savoring the good — one can experience gratitude.*

18 Cheshvan —
19 Shevat —
18 Iyar —
19 Av —

GRASP YOUR JEWISH IDENTITY

DAY 49

19 Cheshvan

20 Shevat

19 Iyar

20 Av

The first man, Adam, was given the task of naming all the creations that surrounded him in the brand-new world God had created.[1] Each of these names reflected the essence of the entity on whom the name was bestowed.[2] Likewise, throughout the Torah, our forefathers and ancestors named their offspring according to the essence and purpose of the child's soul.[3] Even nations, says Rav Dessler,[4] bear names that express their essence, as illustrated by the name *"Mitzraim"* (Egypt), which contains the root word *"meitzar,"* straits.[5]

The ability of a name to convey the essence of its subject is so clear, says the Gemara,[6] that Rabbi Meir would not stay at an inn until he had analyzed the innkeeper's name, from which he determined if the environment would be proper. When invited to a home, Rabbi Yehudah and Rabbi Yose would deliberate upon the name of the prospective host. Once, they came to a house whose owner's name was Balah; they did not go inside, because they inferred from a verse in Yechezkel[7] that the host was a wicked man.[8]

---

1. *Bamidbar Rabbah* 19:3; *Ramban, Bereishis* 2:20.
2. See *Ohr Gedalyahu, Shemos*, p. 2. See also Rav Samson Raphael Hirsch, who states that the Hebrew word *"shem"* [name] defines what a person is supposed to be and what a person is. The word *"shem"* is related to the word *"sham"* [there]. *"Sham"* defines where an item is and *"shem"* defines where a person is.
3. *Ohr Gedalyahu* loc. cit.; ibid., *Moadim U'Lekutim L'Shevi'i shel Pesach*, p. 146, s.v. *K'var amarnu.*
4. *Michtav MeEliyahu*, Vol. 2, p. 17, s.v., *Galus Mitzrayim.*
5. The Jewish people were restricted by the straits of Egypt both physically and spiritually.
6. *Yoma* 83b.
7. 23:43.
8. *Berachos* 7b with *Maharsha's* explanation that God interacts with

The rock-solid pillar of the Jewish identity is built upon the sturdy foundation of this concept. The name *Yehudi*, "Jew," signifies gratitude. Gratitude is the essence of the name by which we are called.[9] This is why, out of the twelve tribes descended from Yaakov, we are called *Yehudim*, after Yehudah alone.

Of course, there is a historic explanation involving the division of the twelve tribes into two different kingdoms, and the ultimate disappearance of all but Binyamin, Yehudah, and Levi.[10] However, there is Divine design in these historic occurrences, and the result of this design is that throughout the world, our people are knows as Jews — *Yehudim*.

The root of this name is *hodaah* — gratitude. Leah gave her son the name Yehudah as an expression of gratefulness to God for His gift to her.[11] However, this was not her first son; it was her fourth. Rashi[12] explains that her gratitude poured forth at this point because with Yehudah's birth, she had been granted more than an equal share of sons among the four wives of Yaakov.[13] As we learned earlier, this sense of having one's expectations exceeded is at the root of the trait of gratitude.

This gratitude is installed as the permanent identity of the Jewish people when Yaakov grants his final blessings

---

our world in accordance with our given name. See *Ohr HaChaim* to *Shemos* 2:10; *Zohar, Bereishis* 58b.

9. See *Divrei Yoel,* Vol. 4, *Parashas Vayakhel,* p. 361, who explains the meaning of our name Yisrael.

10. Ten of the original twelve Hebrew tribes, under the leadership of Yehoshua, took possession of Canaan after the death of Moshe. They were named Asher, Dan, Ephraim, Gad, Yissachar, Menasheh, Naphtali, Reuven, Shimon, and Zevulun — all sons or grandsons of Yaakov. After the death of Shlomo HaMelelch, the ten Tribes formed the independent Kingdom of Israel in the north and the two other tribes, Yehudah and Binyamin, retained the Kingdom of Yehudah in the south. Following the conquest of the northern kingdom by the Assyrians a little over one century before the destruction of the First Holy Temple, the ten Tribes gradually became assimilated.

11. See *Bereishis* 29:35, which states that Leah praised God upon the birth of her son and, therefore, she called him Yehudah.

12. Ad loc.

13. As the mother at that point of one-third of Yaakov's twelve sons, she had been granted more than her rightful share. Eventually, she became the mother of half of Yaakov's sons.

Take It With You

▸ *A name reflects the essence of the person or item named.*

▸ *Leah named her son "Yehudah" because of her hodaah, gratitude, for having been blessed with more than her share of sons.*

▸ *The Jewish people are called Yehudim because gratitude toward God is our essential trait.*

to his sons. He tells Yehudah:[14] "*Yehudah — atah yoducha achecha* — You, your brothers shall acknowledge." *Targum Yonasan ben Uziel*[15] interprets these words to mean that the Jewish people will be called by his name (*Yehudi*), rather than by the name of any other tribe. The name Yehudah contains the letters of God's ineffable Name as well as the root that means "gratitude." *Chidushei HaRim* notes that Jews have come to be called *Yehudim*, after Yehudah, because it is a Jewish characteristic to be grateful to God,[16] with the knowledge that we have been given more than our rightful share.

Thus, gratitude is not only an essential facet of building *emunah* and nurturing love and unity among the Jewish people. It is the essence of the Jewish people's identity, and the key to our successful fulfillment of our mission in the world. Through gratitude, we express the essence of what a Jew is — an eternal *Yehudi*, who proclaims to the world, as did our Matriarch Leah, that God constantly gives us more than our merit could ever earn.

YOU CAN DO IT

Recall and write down one or more times when you received more than you expected. For instance, a task went more smoothly, someone gave you a gift or did you a favor unexpectedly, etc.

---

14. *Bereishis* 49:8.
15. Ad loc.
16. See *Ohr Gedalyahu, Shemos*, p. 2, s.v. *K'siv*, which states that the name of each of God's creations is consistent with the honor of Heaven that it must generate. Accordingly, being grateful to God is a Jew's mission in life.

---

19 Cheshvan —
20 Shevat — לע"נ מיכאל בן שמואל ז"ל
19 Iyar —
20 Av —

CHAPTER 8:
SOLUTION III:
ENDING JEALOUSY
AND HATRED

SPEECH THERAPY

DAY 50

20
Cheshvan

21
Shevat

20
Iyar

21
Av

*Y*onah and Yisrael are two brothers. On their father's birthday, they each bring him a gift. Yonah goes out to his orange grove and picks a bushel of oranges to give his father. "It's nice, it's presentable, and yet, it didn't cost me a fortune," he thinks to himself complacently. "It's good enough."

Yisrael goes out to his pastures, searching among his flocks for the choicest lamb. "No, this one isn't good enough....maybe there's a better one over there...ah, here's the one. The best! I'm sure it would fetch a fantastic price on the market."

Naturally, the father responds with more enthusiasm to Yisrael's heartfelt gift than to Yonah's perfunctory offering. Yonah seethes with envy. One day he meets his brother and lets loose a flood of vitriol.

"You think you're so wonderful! Everything you do is perfect! I won't be happy one day in my life as long as you're around!" the furious Yonah screams, inflaming his own anger with each word.

In the Torah account of Kayin and Hevel, we are never apprised as to what Kayin said prior to killing his brother. We are told only that after Kayin's offering is rejected and God sees Kayin's despondency, He tells him:

> Surely, if you improve yourself, you will be forgiven. But if you do not improve yourself, sin rests at your door. Kayin spoke with his brother Hevel. And it happened when they were in the field, that Kayin rose up against his brother Hevel and killed him.[1]

---

1. *Bereishis* 4:7-8.

What transpired in the field? In *Chochmah U'Mussar*,[2] Rav Simchah Zissel Ziv explains: When God urged Kayin to improve himself, He was urging him to channel his hateful envy into the positive form of envy.[3] "Good envy," says Rav Simchah Zissel Ziv, is the type that inspires one to strive to reach another person's spiritual height.[4] If Kayin had channeled his envy in that direction, God would have forgiven him.

However, in the more common "bad envy," the jealous person does not aspire to improve; rather, he yearns to witness his competitor's fall from grace. Thus, even though Kayin's desire was to have the closeness to God that his brother had, it was not "good envy," because his route to that end was to eliminate the competition rather than to improve himself. God cautioned Kayin that if he remained mired in that catastrophic mind-set, he surely would be consumed by the sin that "rests at your door."

Indeed, Kayin could have pulled himself from the quicksand. Rav Simchah Zissel[5] says that the opportunity to accomplish that feat existed when Kayin spoke with his brother. Kayin could have saved himself by saying pleasing, conciliatory words to his brother; this would have elicited warmth from Hevel, which in turn would have soothed Kayin's fury.

Instead, it seems that Kayin allowed his pain and hatred to charge out of his mouth like an angry bull. His words only incited more anger in his heart, which ultimately resulted in the murder of his own brother.

For some people, however, speaking kindly to the object of one's burning envy might seem like a strategy reserved for saints. In that case, the person can at least refrain from speaking harshly to the other person. Add to that restraint a heaping dose of reason — realizing that the negative thoughts accomplish nothing and that everything comes from God, and one can turn a seem-

---

2. Vol. 2, p. 177.
3. See *Bava Basra* 21a.
4. *Orchos Tzaddikim, Shaar HaKinah*, s.v. Af.
5. *Chochmah U'Mussar*, Vol. 2, p. 177.

Take It With You

▸ *Speaking harshly to the person one envies fans the flames of one's own anger.*

▸ *Speaking kindly to the person one envies soothes one's own anger.*

▸ *If it is too difficult to speak kindly, one can at least refrain from harsh words, and also try to moderate his feelings through reason and emunah.*

ingly insurmountable spiritual challenge into a glowing personal achievement.

YOU CAN DO IT

Next time you see yourself becoming upset, speak in a low voice. Acting opposite of the emotion weakens its power. If you are too upset or if this is not helping, excuse yourself from the conversation.

---

20 Cheshvan —
21 Shevat —
20 Iyar —
21 Av —

TALK IT OUT

DAY 51

The hatred forbidden by the Torah, as we learned previously, hides in the heart, busily spinning a web of negative thoughts and feelings. But what causes hatred to take root there?

The simple answer is "life." Because in life we encounter people who sometimes do hurtful things. They behave or speak without sensitivity. They damage a person's property, family, reputation, or self-image. What is one supposed to feel toward the perpetrators of these acts if not hatred?

Our Creator obviously knew that hatred was within man's emotional repertoire. Therefore, the Torah provides us with a means of productively dealing with the feeling, commanding us:[1] "You shall not hate your brother in your heart."

Usually, when someone is wronged, he seeks redress. He is not inclined to hide his feelings; on the contrary, he may explode with feeling. Keeping one's negative emotions under wraps would seem to be the higher road, requiring self-control and self-sacrifice as well, as the victim chooses not to act on emotion.

Often, however, the motivation for hiding one's feelings is not that lofty. A person may keep quiet out of fear of confrontation, assuming that the wrongdoer might become angry or hurt if he is confronted. The wrongdoer might be someone in a position of authority or a close family member, and the injured party may find it is easier to swallow the damage and move on.

But does he move on? Usually, the feeling of being injured does not heal on its own. A barrier rises between the two parties and subsequent interactions, albeit com-

21
Cheshvan

22
Shevat

21
Iyar

22
Av

---

1. *Vayikra* 19:17.

pletely benign, are interpreted as further insults that reinforce the barrier. This is the tragedy, for anything that builds barriers between Jews thwarts our efforts at achieving unity and hastening the time when the *Shechinah* will again dwell among us.

The Torah urges us to take a more courageous route. Rather than pretending to have forgiven and forgotten, "You shall reprove your fellow, and do not bear a sin because of him."[2] The idea of "reproving" others may not seem like the path to peace; however, the Hebrew word for "reproof" — "*tochachah,*" actually comes from the word "*hochiach*, to prove," which describes the positive outcome of bringing clarity to a situation.[3]

Sincere forgiveness cannot come from papering over the breach with a friendly veneer, but rather, it comes from airing one's grievance. First, a person should wait until his initial emotional reaction cools down. As soon as possible thereafter, he should approach the other person and gently[4] — and privately, so as not to cause embarrassment — express his feelings of hurt.[5]

A person's tone of voice can go far in fostering an atmosphere of reconciliation. If it is non-accusatory, the other party will not jump to defend himself against attack. Instead, his conscience will be awakened and he will hopefully apologize for the pain he has caused or explain that his words were misconstrued and they were not intended to be hurtful.

The Chofetz Chaim provides a model of this peacemaking approach:[6] "When someone wrongs another person...it is a mitzvah to ask him, 'Why did you do this to me?' This will allow him to erase all hard feelings that are in his heart toward another person, by speaking about it to him."[7] By expunging the hatred from one's heart, one protects the spiritual role of this organ — a vessel for feel-

---

2. Ibid.
3. *Daas Torah,* Vol. 2, *Maamar* on *Shemos.*
4. See *Rambam, Hilchos Dei'os* 6:8; see also *Rashi, Arachin* 16b, s.v. *Panav mishtanin.*
5. *Kitzur Shulchan Aruch* 29:13.
6. *Ahavas Yisrael*, Ch. 1.
7. *Mitzvos Hashem, Lo Saaseh,* 142; See *Ramban* to *Vayikra* 19:18.

ings of purity and holiness — from the corrosive taint of hatred.[8]

Talking over one's grievances takes courage, patience, and self-control. But if the Jewish people are ever to coalesce into a loving family, dwelling in happiness and tranquility under the shelter of the *Shechinah,* there is no other option.

YOU CAN DO IT

Write down three "different opening lines" with which you can respectfully begin discussing a grievance with someone you feel has offended you. Speak these lines out loud and role-play several ways the other person might respond.

Take It With You

▸ *The Torah teaches us to give tochachah – reproof — to someone who has wronged us.*

▸ *One meaning of tochachah is clarity, signifying that we must bring clarity to the situation.*

▸ *Clearing the air prevents barriers from arising between Jews, thus advancing unity and bringing us closer to the Geulah.*

---

8. *Ahavas Yisrael*, Ch. 4.

| 21 Cheshvan — |
| 22 Shevat — |
| 21 Iyar — |
| 22 Av — |

LOVE TO GIVE

DAY 52

22
Cheshvan

23
Shevat

22
Iyar

23
Av

I n his famous "Discourse" on lovingkindness, Rav Dessler[1] explores the connection between love and giving. Do we give because we love, or is it perhaps the reverse — that we love because we give?

The usual assumption, says Rav Dessler, is that love causes giving, for we observe that people shower gifts and favors on those they love. There is, however, a strong argument for the opposite perspective: A person loves what he himself has created or nurtured.[2] Whether it is a child he has brought into the world, an animal he has reared, a plant he has tended, an object he has crafted, or a house he has built — a person is bound in love to the work of his hands, for in it, he finds himself.

The tractate *Derech Eretz Zuta* states:[3] "If you want to nurture the love of your friend, make it your concern to seek his welfare." Love flows in the direction of giving.

The emotion aroused by giving is so powerful that the Torah recognizes it as an insurmountable distraction to soldiers heading into battle.[4] Three categories of men are therefore exempted from going out to war: whoever has built a new house and has not yet consecrated it, whoever has planted a vineyard and has not yet redeemed it, and whoever has wedded a woman and has not yet taken her to his home.

It is noteworthy that the Torah treats the homeowner and the vineyard planter in exactly the same manner as the new husband, who has embarked on the most intimate of

1. *Michtav MeEliyahu*, Vol. 1, p. 36.
2. *Bava Metzia* 38a.
3. Ch. 2.
4. *Devarim* 20:5-7.

human relationships. The love a person feels toward the fruit of his labors is directly compared to the love of a man for his betrothed. Their common thread is the power of giving.

Rav Dessler describes a case that he personally observed:[5]

> I knew a couple whose little son was the delight of their lives. War reared its head in their town and they were forced to flee. The young mother was away from home on that day; the father fled with his little boy in one direction while the mother was forced to take the opposite route, and so the family was separated. At long last the battlefronts grew quiet, peace returned, and they were re-united — and what a happy family union that was.
>
> But a remarkable thing came to light...The love of the father for his son was deeper than that of the mother for the son...The cruel fact was that the potential "giving" of all those years was lost beyond recall. It was the father who had reared the child and had lavished on him the thousand-and-one acts of tender care that normally fall to...the mother. The love that springs from all that giving had been nurtured solely by the father.

This phenomenon, says Rav Pam,[6] explains why parents' attachment to their children is stronger than children's attachment to their parents,[7] even though the children are the decades-long recipients of their parents' countless kindnesses. It is the giver's love that intensifies through giving.

That which a person gives to another is never lost, says Rav Dessler. It becomes an extension of his own being, for he sees a part of himself in the person to whom he has given. In effect, he transfers a part of himself to the recipient, which naturally draws them closer. This is the

---

5. *Michtav MeEliyahu* loc. cit.
6. *Rav Pam on Chumash*, Rabbi Sholom Smith (ArtScroll/Mesorah Publ.), p. 94.
7. See *Bava Basra* 80a, *Rashbam*, s.v *Um'shani, ima abrata*.

attachment between one man and his fellow to which we give the name "love."

- *Logically, it would seem that the more a person loves another, the more he gives to the object of his love.*

- *In actuality, it is the giving that fosters the feeling of love.*

- *By giving, a person invests some of himself in the object of his kindness. This creates a strong bond.*

YOU CAN DO IT

Choose one person with whom you feel a lack of warmth and think of a way to give to that person, i.e., a phone call, a small gift, a listening ear.

---

22 Cheshvan —

23 Shevat — לע"נ יהודה צבי בן ר' זאב ז"ל

22 Iyar — Lz'echut Nashim Tzadkaniot all around the world
Dedicated by the nashim of France

23 Av —

REMEDIAL GIVING

DAY 53

Giving not only builds love, it erodes *sinah* — hatred — that has already taken root. The Torah utilizes this phenomenon in an unusual halachah regarding the loading and unloading of animals.

The Torah[1] sets out two obligations — to assist the owner in loading an animal whose burden has fallen off its back, and to help unburden an animal that is unable to rise. If both of these situations occur simultaneously, the animal struggling under its burden takes priority, so that its suffering will be relieved quickly.[2]

That rule holds under all circumstances except one: when a person hates the owner of an animal that needs to be loaded. The Gemara[3] poses a situation in which the animal of one's friend is lying under a burden, while the animal of one's enemy needs to be loaded,[4] and it rules that one should first help his enemy's animal "in order to subdue one's *yetzer hara*."

Ritva[5] explains that subduing the impulse to hate a fel-

23
Cheshvan

24
Shevat

23
Iyar

24
Av

---

1. *Shemos* 23:5; *Devarim* 22:4.
2. See *Shulchan Aruch, Choshen Mishpat* 272:10.
3. *Bava Metzia* 32b.
4. Two cases are discussed in *Bava Metzia* ibid. One is the case of a pack-animal whose load has fallen, and the mitzvah is to help the owner reload it. The other is the case of the overloaded animal, where the mitzvah is both to prevent further suffering to the animal, and to help the owner to load it more effectively. If one is confronted by both cases at the same time, the second one takes precedence, since an additional mitzvah is involved — helping the animal. If one is confronted by two precisely similar cases, but in the one instance the owner is a friend and in the other the owner is an enemy, helping the enemy takes precedence, since there is a specific mitzvah to help one's enemy (*Shemos* 23:5), "so as to conquer one's *yetzer hara*."
5. *Bava Metzia* ibid., s.v. *Ta shema*.

low Jew takes precedence even over the Torah obligation to avoid causing unnecessary pain to a living creature.[6] This is the case, says the Gemara,[7] even in instances where the hatred is permissible.[8]

If the hatred is not forbidden, what is the objective of subduing it?[9] The purpose is to prevent the hatred from escalating, which is not permitted. If a person treats his enemy with hatred — even justifiably — then the enemy will respond in kind, as we learn from the words of *Mishlei:*[10] "Just as water reflects a face back to a face, so is one's heart reflected back to him by another." This will launch an upward spiraling of each party's fury.

Counteracting the hatred also keeps that emotion from settling in one's heart. The Chofetz Chaim[11] warns that if a person does not subdue the type of hatred that is permissible, "one will become accustomed to despise others simply for the sake of hating." [12]

As the Chofetz Chaim states:[13]

If one ponders well the effect of this bitter sin called sinah, it appears that [the sinner] draws an impure spirit into [the organ] upon which his life depends — his heart... Therefore, through this...sin of sinah that is mainly in the heart, the impure spirit will find its way into all his limbs.

Given these facts, the question remains as to why loading one's enemy's animal is the antidote. *Derech Eretz Zuta*[14] supplies the answer: "If one wishes to increase his love for another person, he should exert himself to do the

6. See *Rama, Choshen Mishpat* 272:9.
7. *Pesachim* 113b with *Tosafos,* s.v. *She'raah bo.*
8. Ibid.
9. *Tosafos* ibid. asks: If the *sinah* is permissible, why is there a need to subdue one's evil inclination not to hate?
10. 27:19.
11. Cited in *Daf Digest, Bava Metzia* 32, No. 1549. See *Dibros Moshe, Bava Metzia*, Ch. 2, fn. 77.
12. See *Mishnah Berurah, Orach Chaim, Siman* 1:5, which states that one should not quarrel with people who mock him for his service of Hashem because the attribute of impudence is very abhorrent. It does not befit one to use this attribute at all, even for the service of Hashem, since he would acquire the nature of being impudent, [and utilize it] even where the service of Hashem is not involved.
13. *Ahavas Yisrael,* Ch. 1.
14. Ch. 2.

other person kindnesses." This will serve to counteract ill feelings the person has toward his fellow man.[15]

To bypass a friend in need in order to help an enemy in lesser need forces a person to bend dramatically in the direction opposite his inclination. It is a difficult feat, but Rav Pam[16] explains that just as someone who was gravely ill would do anything to effect a cure, a person who understands the gravity of *sinah* is willing to do what it takes to rid himself of it.

There are many people who think, "That's just not me. I'm not the *chesed* type." In reality, Rav Dessler says,[17] all people have a deep-seated need to share their lives, which naturally involves give and take. The Torah does not ask us to do anything foreign to our nature. It simply teaches how to use the best of our nature to clear all the blockages that compromise the work of our hearts.

YOU CAN DO IT

Do an act of kindness for someone with whom you do not get along. For instance, if there's someone at work for whom you feel an antipathy, give that person your first "good morning."

---

15. See *Yevamos* 63b, where the Gemara tells a story about Rav Chiya, whose wife caused him grief. Nevertheless, whenever he would find an object she might appreciate he would bring it home. Rav said to him, "Doesn't she pain you?" Rav Chiya answered, "Is it not enough that they raise our children and protect us from sin?" In *Alei Shur*, Vol. 2, p. 279, Rav Wolbe explains that the way Rav Chiya was able to live with his wife was through gratitude. By having *hakaras hatov* to his wife, he created positive feelings within himself that enabled him to reduce the pain she caused him by putting it in its proper context.
16. *Rav Pam on Chumash*, Rabbi Sholom Smith (ArtScroll/Mesorah Publ.), p. 93.
17. *Michtav MeEliyahu*, Vol. 1, p. 35, s.v. *Ein adam b'olam*.

---

23 Cheshvan —
24 Shevat — In loving memory of Fay Feinstein ע״ה
לע״נ פיגא בת הרב יצחק וגיטל לייפּער ע״ה
23 Iyar —
24 Av — For Sydney and Pearl Woolf
health and nachas from their whole family
From Dr. David and Tovit Fortinsky and family

Take It With You

▸ *Unloading a burdened animal takes priority over loading an animal, since it relieves the animal's suffering, unless the second animal belongs to one's enemy.*

▸ *The purpose of this is to teach one to subdue his yetzer hara.*

▸ *Giving and helping others counteracts feelings of hatred.*

DO SOMETHING

DAY 54

24
Cheshvan

25
Shevat

24
Iyar

25
Av

A person who does good feels good. Filling one's life with positive interactions — helping others, praying for others, dealing patiently despite annoyance or aggression, cheering someone up, giving encouragement and praise — transforms one's personality.[1] As the *Sefer HaChinuch* teaches:[2] "A person is influenced by his actions."

Obviously, it helps to be born with a kind, patient nature. Nevertheless, even those hard-driving individuals who multi-task their way through each day can find modes of giving suited to their lives. Giving is a mind-set that opens a person's eyes to the thousands of ways in which he can help others.

> In Kelm, the minyan adopted a custom of reciting Maariv on Motza'ei Shabbos almost one half-hour later than the regular time. This was done as a kindness to others, as Eliyahu Rabbah[3] states that as long as even one shul in the city has not yet recited Maariv on Motza'ei Shabbos, the deceased [from the city] are not punished in Gehinnom.[4]

The custom in Kelm, says Rav Yechezkel Levenstein, was an illustration of pure lovingkindness. The *minyan* was "*nosei b'ol im chaveiro* — bearing the yoke with his friend," the deceased of Kelm. Tending to the well-being of others, whether they are in this world or the next, is the antithesis of jealousy, in which one is irked by the other

---

1. See *Matnas Chaim, Maamarim,* Vol. 1, p. 243, s.v. *V'sheinis.*
2. *Mitzvah* 16; see *Mesillas Yesharim,* end of Ch. 7.
3. *Siman* 293:1.
4. Cited in *Ohr Yechezkel, Middos,* p. 55, s.v. *B'Kelm.*

person's well-being.[5]

Kind actions perform another essential role. They turn positive emotions into an actuality.[6] For example, when God promises Avraham to give the Land of Israel to his offspring, Avraham's gratitude does not remain a mere thought or feeling. Rather, he immediately builds an altar to concretize his gratitude.[7] Avraham took action, says Rav Dessler,[8] because without action, his positive feelings might quickly dissipate.

Positive deeds not only transform the doer — they exert a profound influence upon all those in his circle. If he is a teacher, then class after class — hundreds of students over the course of years — can potentially learn from the way in which he interacts. No amount of verbal teaching can come close to the impact of even one real-life display of kindness and integrity.

This was the lesson Reb Shraga Feivel Mendlowitz[9] drew from Rabbi Shimon's statement in *Pirkei Avos*:[10] "I was raised among the Sages and I have found nothing better for oneself than silence." Reb Shraga Feivel explained that Rabbi Shimon is teaching us that in addition to the Torah a student learns from Torah scholars, he can learn both halachah and proper behavior by observing their actions. "*Middos* are caught, not taught," he would often say.

Parents, by virtue of their constant, long-term contact with their children, have the greatest opportunity to teach them, through actions, the proper priorities in life. In both school and at home, the Torah's teachings can best be instilled by example. In fact, Rav Dessler warns that teaching Torah without imparting its spirit of goodness can do far more harm than good:[11]

> *We see the great need to increase good deeds,*

---

5. Ibid., p. 157, s.v. *Hakinah, hataavah.*
6. Ibid., *Shemos*, p. 86, fn 3.
7. *Bereishis* 12:7.
8. *Michtav MeEliyahu*, Vol. 5, p. 453; Vol. 3, p. 127.
9. *Reb Shraga Feivel*, Yonoson Rosenblum (ArtScroll/Mesorah Publ.), p. 109.
10. 1:17.
11. *Michtav MeEliyahu*, Vol. 3, p. 128.

- *A giving nature is developed and enhanced through giving.*
- *Helping others automatically counteracts feelings of jealousy.*
- *Actions turn thoughts and intentions into reality.*

because without this, studying mussar and even learning Torah is dangerous, as Chazal teach:[12] "If he purified himself with actions, then [his Torah] will be a potion of life. If...he did not purify himself with good deeds, then it will be a brew of death."

Actions — positive, loving, helpful actions — are therefore a lifesaver. Not only do they disarm the forces of jealousy that infiltrate our hearts, but they ensure that the Torah we spend our lives pursuing will indeed be our Tree of Life.

YOU CAN DO IT

Begin by giving close to home. Choose one family member who needs help or encouragement. Write down what you will do for this person, and do it every day.

---

12. *Yoma* 72b.

24 Cheshvan —
25 Shevat —
24 Iyar —
25 Av —

"A GOOD EYE"

G ive? I barely have enough for my own family!" said Yaakov, who possessed an investment portfolio worth several hundred thousand dollars. Despite an ample income and comfortable financial cushion, he always feared that somehow, he didn't have enough.

"Give? I'd be glad to," said Yosef. "My business did well this year, baruch Hashem. I'm happy to help out the yeshivah." When he looked at his home, his Shabbos table, his healthy children and loving wife, he felt like the richest man in the world.

25 Cheshvan

26 Shevat

25 Iyar

26 Av

There is a direct connection between a person's feeling of well-being and satisfaction in his lot, and his desire to give to others. That is why the disciples of Avraham Avinu, the paragon of lovingkindness, are described in the Mishnah[1] as those having a "good eye, a humble spirit, and a meek heart." Lovingkindness itself is not mentioned in the list, says Rav Mattisyahu Salomon,[2] because to be a true virtue, it must exist as an outgrowth of a good eye. A good eye sees the good — in life, in the world, and in others. A good eye imbues one's heart with the desire to seek the good in others.

While one might think of a giving nature as arising from a good heart, the Maharal[3] explains that the good eye is yet a higher level. That is because it is possible for the heart to be moved to help someone else, yet harbor jealousy or

---

1. *Avos* 5:22.
2. *Matnas Chaim, Maamarim*, Vol. 1, p. 239.
3. *Nesivos Olam, Nesiv Ayin Tov*, beg. of Ch. 1.

other ill-will toward the recipient. Rav Salomon[4] explains that such a mode of giving is not what the Mishnah is discussing when it describes the "disciples of Avraham." Giving with a good eye means feeling so fulfilled with one's own blessings that one wishes to help others as well. One's heart is like an overflowing spring that nourishes everything around it. This is the spirit, says Rav Solomon,[5] that fueled Avraham's ascent.

By developing the attribute of a good eye toward others, a person uproots from himself the opposite trait — an evil eye. This is the perspective of those whom the Mishnah[6] describe as "an arrogant spirit and a greedy soul, who are among the disciples of [the wicked] Balaam." They follow in the ways of one who was known for his insatiable appetite for other people's money.

The person with a good eye sees giving as an opportunity. If he gives to the local food bank, he finds happiness in the thought of needy Jewish families filling their refrigerators and pantries with food for Shabbos or Yom Tov. Their peace of mind and happiness become his. He is twice blessed — first with his own possessions, and then with the joy he feels in helping others. As *Mishlei* teaches:[7] "He who has a generous eye will be blessed, for he gave of his bread to the poor."

Giving with a good eye is the kind of giving that builds love and unity. Otherwise, giving can actually cause divisiveness. The giver can become resentful if the recipient doesn't seem grateful enough, or if he fails to return the favor when the tables are turned. One who gives with a good eye receives so much satisfaction from giving that he does not feel as though the recipient "owes him." Rather, he feels that *he* gained from the endeavor.

With that spirit, giving can defeat jealousy, thereby uprooting *lashon hara* and *sinas chinam*. When we look at our fellow Jew with a good eye, we are, in reality, seeing

---

4. *Matnas Chaim* loc. cit.
5. Ibid., p. 242, s.v. *Hayotzei mi'devareinu*.
6. *Avos* 5:22.
7. 22:9.

through the crystal clear lens of redemption.[8]

YOU CAN DO IT:

Write down three attributes (material, physical, talents, etc.) with which you have been blessed. Now write down three things you can offer to someone in need.

---

8. See *Matnas Chaim, Maamarim* Vol. 1, p. 242, s.v. *U'mizeh*.

25 Cheshvan —
26 Shevat —
25 Iyar —
26 Av —

Take It With You

▶ *A good eye means perceiving the world and other people as good.*

▶ *A good eye comes from being content with one's lot.*

▶ *One who gives with a good eye has a sincere desire to share his sense of abundance with others.*

JUDGE OTHERS FAVORABLY

DAY 56

26
Cheshvan

27
Shevat

26
Iyar

27
Av

*T*here's Reuven's son, Yaakov, late again for shul," Yosef thought as he glanced at the tall boy edging into his seat one Shabbos morning.

"Reuven just doesn't know how to raise a son," Yosef's internal monologue continued. "A father's got to impress on his son that it's important to be on time!"

Yosef's observation was accurate; Yaakov was always late for shul. However, Yosef's judgment was inaccurate, for Reuven was working mightily to keep his troubled son engaged in Jewish life. That he came to shul at all was a tribute to Reuven's wisdom, love, and effort.

It is easy to predict what will happen next in this story: Yosef will mull over his condemnation of Reuven. Soon, his thoughts will spill out into words: "What's with our neighbor Reuven Pfeferfeld?" he might ask his wife. "It seems like he just lets his son run wild. He showed up in shul today halfway through Mussaf! If that were my son, I'd tell him, show up on time or don't bother coming!"

This is how negative judgment fuels *lashon hara*. What a person thinks, he eventually says. To stop the words from being spoken, one must exert constant effort and vigilance, as if holding the lid down on a volatile substance. Eventually, one's strength gives out and the volatile substance — *lashon hara* — erupts into the air.

The Torah, in fact, commands us to judge others in a positive light:[1] "With righteousness shall you judge your

---

1. *Vayikra* 19:15. *Avos* 1:6; *Rambam, Hilchos Dei'os* 5:7; *Sefer HaMitzvos* to *Rambam, Mitzvas Asei* 177; *Yesod V'Shoresh HaAvodah, Shaar Avodas HaLev,* Ch. 7. see *Mishnah Berurah* 156:4.

fellow." This verse is followed directly by a warning against *lashon hara*:[2] "You shall not be a gossipmonger among your people," confirming the link between how a person judges others and how he speaks of them. Therefore, the Chofetz Chaim[3] urges all those who understand the importance of avoiding *lashon hara* to learn how to judge others favorably.

The way someone judges a situation is a factor in determining whether his words constitute *lashon hara*, says Rav Hutner.[4] He explains that the concept of *lashon hara* is the recital of a true fact without an accurate judgment of what actually occurred.

The story of Moshe Rabbeinu's sister Miriam is the prime example of how *lashon hara* operates. Miriam discusses with Aharon the separation of Moshe from his wife. It is true that the couple has separated. However, Miriam's judgment that the separation is problematic is based on her lack of knowledge as to the requirements posed by Moshe's stature in prophecy.[5] Miriam was thus punished with *tzaraas* (a spiritual malady that manifests itself on an individual's house, clothing, and on his person, where it forms leprosy-like lesions), which God had ordained as the consequence of speaking *lashon hara*.

In the opening story, had Yosef known what a triumph Yaakov's appearance at shul — even at the end of davening — was, he would have had no complaint about Reuven or his son. Had Miriam known that Moshe was doing exactly what God wanted, she would have had no issue to discuss with Aaron. In both cases, it was the rush to judgment, the jump to the *wrong* conclusion, that fueled the *lashon hara*.

The simple fact of life is that no one really knows what is going on inside another person. Even one's children or spouse have many encounters during the day of which other family members are unaware. Therefore, it is literally impossible to judge a person accurately. Judging favorably does not mean blindly accepting unlikely excuses; it

---

2. *Vayikra* 19:16.
3. *Ahavas Yisrael*, Ch. 5.
4. *Iggeres Pachad Yitzchak*, Letter 268.
5. *Kovetz Maamarim*, p. 50.

means opening both eyes to the truth of our own limited knowledge.

In doing so, we open up our lives as well, to receive an incomparable reward — God's compassion. For *Chazal* promise that whoever judges his friend favorably will be judged with favor in Heaven.[6]

YOU CAN DO IT

The next time you find yourself becoming angry at or disappointed in someone, make a commitment to refrain from reacting right away. At a cool-headed moment, write down numerous possible explanations for the person's actions.

---

6. *Shabbos* 127b; *Sefer HaYirah.*

26 Cheshvan —
27 Shevat —
לע״נ חי׳ גיטל בת ר׳ אברהם יצחק ע״ה — 26 Iyar
27 Av —

JUDICIAL ETHICS

DAY 57

Once it has been established that there is an obligation, based in the Torah, to judge others favorably, the next question is, how? How does a person go about satisfying this requirement? Does it mean turning a blind eye to real evil? How do we discern between favorable judgment and the rationalization of wrong?

The framework for judging others depends on the spiritual stature of the person being judged. There are four categories relevant to this discussion: The *tzaddik* (saintly individual), the average person, the person one does not know, and the *rasha* (evil person).

27 Cheshvan

28 Shevat

27 Iyar

28 Av

The *Tzaddik*:

- A person should assume that the righteous person is doing good, even if an explanation would be far-fetched or the unfavorable judgment appears reasonable. [1]
- Example: *If you were to see a Torah scholar enter a nonkosher restaurant, you should assume he did so for a valid reason. If you are in a situation in which you see a God-fearing person eat something nonkosher, you should assume that he has a health issue that necessitates his doing so.*

The Average Person:

- An average individual must be judged favorably to the extent that if you observe an act that can be interpreted in either a positive or negative way, it should

---

1. *Rambam, Peirush HaMishnayos, Avos* 1:6; *Shaarei Teshuvah, Shaar* 3, *Os* 218.

be interpreted favorably.[2]

- Example: *You see an average person putting a box of cereal into his shopping bag in a way that could be stealing, or could be something innocent (he is exchanging an already paid-for product). You must give him the benefit of the doubt.*

The Stranger

- Regarding someone whose spiritual status is unknown, if one observes him doing or saying something that would be good if interpreted one way, or bad if interpreted another way, one should take the favorable approach.[3] If the action lends itself strongly to a negative interpretation, then the onlooker is not commanded to judge him favorably. However, it is considered praiseworthy to do so.[4]
- Example: *A late-model car parks in front of your house and a well-dressed man comes to your door asking for money toward his child's medical expenses. You could assume that he is either truly needy and that his clothing and car have been borrowed, or that he is a fraud. You should assume his truthfulness.*

The *Rasha*[5]

- If the habitual wrongdoer commits an action that could be interpreted positively or negatively, there is no obligation to judge him favorably.[6] Rather, one can presume that he has indeed done wrong. Even if his actions lend themselves to a favorable interpretation, one can still suspect that he was doing wrong.

---

2. *Chofetz Chaim*, Intro., *Asin* 3 with *Be'er Mayim Chaim*; *Shaarei Teshuvah* loc. cit.; *Smag, Mitzvos Asei, Mitzvah* 106; *Meiri, Avos* 1:6. See also *Rashi, Shevuos* 30a, s.v. *Havei dan*.
3. *Rambam, Peirush HaMishnayos, Avos*, Ch. 1; *Chofetz Chaim* loc. cit. See *Rav Bartenura* on *Avos* 1:6.
4. *Rambam* loc. cit.
5. See *Shaarei Teshuvah, Shaar* 3, *Os* 218 for definition of a "rasha."
6. *Shaarei Teshuvah*. See *Rambam* loc. cit.; *Rav Bartenura* loc. cit.; *Yad Yechezkel, Parashas Emor*, p. 187, s.v. *Gemara Yevamos*. However, see *Likutei Maharan, Mahadura Kamma, Siman* 282.

- Example: *A person is known as a compulsive thief, and you see him doing something that could be innocent, or could be thievery. You may presume that he is indeed stealing.*

The reason for these precautions regarding the proven *rasha* is that the Torah does not promote irrational naïveté. A person who regularly sins can be assumed to be continuing in that fashion unless he demonstrates consistent change. For everyone else, however, we offer that which we want for ourselves — a kind eye and a gracious heart.[7]

YOU CAN DO IT

Ask yourself this question: What approach do you take when judging the acts or words of others? Does it conform to the approaches for a righteous or an average person? Work on yourself to judge favorably.

Take It With You

▸ *Whether one judges others favorably depends on the spiritual status of the person being judged.*

▸ *A tzaddik is assumed to be doing right even if his act gives the appearance of sin.*

▸ *For an average person, if his act is open to interpretation, it should be interpreted as good.*

▸ *A person who is known to be a sinner is not given the benefit of the doubt.*

---

7. *Rambam* loc. cit.

EXPAND THE INNER CIRCLE

DAY 58

28
Cheshvan

29
Shevat

28
Iyar

29
Av

*T*he immigrant worked long hours to make a living and pay his children's yeshivah tuition. Several of his sons became great Torah scholars, renowned throughout the world for their wisdom and learning. Was the father jealous? Did he resent having had to forego his own learning so that his sons could achieve greatness? Not at all; his children were his crowning achievement.

This example illustrates the Gemara's[1] statement that "there is not a father who is jealous of his son." Love binds the father to his child with such closeness that the father experiences the child's successes as his own.

For the same reason love drives out jealousy, it can also drive out negative judgment. For example, if a person saw a beloved friend walk into a neighbor's house and walk out carrying a silver menorah, he would assume his friend had permission to borrow the item. However, if he would see a complete stranger performing the same actions, he would assume, albeit mistakenly, that the stranger was a thief. Love, says Rav Chaim Friedlander,[2] influences a person to judge the loved one's actions favorably.

Thus, the cure to negative judgment is to cultivate a loving attitude toward all the people in our lives. That means undertaking a great stretching exercise, daily reaching beyond our own immediate radius of close friends and relatives, to forge positive connections with people we do

1. *Sanhedrin* 105b.
2. *Sifsei Chaim*, Vol. 1, p. 228, s.v. *Hamistakel.*

not yet love.

Before one can begin to do that, however, one must come to the realization that doing so is within his power. In *Michtav MeEliyahu*,[3] Rav Dessler explains that every person possesses some spark of the desire to give.[4] However, if he expresses that desire only toward the people nearest and dearest to him, the desire remains just a spark. His world remains divided into two teams —"them and us." "Them" are the outsiders, with whom "survival of the fittest" rules the relationship. "Us" are the closest family and friends, to whom the commandment "Love your neighbor" is applied.

By limiting the ranks of the "us" team, a person suffers unnecessarily from a paucity of positive interactions in his life. He is like someone who limits his income to the poverty level so that he won't have to pay taxes; he saves himself from having to give away anything, yet he forfeited a better life.

The circle of "us" is endlessly expandable, and the means to do it is through giving, as we learned on Day 52. All those individuals relegated to the "them" category are simply those to whom one has yet to give. If a person were even to offer that stranger a smile and a hello, a brief moment of small-talk that acknowledges his existence, he would begin to change the nature of the relationship. The barriers would begin to erode and soon there would be yet another person in whom one's effort and caring has been invested, and thus, another person who is a part of oneself.

Someone who has been granted the merit to reach this sublime level can understand the command:[5] "You shall love your neighbor as yourself," in its literal sense: "As yourself — without distinction; as yourself — in actual fact. By giving of yourself to another you will find in your soul that you and he are indeed one: you will feel in the

---

3. Vol. 1, pp. 44-45.
4. Rav Dessler explains that it is essential that this should be so, for the world depends on it for its very existence; without that vestigial spark of giving, no one would marry or have children.
5. *Vayikra* 19:18.

Take It With You

▶ *Sincere love eliminates jealousy, for a person feels that the beloved person's success is his own.*

▶ *For the same reason, love counteracts negative judgment.*

▶ *A person can promote positive judgment by expanding the circle of people he loves, and giving to others.*

clearest possible manner that he really is to you 'as yourself.'"

YOU CAN DO IT

Add to your "us" team by reaching out to someone outside your immediate circle.

---

28 Cheshvan —
29 Shevat —
28 Iyar —
29 Av —

BEHIND CLOSED DOORS

DAY 59

29-30
Cheshvan

30
Shevat

29
Iyar

30
Av

*R*ena was a pillar of kindness in her community. Every school, shul, and organization she belonged to benefited from her energy and creativity, which she applied to organizing highly successful fundraising functions. Her home was the frequent site of parlor meetings and community events.

But when the doors closed and the family was alone in their home, the giving ended. Rena's perfectionist nature turned her into a demanding wife and mother. No one dared to forget anything she had told them to do, nor make any kind of mistake that she might discover. She forgot nothing, and forgave very little indeed.

In previous days, we discussed how to expand the circle of loved ones so that our fellow Jews receive the benefit of our favorable judgment and willing hands. Putting distance between ourselves and others creates a climate for divisiveness. On the other hand, people sometimes display even worse cruelty to those to whom they are closest. In the false belief that they can show their "real selves" to their nearest family, they fan the fires of hurt and enmity every day, destroying Jewish unity at its very root.

Rav Binyomin Zilber was visited by a man who requested a blessing for shalom bayis, but Rav Zilber demurred. He explained to the man that shalom bayis depended on a person's own willingness to be "mevater al hakol" — to always step into his wife's place, view the situation from her point of view, and concede to her. With this approach, he said, the man would create his own shalom bayis.[1]

"Being *mevater*" — conceding to the other person — is a key to maintaining a peaceful home. Rav Mattisyahu Salomon explains:[2] "The *middah* of being *mevater* plays a very big role in a successful marriage. Situations of potential conflict often arise in a marriage, and the willingness of both partners to step back from what they think are their rights and allow the other to have his way can only promote love and harmony in the home. Sometimes, you can fight for your rights and demand justice, but even if you prevail, you may pay a steep price for your victory. It would be far wiser to be *mevater*."

Most people, however, may not be prepared to walk away from what they perceive as their due. It is a trait that needs to be developed gradually, and one way to do so is by applying the principle of *vatranus* to everyday mishaps. The Midrash[3] teaches that one can become a *vatran* by refraining from anger if someone inadvertently spills something in his house or rips his clothing.

Because this trait is so essential to a couple's marital harmony, parents can give their children an enormously valuable gift by training them in this way. Rav Mattisyahu Salomon offers an example:[4]

> Being mevater [may] involve a situation where a child has something to which he is completely entitled, and another child grabs it away unjustly... The parent tells the child, "It really is yours, and if you want you could take it back, but be mevater...Instead of fighting, let him have it for a while."[5]

---

1. "Hakhel Daily Community Awareness Bulletin," Kislev 15, 5770/ December 1, 2009.
2. *With Hearts Full of Love*, Rabbi Mattisyahu Salomon, Adapted for Print by Rabbi Yaakov Yosef Reinman (ArtScroll/Mesorah Publ.), p. 180.
3. *Bamidbar Rabbah* 9:2.
4. *With Hearts Full of Love* loc. cit.
5. Rav Salomon adds that if the child in this scenario is yours, your first obligation before you ask him to be *mevater* is to tell the grabber not to take something that doesn't belong to him. But if the grabber is not your child or if he is too young to understand, then it is appropriate to ask your child to be *mevater*.

You acknowledge that the child is within his rights, you ask him to forfeit his rights in this situation for the sake of peace...That is chinuch in being mevater... And when children see that their parents are mevater to each other, the chinuch benefits will serve them well when they grow up and get married and in all situations in life.

YOU CAN DO IT

Right now, today, think of an ongoing conflict in your life. Write down the advantages and drawbacks of giving in. On the advantage side, give special weight to the benefit of shalom. Once you have assessed the situation, try to find the courage to give in on this issue.

Take It With You

▸ *Being a "vatran" means looking at a situation from the other person's perspective and conceding to him for the sake of peace.*

▸ *Vatranus is essential to a peaceful relationship between husband and wife.*

▸ *Parents can teach their children — especially by example — to "be mevater" with possessions and privileges that rightfully belong to them.*

29-30 Cheshvan —
30 Shevat —
29 Iyar — לזכות ברכה והצלחה בכל
לכל בני משפחתנו ולכלל ישראל
ע"י משפחת פירסט
30 Av — In honor of the wedding of
Talia Waizman & Eitan Herskovitz
May we see much nachas.
Dedicated by their grandmother, Kaaren Staschower

GETTING OVER IT

DAY 60

1
Kislev

1
Adar

1
Sivan

1
Elul

*C*haim's family is moving to a house five blocks away. His neighbor, Baruch, has a van that generally sits idle in the driveway. Chaim asks to borrow the van to transport some cartons to the new house. Without explanation, Baruch refuses. Chaim begins to shlep the items in his own small car, making numerous trips back and forth. Every time he comes to pick up more cartons, he sees Baruch's van sitting in the driveway, while Baruch sits on his porch watching Chaim labor.

The next morning, there is a knock on Chaim's door. It's Baruch. "Do you mind if I come in and use your fax machine?" Baruch asks. "I need to get these papers to my bank, but it's such a hassle to park there."[1]

There is no doubt that the Torah forbids Chaim to refuse the favor. His refusal would violate the prohibition against taking revenge.[2] Therefore, the Rambam[3] offers another option — an option which, rather than fanning the flames of divisiveness within the Jewish nation, will strengthen the essential bond of unity: "It is worthy for a person to be *maavir al midosav* on all things in this world."

This option is accompanied by a remarkable incentive cited in the Gemara:[4] "*Kol hamaavir al midosav, maavirin mimenu kol pesha'av* — A person who overlooks wrong-doing against him will have all his sins removed from him."

Every Jew who believes there is judgment in the Next

---

1. Adapted from the classical example of *Yoma* 23a. See also *Matnas Chelko* on *Mesillas Yesharim*, p. 138.
2. *Vayikra* 19:18.
3. *Hilchos Dei'os* 7:7.
4. *Rosh Hashanah* 17a; *Megillah* 28a.

World should read and re-read the Gemara's incentive. If, before one dies, he has been unsuccessful in doing *teshuvah* properly, he can still merit Gan Eden. Being a *vatran* has the capacity to atone for one's *aveiros,* while other mitzvos cannot do so.[5]

Nevertheless, overcoming the desire to express one's indignation takes serious effort. *Mesillas Yesharim*[6] explains that "hate and revenge are very difficult for man's spiteful heart to escape, for in view of his being extremely sensitive to insult and suffering great anguish because of it, revenge, being the only thing that will give him rest, is sweeter than honey to him."

Yet, a person who develops the ability to "let it go"[7] is able to usher his heart past the resentment that another person's behavior may arouse. He integrates the loss or insult into his life, realizing that it, as everything else, has come to him from God.[8]

The person who follows this path is not outfoxing Divine justice. Rather, this principle conforms precisely to the basis of Divine justice, which is described as "measure for measure."[9] Upon that basis, it makes perfect sense that if a person has overlooked the honor or favors others

---

5. *Rashi, Rosh Hashanah* 17a, s.v. *Maavirin lo; Michtav MeEliyahu,* Vol. 4, p. 243, s.v., *Mi mimenu.* The Chofetz Chaim writes that if someone has embarrassed or humiliated you, you should not hate him. Although he has committed a transgression, he has actually rendered you a service — for when a person suffers humiliation in silence, it atones for any sins he may have.

   See *Shemiras HaLashon, Chasimas HaSefer,* Part 1, Ch. 6, s.v. *Kein b'inyan zeh,* which states that by being *maavir al midosav* one saves himself from numerous sins, as it is difficult for one to know clearly all the laws of the Torah involving interpersonal relationships.

6. Ch. 11, s.v. *Gam ha'sinah.*

7. *Rashi, Rosh Hashanah* 17a, s.v. *Hamaavir al midosav.*

8. *Sefer HaChinuch, Mitzvah 241,* cited in *Matnas Chelko* on *Mesillas Yesharim,* p. 138, s.v. *U'b'Sefer HaChinuch.* See *Chofetz Chaim al HaTorah, Parashas Mishpatim; Shem Olam, Shaar Shemiras HaShabbos,* Ch. 3 (all cited in *Matnas Chelko* on *Mesillas Yesharim,* pp. 138-139). See also *Rambam, Hilchos Dei'os* 7:7, who cites another reason why one should be a *maavir al midosav.*

9. *Shabbos* 105b. See *Mesillas Yesharim,* Ch. 19, s.v. *V'amru od v'nosan; Mishnah Berurah* 606:8, with *Shaar HaTziyun, Os* 8. See also *Michtav MeEliyahu* Vol. 5, p. 70, where Rav Dessler states that *middah k'neged middah* is the reason the person's sins are overlooked.

▸ *The Gemara
promises
that one
who over-
looks
wrongs
will receive
the same
treatment,
measure for
measure,
when his
time comes
for Divine
judgment.*

▸ *Letting go
of one's
grievances
has great
protective
power for
an individ-
ual and for
the Jewish
people.*

justly owe him during his time on earth, God will overlook that person's spiritual debts when the time arrives for his final judgment.

> *During the Six Day War in 1967, a shell hit the roof of the building where Rav Chaim Shmulevitz and his students were huddled for safety, but did not explode. Rav Chaim said, "You may all think this was in the zechus of our Torah. However, we were saved in the merit of a women here, whose husband had abandoned her many years ago without giving a get. Nevertheless, she said she would forgive him if Hashem would have mercy on the students."*[10]

As individuals and as communities, we have everything to gain by following this path. As we will see, it is not only the path to Divine forgiveness, but the path to redemption as well.

YOU CAN DO IT

Choose a situation you find mildly irritating. For example, Some-one has infringed on your rights. You come to work and are pre-pared to pull into your designated parking space. But, someone else has parked his car in your spot. See if there is an open spot you can use and don't even mention what happened to anyone. Hold back from criticizing. Think about the reward for vatranus.

---

10. Heard from Rav Avraham Ausband, Rosh Yeshivah of Yeshivah Telshe Riverdale, NY.

GETTING OVER IT, PART II

DAY 61

In a world of right and wrong, reward and punishment, the concept of putting aside one's indignation raises a question: What is wrong with being indignant about an insult or injury? Is that not, in the reality of this world, the basis of justice?

Why, in fact, does the Gemara[1] blame the destruction of the Beis HaMikdash partly on the fact that the Jewish people insisted on pressing charges against each other for every legal right? If they had the rights, why should they not bring suit for them?

The problem, says the *Divrei Shaul*,[2] arises from the fact that strict justice is often born from *sinas chinam*. One who harbors hatred against another person is far more likely to be demanding his "rights" in court due to his hatred of his enemy rather than his love of justice.

Rav Elyah Lopian[3] explains that as long as the Jewish people were willing to go beyond the letter of the Torah law, showing mercy for one another's sake, God dealt likewise with them.[4] However, when their *sinas chinam* incited them to demand every last ounce of redress, with no mercy shown for the defendant, then God judged the Jewish people in the same spirit. He exacted precise recompense for their sin of *sinas chinam*, and thus the sec-

2
Kislev

2
Adar

2
Sivan

2
Elul

---

1. *Bava Metzia* 30b.
2. Cited in *Megadim Chadashim* to *Shabbos*, p. 305, s.v. *V'ra'isi*.
3. *Kuntres Shevivei Lev* (back of *Lev Eliyahu*), p. 292, s.v. *Maseches Bava Metzia*.
4. See *Michtav MeEliyahu*, Vol. 5, p. 70, where Rav Dessler adds a second reason why heaven "passes over his sins." Someone who is *maavir al midosav* connects himself to the community. Therefore, he is judged as part of that community, which is always more meritorious than one who stands in judgment on his own.

ond Beis HaMikdash and Jerusalem were destroyed.

Conversely, the promise of redemption rests on the trait of relinquishing one's grievance, the power of which is touchingly portrayed in the Midrashic[5] account of Rochel Imeinu's plea to God to end the exile. Although the Forefathers and Moshe Rabbeinu each have an opportunity to present an argument in their children's behalf, only Rochel succeeds, and she does so by stating:

> If I, a mere mortal, was prepared not to humiliate my sister…how could You, the eternal, compassionate God, be jealous of idols — which have no true existence — that were brought into Your home? Will You cause my children to be exiled on this account?

Rochel was willing to relinquish her rightful place as Yaakov's first wife to her sister Leah. She did not insist on her "rights," so as not to subject her sister to embarrassment. This is what bestowed upon her the standing to make a convincing argument to God. Thus, in this Midrash,[6] the trait of overcoming one's grievance becomes the basis upon which God promises the end of the exile: "There is reward for your actions… Your children will return to their borders."

Today, as the exile continues, we suffer from the same passion for "justice" that beset the generation of the second Beis HaMikdash. But we can change.

When the injustices of life prickle at your heart and you are filled with the desire to "set things right," the best strategy is to think of the final outcome. Have you still got a few sins on your record? If so, being *maavir al midosov* is the ideal solution.[7] Drop the matter and move on.[8] God will reciprocate in both this world and the Next.[9] Heavenly mercy and compassion will be aroused.[10] You will be freed

---

5. *Eichah Rabbah, Pesichah* §24.
6. Ibid.
7. *Michtav MeEliyahu*, Vol. 4, p. 243, s.v. *Mi mimenu*.
8. *Rashi, Rosh Hashanah* 17a, s.v. *Hamaavir al midosav*.
9. However, see *Sichos Mussar* (Rav Chaim Shmulevitz), *Shaarei Chaim, Maamar* 100, p. 422, "Likras Yom Hadin" [5732, Maamar 38], which states that the benefit of being a *maavir al midosov* applies only if it comes about through humility.
10. *Shaar HeZechirah,* Ch. 2.

from the hatred in your heart, and will help to move the entire world closer to redemption.[11]

YOU CAN DO IT

Imagine arriving in Heaven with a clean slate — all your imperfections, insensitive remarks, and foolish actions suddenly wiped away! Now wipe the slate clean here on earth for someone in your life.

---

11. See *Eitz Yosef* on *Taanis* 25b, s.v. *Ela* (found in *Iyun Yaakov*).

---

2 Kislev —
2 Adar — Judy Pressman לע"נ יוכבד בת ר' אלחנן ע"ה
By the Pressman, Hefter, Goldberg and Rothenberg families
לע"נ רחל שרי בת אלכסנדר משה ע"ה **— 2 Sivan**
לע"נ זיסל בת אריה דב ע"ה
לע"נ ברוך מרדכי בן כלב ז"ל
Dedicated by Alex Goldsmith
2 Elul —

Take It With You

- *Being "maavir al midosav" is the quality of someone who overlooks his indignation at a wrong done to him.*

- *The Gemara promises that God will wipe away the sins of anyone who makes concessions to his fellow man.*

- *This promise is based on the concept of "measure for measure." God overlooks the sins of those who overlook their fellow's sins.*

- *Exacting one's due stems from sinas chinam and brought about the destruction of the second Beis HaMikdash.*

GET READY TO "LET IT GO"

DAY 62

Even with the promise of a life of harmony, a promise of reciprocity in both this world and the Next, and knowing that you helped to move the entire world closer to redemption, conceding to others demands tremendous effort. Like all self-improvement, it is best approached in small, steady steps. Rabbi Dessler[1] offers ten concepts to enable a person to transform himself into one who is able to let go of resentments, grievances, and anger.

(1) **Warmth:** Deal with others in a warm, friendly, concerned manner. Don't be "all business."

(2) **Honor:** Everyone thinks they are superior to you in some way; and they are probably right. By acknowledging the other person's pre-eminence in a specific area, you arouse his positive feelings.

(3) **Common Interest:** Most people seem more interested in their own needs than in yours. Look for and emphasize areas in which you have needs in common.

(4) **Actions:** Don't only try to do, but also *want* to do for others. If you truly want to act, you will find ways to overcome most obstacles, and doing the deed will enrich you.

(5) **Avoid Controversy:** Be careful not to enter into heated disputes with your friend. If you know you have strong, differing opinions on certain subjects, avoid those subjects, because these arguments, even when they are not personal, erect barriers between you.

(6) **Me, Me, Me:** Do not talk excessively about yourself. Talk to your friend about himself, and he will be interested in listening. (To most people, there is nothing

---

1. *Michtav MeEliyahu*, Vol. 4, p. 244, s.v. *Machmas chashivus.*

more pleasant than their own name.)

(7) **Pay Attention:** Listen attentively to others. Make an effort to remember people's names and details, and they will respond to your attentiveness.

(8) **No Lectures:** Do not openly criticize your friend because he will only become defensive and reject your statements. People do not readily admit to their faillings in their hearts.

(9) **Admit Truth:** When speaking to your friends, agree to the truth in their statements rather than holding on to your side for the sake of "winning." Why create friction?

(10) **Understanding Is Crucial:** Remember what wise doctors say: It is better to understand the patient than to understand the disease. That is because a large portion of every sickness, and sometimes the entire sickness, results from the spirit of the patient. When you succeed in curing this through loving and befriending him more, the sickness will pass.

How do these "people skills" nurture a more forgiving approach toward others? Rav Dessler explains that they train a person to aggrandize the other person rather than himself and to adopt the other person's perspective. At that point, it is not so large a leap to admit that it is not worth stirring up the fires of hatred and envy between one Jew and another over one's own slight or loss.

▸ *Relinquish-ing one's indigna-tion does not come naturally to most people.*

▸ *Rav Dessler prescribes methods that train a person to aggran-dize others rather than himself.*

▸ *From that perspective, one can more eas-ily find the strength to see things the other person's way.*

Take It With You

YOU CAN DO IT

Choose two of Rabbi Dessler's suggestions that you feel you can implement more often. Try using them today.

---

3 Kislev —

3 Adar — In loving memory

לע"נ ר' מיכאל בן ר' הערש יוסף ז"ל

Dedicated by his son-in-law and daughter,

ברוך יעקב ובילא שבע ברנר

3 Sivan —

3 Elul —

WALK IN GOD'S WAYS

DAY 63

4 Kislev

4 Adar

4 Sivan

4 Elul

*M*oshe wanted desperately to be a good father. He pored over books on parenting and sefarim on chinuch. He sought advice from rabbanim and rebbeim. But when faced with a trying situation, his initial response was to emulate what his father had done. His father — insightful, encouraging, and firm in his convictions — was everything Moshe wanted to be.

Character development requires consistency and constant encouragement. In fact, Rav Yisrael Salanter[1] taught that it is easier to learn all of Torah than it is to correct one character flaw. Therefore, even the firmest resolution to become a peace-maker and a giver, backed by all the *mussar* to be found on *sefarim* shelves around the world, may still leave a person facing confusing forks in the road.

The most effective way to steer the course of one's life is to follow an exemplary role model, the way Moshe in the story above followed the example of his father. For a Jew, that strategy is spelled out in the mitzvah: "*V'halachta bidrachav*[2] — and you shall walk in His [God's] ways."[3]

One of the lesser-known mitzvos,[4] "*V'halachta bidrachav*" teaches that as God is merciful, we are required to

---

1. *Ohr Yisrael, Os* 30.
2. *Rambam, Hil. Dei'os* 1:5 cites *Devarim* 28:9. See *Mesillas Yesharim*, Intro., s.v. *U'mah she'Moshe*, which cites *Devarim* 10:12: "Now, O Israel, what does Hashem, your God, ask of you? Only to fear Hashem, your God, to go in all His ways." See *Devarim* 13:5: "Hashem, your God, shall you follow." See *Sefer HaMitzvos L'Rambam, Mitzvas Asei* 8, and *Mishnah Berurah* 156:4 for an explanation.
3. *Mesillas Yesharim* loc. cit. See also *Sotah* 14a, *Shabbos* 133b.
4. *Mitzvah* 611. See *Rambam, Hil. Dei'os* 1:5-6. See also *Pachad Yitzchak, Yom HaKippurim, Maamar* 31, *Os* 6, where Rav Hutner explains that the mitzvah of "*V'halachta bidrachav*" is between man and God and not between man and his fellow man.

be merciful; as He is compassionate, righteous, and holy, so must we be. Our potential to act in Godly ways arises, according to the *Nefesh HaChaim*,[5] from our status as a *tzelem Elokim* — a being created in God's image. Invested with this spark of Godliness, man possesses what no other living being possesses — a capacity for giving and compassion.[6]

Because this capacity for giving is embedded in man's soul, giving should come naturally. However, until we apply that capacity, it remains nothing more than potential. "*V'halachta bidrachav*" goes far beyond a spontaneous impetus to do someone a favor. It is the policy that governs all of one's interpersonal relationships, even when one feels overwhelmed, slighted, or wronged.[7]

According to the *sefer Tomer Devorah*, the Thirteen Attributes of Divine Mercy set the template for fulfilling "*V'halachta bidrachav*." For example, *Tomer Devorah*[8] points out that even when a person sins, God still sustains him: If he were eating nonkosher food, God could cause him to lose the power to swallow. Instead, Hashem allows him to act in a manner than runs contrary to His will until the individual does *teshuvah*. In emulating God, therefore, we are called upon to benefit even those who hurt us.[9]

> At the peak of acrimony in a hostile divorce, the husband, whose uncontrollable temper was the impetus for the breakup, was stricken with a serious illness. His abusiveness had alienated his entire family and lost him his job, and now, he found himself in a hospital bed, sick and alone, as Shabbos arrived. Suddenly, a delivery man arrived bearing a hot Friday night seudah. Unbeknownst to him, it had been ordered by his ex-wife and her family, for although they could not go forward as a united family, neither

5. *Shaar* 1, Ch. 3.
6. See *Ohr Gedalyahu, Shemos*, p. 9, s.v. *Amru Chazal.*
7. See *Matnas Chelko* on *Mesillas Yesharim*, Ch. 19, p. 220, s.v. *Ba'nefesh*, which states that the mitzvah of "*V'halachta bidrachav*" requires that one strive to give his neighbor as much satisfaction as possible.
8. Ch. 1, s.v. *Mi Keil kamocha.*
9. See *Mesillas Yesharim*, Ch. 22, s.v. *Ha'chelek hasheni.*

Take It With You

could they leave a fellow Jew alone and bereft in his sickbed.

There are situations in which we have been victimized and humiliated. We are filled with righteous indignation against the sinner and we know with absolute clarity that he is wrong and we are right, in the same way that a person who sins is wrong, and God is right. In such situations, the mitzvah of *V'halachta bidrachav* is our guide, and it leads us toward sustaining our effort to help the other person come to good.

Doing so, says *Tomer Devorah*,[10] is a *segulah* that will unlock heaven's mercy and "illuminate the world."[11]

YOU CAN DO IT

Next time you are upset at someone, do not hold back from doing him or her a favor. Follow in Hashem's ways and do good.

---

10. End of Ch. 1.
11. See *Matnas Chaim, Maamarim* ,Vol. 1, p. 141.

CHAPTER 9:
SOLUTION IV:
V'AHAVTA L'REI'ACHA
KAMOCHA

YOUR REALITY

DAY 64

5
Kislev

5
Adar

5
Sivan

5
Elul

After a frustrating day at work, you're stuck in traffic and growing more tense by the moment. How are you supposed to remember to pick up the dry cleaning? How are you supposed to recall that your wife needs her suit for a job interview in the morning?

When you arrive home without the suit, your wife is upset. "You know how important this interview is," she complains. "Now what am I supposed to do? I don't have anything else to wear!"

"You reminded me about it at 6 this morning. It might as well have been a month ago!" you say in your own defense. "Do you know how much I have on my mind right now?"

People love themselves. When they make mistakes, they are full of graciousness and understanding for themselves, taking into consideration all their good intentions, all the events that conspired to make the mistake happen. A person who can supply that same understanding to the one who causes *him* damage or hurt lives up to the commandment, *"V'ahavta l'rei'acha kamocha* — love your neighbor as yourself."

If the wife in the story above were to rise to that level, every transgression of the Torah's *mitzvos bein adam l'chaveiro* that might spring from this incident would be avoided. Instead of *onaas devarim*, the wife might provide sympathy for her husband's exhausted state. There would be no potential for *lashon hara,* for the wife would have no negative thoughts about her husband, and therefore, nothing negative to say. There would be no *sinas chinam,* for their empathy for each other would have defused any hostility.

In short, *V'ahavta l'rei'acha kamocha* is the master key that unlocks all the other manifestations of *achdus* discussed in earlier days. With it, the *middos* necessary to hasten the *Geulah* are at our fingertips, and without it, we keep running through the same tragic *galus* script of divisiveness and national disaster.

It's all about one's perspective, as Rav Dessler elaborates:[1]

> One should accustom himself to viewing the next person as if he is looking at himself. All the anger, all the hatred, all the arguments and disagreements with another come because one views himself in a different light.

He gives an example of a poor person who asks a wealthy man for a large sum of money. The wealthy man regards the request as "a chutzpah" and becomes angry. The poor person, embarrassed and saddened, sees the wealthy man as selfish. But if each had tried thinking from the other's perspective, negative feelings and words would be avoided.

In fact, the Torah commands us to lend money to people in need, as the verse says:[2] "When you will lend money to My people, to the poor among you." Regarding the phrase "the poor among you," Rashi expounds.[3] "Look upon yourself as if you were poor." If you visualize the response *you* would want if you were seeking the loan, you will react properly.

> Someone on your block makes a simchah and forgets to send you an invitation. As much as you try to rationalize, you feel hurt.
>
> Now you are making a simchah. The invitation to your best friend from high school gets lost in the mail. She is hurt and angry. When you finally hear about it months later, you're astounded. How could she imagine you would not invite her? Doesn't she know how much can go wrong in making a simchah?

---

1. *Michtav MeEliyahu*, Vol. 4, p. 243.
2. *Shemos* 22:24; *Ahavas Chesed*, Ch. 1.
3. Ad loc.

- *Most people love themselves and excuse their own mistakes and flaws.*

- *Providing that same understanding to others is key to fulfilling "V'ahavta l'rei'acha kamocha — love your neighbor as yourself."*

- *Experiencing another's reality fosters achdus and redemption.*

Both realities are true. By trying to experience the other person's reality, love among Jews can thrive, bringing *achdus* and redemption into our world.

YOU CAN DO IT

Spend a few moments focusing on the various struggles your spouse or friend encounters each day.

---

5 **Kislev** —In memory of אבי מורי ליבוש בן שמעון ז"ל
P.K. and JoD Koenigsberg and family
5 **Adar** —
5 **Sivan** —
5 **Elul** — לע"נ ר' אברהם ניסן בן אהרן גדול הכהן ז"ל
ור' שלמה יצחק בן חיים יוסף מאיר ז"ל
ופעסיל גיטל בת ישעי' יצחק הכהן ע"ה
Dedicated by Mendy and Leah Elefant

GAME CHANGE

DAY 65

*T*here is a popular concept called the "I-You Game." It is played by almost everyone in the world, many times a day. Here is how it is played:

Each player is "I." Whatever "I" do is done with good reasons and good intentions. "I" am the white piece in the game. The other person is "You." "You" do wrong-headed things. "You" are far less competent and intelligent than "I," and "I" feel free to say so, especially when "You" are not there to hear it. "You" are the red game piece.

This game plays out countless times a day. "I" am in the middle of a telephone call when the doorbell rings. "I" am justified in putting my friend on hold while "I" tend to the important individual at the door — the repairman for whom "I" have been waiting all day.

"You" put me on hold to tend to your child and "I" just cannot understand what is taking so long. When "You" come back to my call, "I" might sound a little colder than "I" sounded before, just to give "You" a hint of my disapproval.

The *"I-You Game"* is a phenomenon that plays itself out in a variety of ways, especially in the context of a family:

- *If I stick to something, I call it perseverance. If my child or spouse sticks to something, I call it stubbornness.*
- *If I ask for my spouse's help with a problem, I call it consulting. If my spouse seeks out my help, I call it complaining.*
- *If I forget something, I call it absent-minded. If my*

6
Kislev

6
Adar

6
Sivan

6
Elul

Take It With You

▸ How we perceive others' actions is different from how we perceive our own actions.

▸ What we see as positive traits in ourselves are often perceived as negative traits when they appear in others.

▸ Working to bridge the gap between our self-love and the love we feel for others trains us to be able to fulfill V'ahavta l'rei'acha kamocha.

spouse forgets something, I call it uncaring.

- If I raise my voice, I call it exerting authority. If my child raises his voice, I call it a bad temper.
- If I behave in an unusual way, I call it unique. If my child behaves in an unusual way, I seek a psychological evaluation.

The solution to this dichotomy is to follow Rav Dessler's suggestion:[1] "To accustom ourselves to see others in the same way that we view ourselves." The words "accustom ourselves" indicate the need to build a new habit. Our first impulse is to frame the situation around our own emotions. "Why is this guy in front of me going so slowly? What's wrong with him! He shouldn't be driving!"

To accustom ourselves to a new way of reacting and interacting, it's necessary to push ourselves past the initial, personal reaction, and first consider the other person's reality as if it were our own. Maybe the driver is so slow because he's lost. Perhaps he's a new driver like your daughter, or an elderly driver like your father, who needs to be extra cautious. Those thoughts alone are enough to cool one's anger and thereby fend off the negative interactions (the blaring horn blast) that might otherwise follow.

In each new round of the "I-You Game," our goal must be to ultimately replace red pieces with white. This change is how you — and the Jewish people — win the ultimate game.

YOU CAN DO IT

When you feel frustrated think of one or two positive slants on the other person's actions.

---

1. *Michtav MeEliyahu*, Vol. 4, p. 243.

לע"נ גאלדא חנה בת ר' חיים אלטר ע"ה — 6 Kislev
Dedicated by her family
6 Adar — In memory of Yaakov ben Avrohom a"h
Dedicated by his loving family
6 Sivan — In memory of Aliza bas Zakieh a"h
Dedicated by Nissim Farhi
6 Elul —

ONE FOR ALL

DAY 66

O ne of the best-known stories in the Gemara is the famous incident involving Hillel and Shammai:[1] A gentile approached Shammai and stated that he would convert to Judaism "on the condition that you teach me the entire Torah while I am standing on one foot." Shammai refused the request and sent the man on his way.

The gentile then approached Hillel with the same request. Hillel encapsulated the Torah in one statement: "What is hateful to you, do not do to your fellow." Why did Hillel phrase his statement in the negative, stating "what *not* to do," rather than echoing the Torah's affirmative commandment:[2] "Love your neighbor as yourself"?

The answer to this question provides the foundation for the phenomenon we discussed in the previous two days: the difference between how we perceive others and how we perceive ourselves. Rav Elyah Lopian[3] explains that the treatment that is "hateful to you" is to be judged harshly by others. If you refrain from doing this hateful thing to your fellow, you will automatically be showing him the same love you show yourself.[4]

According to Ramban,[5] the mitzvah of "Love your

7
Kislev

7
Adar

7
Sivan

7
Elul

---

1. *Shabbos* 31a.
2. *Vayikra* 19:18.
3. *Lev Eliyahu*, Vol. 2, *Parashas Beshalach*, s.v. *V'al peirush zeh*; see ibid., Vol. 1, p. 253, where Rav Lopian states: "Do for others what you would want them to do for you; and do not do to others what you do not want them to do to you."
4. See *Sichos Mussar*, end of *Maamar* 82, p. 358 (*Maamar* 29, 5732), s.v. *V'hateshuvah l'kach*.
5. *Vayikra* 17:17. One cannot love another as he loves himself. Besides, the Gemara (*Bava Metzia* 62a) states that a person's life takes precedence over that of another. See *Sanhedrin* 45a, *Tosafos*, s.v. *Barur lo*; *Maharsha*, *Shabbos* 31a, s.v. *D'alach sani*.

neighbor like yourself" requires us only to be concerned about people, to show them warmth and comfort, and to provide them with what they need — be it financial, spiritual, physical, or emotional help. It also requires that we rejoice for one another's good fortune and feel one another's pain.[6]

The gentile's question, however, raises yet another issue. He was seeking an insight that would cover the entirety of the Torah. How did Hillel's answer satisfy his request?

Hillel's answer works because it reveals God's plan to create a nation that would be a mosaic, rather than a monolith. God gave the entire Torah to the Jewish people to fulfill, and yet, there are many mitzvos that only certain categories of Jews can fulfill. For example, a penniless man cannot fulfill the mitzvah of giving charity. This dilemma, says the *Anaf Yosef*,[7] was at the heart of the gentile's question. He was asking how he would be able to fulfill commandments that apply to a Kohen, to a Levi, to a wealthy man, and so forth.

The *Anaf Yosef* explains that Hillel's answer expressed the vital role of unity in a Jew's complete service to God: "Because if there is love between him and other members of the Jewish people, then we are considered 'one body' and can actually combine in fulfilling all the mitzvos."

The numerical equivalent of the Hebrew words for "love — ahavah" (*aleph, hei, veis, hei*) and for "one — echad" (*aleph, ches, dalet*)[8] are the same: 13. This succinctly conveys the message that real love — *ahavah* — exists where we are one — *echad*.[9]

---

6. *Ohr Yechezkel, Middos,* p. 122. The Alter of Kelm (*Kisvei HaSaba MiKelm,* p. 13) states that with *V'ahavta l'rei'acha kamocha* one can perform thousands of mitzvos every minute, because for every single Jew that one loves, he is performing a separate *mitzvas asei.* Also see *Yesod V'Shoresh HaAvodah* 1:7-8; see *Love Your Neighbor* (by Rabbi Zelig Pliskin) for a list of opportunities to fulfill this mitzvah.

7. *Shabbos* 31a.

8. *Aleph* = 1, *ches* = 8, *dalet* = 4, totals 13. *Aleph* = 1, *hei* = 5, *veis* = 2, *hei* = 5, totals 13. Cited in *Ohr Gedalyahu, Shemos,* p. 126, s.v. *K'mo she'haya; Michtav MeEliyahu,* Vol. 2, p. 91, s.v. *Ulam.*

9. *Mesillas Yesharim* (end of Ch. 19) writes: "*Hakadosh Baruch Hu*

What does it mean to be "one body"?[10] Schoolchildren often learn this concept through the analogy to a person who accidentally cuts his left hand while preparing food.[11] Certainly, he would not then take revenge against his right hand by cutting it, for this would only hurt him more. Though it is simple enough for a child to understand, this analogy tells the whole tale. By striking out at a fellow Jew, we do the most grievous harm possible to the body of the Jewish nation, keeping it trapped in exile. If instead we salved each other's wounds, how much pain could be spared!

YOU CAN DO IT

Choose someone with whom you are close. Think about what would give this person happiness or comfort. It could be concrete help, a warm smile, a piece of advice, or chizuk (see Alei Shur, Vol. 2, p. 198). If possible, give the person what he or she needs.

---

only loves those who love their fellow Jew, and the more one increases his love for fellow Jews, the more *Hakadosh Baruch Hu* loves him."

10. See *Kovetz Igros Chazon Ish*, III:62, where the Chazon Ish explained that just as each of a person's limbs and organs have specific uses — eyes see, ears hear, and hands carry out physical activities, so too the Jewish people is like one body consisting of many different parts, in which each person has his own individual mission in life. See *Tomer Devorah*, which states that "all Jewish souls are linked together, each one has a portion...when one sins he damages himself and the portion that his friend has." See also *Sifsei Chaim*, Vol. 1, pp. 103-104.
11. *Yerushalmi Nedarim* 9:4.

| 7 Kislev — |
| 7 Adar — |
| 7 Sivan — |
| 7 Elul — |

Take It With You

▸ *Everyone hates being judged harshly. Therefore, if one refrains from doing to others what is hateful to himself, he leads himself to love others.*

▸ *Loving one's fellow Jew requires one to feel for them, help them with their needs, and rejoice in their successes.*

▸ *By loving our fellow Jew, we attach ourselves to the body of the Jewish people.*

▸ *By being part of this diverse, yet unified body, we are able to have a portion in the performance of other Jews' mitzvos.*

GATHER TOGETHER

DAY 67

8
Kislev

8
Adar

8
Sivan

8
Elul

*A*sk a group of Ashkenzic yeshivah children what Mashiach will be wearing. The answer will no doubt reflect their image of a talmid chacham: a frock coat, a large black hat, and he will have a long white beard. Ask a group of Sefardic children, and the description will match that of a revered Chacham. Chassidish children will describe him with long peyos, a shtreimel (fur hat), and a bekeshe (long coat).[1]

Now ask yourself: How will we recognize Mashiach if we recognize holiness only in our own image? Even on the most practical level, unity is a prerequisite for the arrival of Mashiach. Without it, there is no hope of having the entire nation recognize one leader.

The Torah reveals the vital role of unity as Yaakov Avinu bids his sons farewell shortly before his death: "Assemble yourselves and I will tell you what will befall you in the End of Days. Gather yourselves and listen.[2]

Ramban[3] explains that "...in the End of Days" refers to the days of Mashiach. With these words, Yaakov also reveals to his descendants the condition that must precede the End of Days: "Gather yourselves" as one. The unity of Israel is the preparation and condition for the Ulti-

---

1. See *Netzach Yisroel*, Ch. 41, where Maharal explains that the character of Mashiach encompasses the virtues of every human being. Therefore, one who studies about Mashiach will naturally be drawn to seeing his own personality. That explains why, in *Sanhedrin* 98b, the Sages who attempted to determine Mashiach's name concluded that it was the same as their own. Each one is simply stressing the aspect of Mashiach's personality with which he is most familiar.
2. *Bereishis* 49:1-2.
3. Ad loc.

mate Redemption.[4]

This is the message that echoes over and over again throughout the ages:

The prophet Yirmiyah promises his exiled nation: Israel will be redeemed when they shall be a singular band, as it is said, "In those days and at that time, says God, the Children of Israel will come, they and the Children of Yehudah *together...*[5] to the land I have given as a legacy to your fathers."[6] Another Midrash offers this glowing image: "When they are bound together they shall greet the Face of the *Shechinah*!"[7]

Even in our daily *Shemoneh Esrei,* as we plead for redemption, our prayer is phrased in terms of joining together, reuniting with the joy of a family that had been driven apart by the winds of history: "*V'kabetzeinu yachad mei'arba kanfos ha'aretz,*" Gather us in — *yachad,* together — from the four corners of the earth.

What is this ingathering? It is the outcome of love and longing for one another. Despite the fact that our physical bodies and personal aspirations are distinct, our Jewish soul is one[8] and longs to unite, just as a dispersed family rejoices in its reunion at a family *simchah.* They may not all agree with one another's point of view or lifestyle, but that does not diminish the joy of having every one there to dance, rejoice, and pose together in a family picture that has no pieces missing.

In his patriarchal advice to his sons, Yaakov Avinu urges his children to preserve this spirit among themselves. The Midrash expounds:[9]

> *Though it is not known when the Day of Judgment will be, I do tell you that the hour you gather and assemble together you shall be redeemed, as it is said, "I will surely gather all of you, O Yaakov ...," for*

---

4. *Bereishis Rabbah* 98:2.
5. *Yirmiyah* 50:4.
6. Ibid. 3:18.
7. *Tanchuma, Nitzavim,* end of §1.
8. *Ohr Yechezkel, Middos,* p. 122, s.v. *Amnam.*
9. *Aggadas Bereishis,* Ch. 83. See *Midrash HaGadol* on *Bereishis* 49:1; and see *Sifre, Vezos HaBerachah* §346.

then, immediately, "their king will pass in front of them with Hashem at their head."[10]

This is a vision that many of us cynically assume cannot happen. Yet it *must* happen, and *will* happen when we finally learn to see ourselves in one another. When we realize that in every segment of Torah Jewry, hearts beat with the same desires: for peaceful Jewish homes; children who serve God with joy; thriving, supportive communities; and a meaningful connection to God. Beneath the clothes, beneath the skin, beneath our differences, we are indeed *"kamocha."*

YOU CAN DO IT

Identify three positive qualities possessed by someone outside your circle. Contemplate that there is good in everyone.

---

10. *Michah* 2:12-13.

---

8 Kislev —
8 Adar — L'iluy nishmas Tzivia bas Menachem Mendel a"h
8 Sivan — L'iluy nishmas Chaya Miriam bas Zev Halevi a"h
Dedicated by her loving family
8 Elul —

FOR A SACRED
PURPOSE

DAY 68

Sadly, throughout history, our greatest unity has occurred in the face of a dangerous common enemy. As Haman declared, "There is a certain people scattered and dispersed... let it be recorded that they be destroyed."[1] We "scatter and disperse," splintering into subsects defined by our differences, until our enemies step in, brutally reminding us that we are not as different as we thought we were. They cause us to forget the distractions and divisions rooted in the material world and to see ourselves as they do — as Jews, whose primary allegiance is to God.[2]

The atrocities perpetual during World War II bitterly reminded us of this truth, making no distinctions in their destruction. Today, radical Muslim attackers provide us with another course in unity. We cry over each spilling of Jewish blood, whether it flows from yeshivah students gunned down in their *beis medrash* or families enjoying a Seder in a hotel dining room. Somehow, whoever we are, we recognize all Jewish blood[3] as our own.

There is, however, another script for Jewish unity. There was another time when our hearts were united, and that is when the Jews approached Mount Sinai to accept the Torah. The well-known Torah verse states:[4] "Israel encamped there, opposite the mountain." Rashi[5] explains that the verb "*vayichan* — and [Israel] encamped," is written in the singular, in contrast to the previous verbs, to

9
Kislev

9
Adar

9
Sivan

9
Elul

---

1. *Esther* 3:8-9.
2. *Ohr Yechezkel, Middos*, p. 123, s.v. *V'hachi nami*.
3. *Devarim* 12:23: "...*Ha'dam hu hanefesh*"; *Ibn Ezra* ibid., and on *Vayikra* 17:7. See *Pesachim* 16b, *Sanhedrin* 59a.
4. *Shemos* 19:2.
5. Ad loc.

teach that the huge multitude encamped like a single person, with a single aspiration.

The Midrash expounds:[6] "*Hakadosh Baruch Hu* said: 'Because the Jewish people hate disagreements and love peace and they encamped as one, now I will give them the Torah.'"

Only seven weeks earlier, the Jews were a spiritually bankrupt band of slaves leaving their Egyptian masters. How were they able to ascend to this exalted level in so short a time? The simple answer is that, in their desire to come close to God, they shed their egos. Rav Gedaliah Schorr[7] explains that they removed their "sense of self" that gets in the way of unity. He writes[8] that their desire for God enabled them to completely subjugate themselves to Him. Freed from their emotional armor, they melded easily, achieving the sublime unity that can be reached only in the service of a spiritual purpose.[9]

The same dynamic brought the Jews together to fend off the national catastrophe planned by Haman. Mordechai tells Esther,[10] "Go and gather all the Jews." Maharal[11] explains that the fact that the Jews gathered together to reach out to God resulted in complete *teshuvah*, which in turn resulted in salvation.

There is a model of Jewish marriage that counselors use to help couples understand the goals of their union. It is a pyramid, with each spouse at one corner of the base and God at the pinnacle. The greater the distance from God that they stand, the farther apart

---

6. *Maseches Derech Eretz, Perek Shalom, Halachah* 5.
7. *Ohr Gedalyahu, Shemos,* p. 126, s.v. *K'mo she'haya.*
8. Ibid.
9. See *Ohr Yechezkel, Middos,* p. 122, s.v. *U'b'beur ha'inyan.* See also *Rashi, Bereishis* 46:26, where the Torah uses the singular word "*nefesh*" soul: "All the persons ('*nefesh*') coming...to Egypt...sixty-six persons"; and see *Shemos* 1:5: "All the persons ('*nefesh*') who emerged from Yaakov's loins were seventy," to portray the people who originally went down into Egypt. Despite the fact that the people were a diverse group composed of different tribes, the Torah calls them "*nefesh*" in the singular because in order for a nation to remain united in exile, a spiritual purpose is required.
10. *Esther* 4:16.
11. *Ohr Chodosh,* cited in *Ohr Gedalyahu, Devarim ,* p. 163, fn. 3.

are the spouses. As they climb spiritually — toward the pinnacle — they come ever closer to each other.

This model works for us as a nation, too. When our striving is toward God, the distance between us diminishes.[12] Rather than having our unity thrust upon us by our enemies, we can embrace it, and thereby stand ready to be redeemed.

YOU CAN DO IT

The next time you are involved in a disagreement, ask yourself what Hashem would want you to do in this situation.

Take It With You

▸ *Throughout history, persecution has been the chief cátalyst for Jewish unity.*

▸ *The unity evident at Mount Sinai prior to receiving the Torah illustrates another, positive model of achieving Jewish unity.*

▸ *The key element in building unity is striving together toward spiritual goals.*

---

12. *Ohr Yechezkel, Middos,* p. 123, s.v. *V'hachi nami.*

STRATEGY 3:
HONOR SHABBOS
PROPERLY

❧

STRATEGY 4:
PRAY FOR THE
GEULAH

❧

STRATEGY 5:
THE POWER OF
TZEDAKAH

CHAPTER 10:
REVEALING HASHEM'S PRESENCE: SHABBOS, TEFILLAH AND TZEDAKAH

DAY 69

THE ONE-DAY "SEGULAH"

10
Kislev

10
Adar

10
Sivan

10
Elul

*H*onor your father and your mother, so that
your days will be lengthened. . ."[1] This is
the Torah's promise. The same reward is
achieved through performing the mitzvah of "shi-
luach hakein"— sending the mother bird away from
her nest before removing her eggs — as the Torah[2]
states.

People eagerly pursue these mitzvos for their promise
of a magnanimous return on the time and effort invested.[3]

As remarkable as these rewards seem, Shabbos, the
Jewish people's weekly encounter with a purer distilla-
tion of holiness, is perhaps the most remarkable *segulah*
of all. It has the power to bring about nothing less than
the immediate arrival of the Final Redemption, a blessed
shortcut around all the wars, confusion, and tribulations
associated with the End of Days. The Gemara[4] itself is the
source for this *segulah*:[5]

"If the Jewish people would only observe two Sabbaths
then they would be redeemed immediately."[6]

The *Talmud Yerushalmi*[7] makes an even bolder prom-

---

1. *Shemos* 20:12.
2. *Devarim* 22:7.
3. However, see *Rabbeinu Bachya, Shemos* 20:12, which states that
the promise of long life for honoring parents is to recompense us
for time spent honoring our parents.
4. *Shabbos* 118b.
5. See *Divrei Yoel*, Vol. 8, p. 200, s.v. *V'yisba'er ha'inyan*.
6. See *Tosafos, Yoma* 13b, s.v. *Ad she'yichlu; Maharsha* ibid., s.v. *Ein
ben Dovid; Maharatz Chayes* ibid., *Chasam Sofer* ibid.
7. *Taanis* 1:1: "Though I have set a limit to 'the end,' that it will happen in its time regardless of whether they will do *teshuvah* or not...
Mashiach will come if they keep just one Shabbos, because the
Shabbos is equivalent to all the mitzvos." See also *Shemos Rabbah*

ise, stating that if the Jewish people keep just *one* Shabbos properly, Mashiach will come immediately.

There are various ways to reconcile the two promises:

- *Zohar*[8] states that the night of Shabbos counts as one Shabbos, and the day that follows is the second Shabbos.

- *Yismach Moshe*[9] explains that only one Shabbos is needed. However, every Shabbos influences the weekdays that follow, and those weekdays then influence the Shabbos that follows them.[10] Therefore, we must observe the first Shabbos perfectly so that it will elevate the week that follows. The Shabbos capping that elevated week will achieve the level of perfection needed to bring redemption.[11]

- *Michtav MeEliyahu*[12] identifies the "two Sabbaths" as two levels of sanctity: The "outward Shabbos" is one in which the individual is still clinging to material concerns as God sends Shabbos down upon him as a gift from Above. The higher level is the "internal Shabbos," experienced by one who is imbued with the spirit of Shabbos even before it arrives. Both levels are required for immediate redemption.

- *Divrei Yoel*[13] interprets "two Sabbaths" as the actual day of Shabbos and *"tosefes Shabbos"* — that part of the weekday[14] one adds to Shabbos[15] by accept-

---

25:12.

8. Introduction to *Zohar* 5b, cited in *Divrei Yoel*, Vol. 4, p. 367, s.v. *V'yevuar*. See also *Ben Yehoyada, Shabbos* 118b, s.v. *Meshamron*.

9. *Parashas Ki Sisa*, cited in *Divrei Yoel*, Vol. 3, p. 362, s.v. *V'yisba'er*.

10.*Ohr Gedalyahu, Bereishis*, p. 18, s.v. *B'Gemara Shabbos*; and *Shemos*, p. 71, s.v. *B'Midrash*.

11. See *Pri Tzaddik, Bamidbar*, p. 78; *Sfas Emes, Vayikra*, p. 30; and *Pachad Yitzchak, Shabbos, Kuntres HaReshimos* 2.

12. Vol. 4, p. 143, s.v. *Il'malei*.

13. Vol. 6, p. 160.

14. Various minimum amounts of time include 2 minutes to 15 minutes. See *Eretz Tzvi, Siman* 70; *Igros Moshe, Orach Chaim*, Vol. 1, *Siman* 96; *Avnei Nezer*, Vol. 4, *Siman* 98; *Minchas Elazar*, Vol. 1, *Siman* 23; *Maharshag, Siman* 38. See also *Siddur Yaavetz; Mishnah Berurah* 261:22 and *Beur Halachah*. See also *Chayei Adam* 5:2. See also *Kaf HaChaim* 261:16, which states that *tosefes Shabbos* applies to both men and women.

15. *Orach Chaim* 261:2.

▸ The Talmud promises that if the Jewish people keep one Shabbos properly, they will merit immediate redemption.

▸ On Shabbos, we refrain from activities related to material pursuits, confirming that God runs the world.

▸ Each week, Keeping Shabbos reawakens us to God's mastery over everything — the belief necessary to merit redemption.

ing it before sunset and observing it for a period beyond sunset of the next day.[16] By giving "extra" to Shabbos,[17] we merit, measure for measure, that God gives us "extra," bringing the redemption even if we are not worthy.[18]

Regardless of whether one or two Sabbaths are required, Shabbos observance is securely bound to sanctification of God's Name, and thus, the *Geulah. Chazal*[19] teach that "Whoever keeps the Shabbos is considered to have kept the whole Torah ..." The Chofetz Chaim[20] explains that this equation works because "the root...is to know that...Hashem created everything. He is Master over everything..." Shabbos is an eternal sign that eloquently declares this fundamental truth.[21]

Weekday activities plunge a person into a material world in which God's "Hand" is hidden. The result is a weakened bond between the individual and Hashem. When we refrain from work on Shabbos, we regain clarity and understanding as to the message of the Final Redemption — that Hashem is the Creator and Sustainer of life.

---

16. See also *Mishnah Berurah* 261:19, and see *Rosh Hashanah* 9a for the source of this mitzvah.
17. *Divrei Yoel*, Vol. 5, p. 349, s.v. *V'zos.*
18. Ibid., p. 348, s.v. *V'hinei.*
19. *Shemos Rabbah* 25:12; *Midrash Aggadah* 15:34.
20. Introduction to *Mishnah Berurah*, Vol. 3, *Hilchos Shabbos.*
21. *Chayei Adam, Hilchos Shabbos* 1:1. See also *Ramban, Devarim* 5:15, and *Maggid Mishneh, Hilchos Shabbos* 30:15.

10 Kislev —
10 Adar —
10 Sivan —
10 Elul —

WHAT'S IN A GREETING?

*S*habbos is greeted. Shabbos is escorted when she leaves. Shabbos is described in human terms — "Come, Bride, Come, Bride, Shabbos, the Queen."[1] No other Yom Tov is personified in this way: beckoned, greeted, and sent off like an honored guest. What makes Shabbos different?

The answer to this question provides an important insight into what makes Shabbos observance so vital in terms of hastening the Final Redemption.

In *Nefesh Shimshon*,[2] Rav Pincus, citing the Brisker Rav,[3] explains that *Kabbalas Shabbos* — the prayer service that greets the Sabbath — is derived from the Jewish people's greeting of the *Shechinah* as they stood at Mount Sinai to accept the Torah. Shabbos is the Jewish people's weekly visit with the Divine Presence. It is a foretaste of the closeness we will have with the *Shechinah* in the Messianic era. Therefore, our ability to relish Shabbos in its fullest sense is a reliable indicator of our readiness to live with the full manifestation of the *Shechinah* returned to our midst.

Shabbos is unlike most other mitzvos. The vast majority of commandments demand nothing more of us than to fulfill them and in so doing, to obey God's will. Shabbos is a different kind of mitzvah, most closely comparable to the mitzvah of the *Shalosh Regalim* — the three holidays on which the Jewish people were commanded to make a pilgrimage to the Beis HaMikdash.

---

1. See *Shabbos* 119a.
2. *Shabbos Kodesh*, p. 8.
3. *Griz al HaTorah, Parashas Yisro.*

Take It With You

The Torah states:[4] "Three times a year, all your males shall appear before Hashem, your God, in the place He will choose." Here, the purpose is not just to fulfill God's will, as is the purpose of mitzvos such as eating kosher or refraining from *chametz* on Pesach. The mitzvah of Shabbos requires certain actions, whose main purpose is for the Jewish people to forge a close personal relationship with God.

In the days of the Beis HaMikdash, there was an earthly address for God's presence. Surrounded by sanctity and open miracles, a person was fully aware that God exists. When Mashiach arrives, that special relationship will be rekindled, and we will again be able to vividly "see" God's active presence in our daily lives. In our day, the mitzvah of Shabbos, observed with the utmost purity, has the power to convey to us a clear sense of this kind of proximity to the *Shechinah*.

As Rav Pincus states:[5] "When we greet Shabbos, we are actually greeting the *Shechinah*. By understanding this point, we come to understand why Shabbos must be prepared for, greeted joyfully, kept foremost in our minds as she pays her weekly visit, invited to linger even after her time is up, and then, at last, sent off with all due honors."

The fact that the Jewish people still observe Shabbos thousands of years after its inception on the seventh day of Creation might seem like merit enough to bring the redemption. After all, centuries of tremendous sacrifice have gone into protecting the sanctity of our Shabbos Queen. However, it is not obedience to the commandment alone that brings the merit. It is the vibrant, all-consuming embrace of Shabbos — a greeting that tells God how very dearly we love to be in the *Shechinah's* presence.

---

4. *Devarim* 16:16.
5. *Nefesh Shimshon, Kedushas Shabbos*, p. 10.

11 Kislev —
לע״נ בן עמי הלוי בן משה אהרון הלוי ז״ל — **11 Adar**
Dedicated by Tzivia Fisher
11 Sivan —
11 Elul —

ALL FOR SHABBOS

*M*arried for 60 years, Miriam and Eliezer demonstrated inordinate care for each other. Miriam cooked each meal with Eliezer in mind: What did he like? What was healthy for him? If she heard good news or a cute story about their grandchildren, she couldn't wait to share it with him, to see him smile. Eliezer, in turn, lavished hundreds of acts of thoughtfulness upon his dear wife. All his plans and activities revolved around her needs.

12 Kislev

12 Adar

12 Sivan

12 Elul

God's "marriage" to the Jewish people[1] has endured for thousands of years, and yet His display of love never fades. Shabbos is a radiant symbol of that love. In fact, the Chofetz Chaim would often compare Shabbos to a wedding ring given by God to the Jewish people. When Shabbos coincides with any Jewish holiday, we add the word "*b'ahavah*" — with love — to our prayers, because Shabbos is our tangible experience of God's love.

But what is our role in this loving relationship? If we are like Sarah and Eliezer in the above story, then everything we undertake should be done with our Beloved in mind. We fulfill this role by preparing for Shabbos.

The Rambam[2] describes the exultation of those to whom the sanctity of Shabbos was palpable: "The earlier Sages would gather their students on the eve of Shabbos and don their cloaks and say: 'Come, let us go out to greet Shabbos, the Queen!' "

However, preparation for Shabbos can and indeed

---

1. See *Rashi, Bamidbar* 7:1; *Rambam, Hil. Teshuvah* 10:3.
2. See *Hilchos Shabbos* 30:2.

should overflow into other days of the week. Just as Miriam stored away tidbits of news to delight her husband, a Jew can keep Shabbos in mind all week by storing away special items — good food, new clothing, fresh flowers, special desserts — for Shabbos.

Mishnah Berurah teaches that when purchasing something for Shabbos, one should say *"likavod Shabbos kodesh* — In honor of the holy Shabbos;"[3] to fulfill the mitzvah: "Remember the Shabbos day to sanctify it."[4] The mitzvah to "remember" can be fulfilled through anything one does especially for Shabbos. Taking a haircut, having one's suit cleaned, shopping, cooking — all are acts of love, reciprocating the love God lavishes upon us through His gift of Shabbos.

Each step in preparing for Shabbos endows our mitzvah with greater value. Rav Dessler,[5] quoting Rav Yeruchem Levovitz, states that preparation is the essence of all mitzvos, for it demonstrates the degree of wholeheartedness with which one performs God's will.

Yet, Shabbos is special, because its unique preparation gives us many opportunities each week to nurture and expand our personal relationship with the *Shechinah* that Shabbos affords. This concept is amply illustrated by the many great scholars who interrupted their Torah studies to participate in Shabbos preparations. The Gemara[6] relates that in order to have the finest selection for Shabbos, Rav Abba bought meat from thirteen butchers on Friday. Rav Abahu sat on a stool and fanned the fires used to cook the Shabbos meals. There are many more examples, both ancient and modern.

Having the table set before Shabbos arrives is another tangible way to honor it. To leave our regal "guest" waiting while we scurry about setting the table indicates a lack of proper esteem. The Gemara teaches that being lax in preparing one's home for Shabbos can set off a

---

3. See *Shemos* 20:9-10 and *Rashi* ibid. for how one can observe Shabbos in attitude.
4. *Shemos* 20:8.
5. *Michtav MeEliyahu*, Vol. 5, p. 191.
6. *Shabbos* 119a.

downward spiral for the coming weeks.[7]

After Shabbos, too, we demonstrate our love by asking our guest to stay longer. The Gemara[8] states that one should set the table at night, after Shabbos ends, even for a very small meal. This is a royal send-off, says Rashi[9] — the *Melaveh Malkah* — a fitting farewell for Shabbos, our Beloved Queen.

> 12 Kislev —
> 12 Adar —
> 12 Sivan —
> 12 Elul —

Take It With You

▸ *Shabbos demonstrates God's show of love for us. We reciprocate by showing our love for Shabbos.*

▸ *Preparations for Shabbos demonstrate our love of the mitzvah to "remember" Shabbos and our love of God.*

▸ *As we prepare throughout the week, we reinforce the bond with God that Shabbos affords us.*

▸ *Having a meal after Shabbos provides a fitting "escort" for its departure.*

DAY 72

INSIDE SHABBOS

T he connection between Shabbos — a sanctification of time — and the Beis HaMikdash — a sanctification of a place — emerges clearly with the following verse:[1] "You shall observe My Sabbaths and you shall revere My Sanctuary."[2]

13
Kislev

13
Adar

13
Sivan

13
Elul

Why are these two entities intertwined in one verse? Rabbi Elyah Lopian[3] makes the following observation: The Rambam[4] states that the sanctity of the Temple Mount — the site of the Beis HaMikdash — endures forever, even though the building has been destroyed. The two-part mitzvah quoted above teaches a two-part lesson. Shabbos provides the model for the eternal holiness of the Beis HaMikdash; in turn, the Beis HaMikdash provides a model for the deep reverence one must show upon entering Shabbos.

Rav Lopian observes:

> If the Torah is so concerned lest we enter the Temple area in a state of unpreparedness, or lest we behave disrespectfully when even facing that place, how careful must we be with regard to the sanctity of Shabbos.

We fulfill the mitzvah to "Safeguard the Sabbath day"[5] by refraining from thirty-nine categories of *melachah* (creative activity), derived from the forms of labor required in the building of the Mishkan. We also refrain from other activities, which may be halachically permit-

---

1. *Vayikra* 26:2.
2. *Rambam, Hilchos Beis HaBechirah* 7:7.
3. Cited in *Inspiration and Insight*, Translated and Arranged by Rabbi Shimon Finkleman (ArtScroll/Mesorah Publ.), p. 30, fn. 1.
4. *Hilchos Beis HaBechirah* 6:15.
5. *Devarim* 5:12.

ted, but are not fitting or appropriate on this special day.

Beyond the thirty-nine *melachos,* the mitzvah of "Remember Shabbos" provides the spice and spirit that determine whether Shabbos is experienced as a rejuvenating wellspring or as a burdensome interruption of real life. How one dresses, how one speaks, what topics one thinks and talks about are all important ingredients in developing and dwelling within a distinct, sacred Shabbos consciousness.

For example, a person is profoundly influenced by what he is wearing. Dressed in rags, one feels downcast and humiliated. Dressed in work clothes, one is primed for accomplishment. By donning fine clothing reserved just for Shabbos, a person instantly clothes himself in a spiritually elevated Shabbos frame of mind.[6]

Dressing regally does not have the desired impact, however, for people who are still pondering and discussing their business, new purchases, household tasks, post-Shabbos plans, and so forth. Doing so is not only forbidden,[7] but is also illogical; one devalues with his own actions the pristine gift God has given him. The *Mishnah Berurah*[8] states that a person who refrains from speaking about weekday matters on Shabbos will be called "holy."

Rather than dragging weekday concerns across the threshold into Shabbos, a person can use his words to fulfill the mitzvah of "Remember Shabbos." The Shelah HaKadosh[9] says that by greeting someone with a *"Gut Shabbos"* or *"Shabbat Shalom,"* rather than "Hello," or "Good morning," one has fulfilled the mitzvah.

> *Chazal*[10] *relate that God told Moshe: "I have a precious gift in My treasury…Shabbos is its name. Go and tell Israel I wish to present it to them."*
>
> *This is a gift so divine that it could not even be absorbed by the neshamah given to man; therefore,*

---

6. See *Mishnah Berurah* 262:2.
7. *Orach Chaim* 306:1. The general rule is that anything that cannot be done on Shabbos should not be spoken about.
8. 307:5.
9. Cited loc. cit.
10. *Shabbos* 10b; *Beitzah* 16a.

Take It With You

▸ *Just as one must enter the Beis HaMikdash with reverence, one must enter Shabbos with reverence.*

▸ *A person's mode of dress and speech should reflect the special sanctity of the day.*

▸ *The Jewish people's clear separation of Shabbos from the weekdays will lead to a clear separation of Israel from the nations of the world, and thus to redemption.*

God grants us a "neshamah yeseirah"[11] (an extra neshamah) on Shabbos, to expand our spiritual capacity and enable us to "drink" in all that Shabbos offers.

When the Jewish people rise to this level of Shabbos observance, we will experience a true *"Havdalah."* This prayer, which concludes Shabbos, praises God Who "separates between...Israel and the nations, between the seventh day and the six weekdays." Maharal[12] explains that when the Jewish people clearly, absolutely distinguish Shabbos from the weekdays, we will become clearly and absolutely distinguished from the nations of the world. Thus, redemption will arrive.

---

11. See *Rashi, Taanis* 27b, s.v. *Neshamah yeseirah; Beitzah* 16a, s.v. *Neshamah yeseirah.*
12. *Chidushei Aggados, Shabbos* 118b, s.v. *V'od yeish lecha la'daas.*

לע"נ דוד צבי בן הרב אברהם מאיר ז"ל — 13 Kislev
13 Adar —
13 Sivan —
13 Elul — In honor of our parents,
Mr. & Mrs. Mitcheal Bloom
On their sixtieth wedding anniversary

DAY 73

PRAY! PRAY! PRAY!

There is no Jew who davens from a *siddur* who does not pray for the *Geulah*. This plea is featured in our primary prayer, the *Shemoneh Esrei*, numerous times, phrased in numerous ways, proposed from numerous angles. Right from the start, we identify God with the words: "*U'meivi goel livnei v'neiham*, the One Who brings the redeemer to their (the Forefathers') children..." We then laud God's power to restore the dead to life — a component of Messianic times.[1]

As we proceed, we recite a prayer for complete redemption, one for a gathering of the exiles, one for God to establish His reign of righteousness, one for retribution against our enemies, one for the rebuilding of Jerusalem, one for the rise of King David's power, one for the return of the sacrificial service to the Beis HaMikdash, one for the return of the *Shechinah,* and finally, in our closing meditation, we once again ask for a rebuilding of the Beis HaMikdash so that we can serve God "as in the days of old."

We see from this inventory that far more of the *Shemoneh Esrei* is devoted to praying for the redemption than is focused on personal needs such as health, wealth, and wisdom. Considering the fact that a great majority of the believing Jews in this world have been reciting these prayers three times a day for close to 2,000 years, a strong question emerges: What have we accomplished?

14
Kislev

14
Adar

14
Sivan

14
Elul

---

1. *Beis Elokim, Shaar Tefillah,* Ch. 17.

Mabit[2] writes that every prayer a Jew recites regarding the destruction of the Beis HaMikdash has influence. Every prayer helps bring about the end of the exile and the beginning of the ingathering of the *galus* of Jews. Rav Mattisyahu Salomon relates the following potent proof of the cumulative power of prayer:[3]

> *In 1991, when the Soviet Union collapsed, we merited the beginning of the ingathering of the exile of Jews from that region of the world. How did that happen?*
>
> *For years, Jews the world over prayed and cried for Russian Jewry trapped behind the Iron Curtain. In the most miraculous and astounding way, God utilized the millions of prayers to bring down the Soviet Union. When the right time came, it was "miraculously" over.*

Rav Salomon explains that all these prayers for the Soviet Jews were like waters building up behind a dam. From the other side of the dam, it would have appeared that nothing was happening. Yet the salvation of the Soviet Jews was in the making, building momentum with each additional plea from a sincere Jewish heart. "When the right time came, it was over," and so it shall be for us.

The following reveals the impact of these prayers:[4]

> *Recently a graduate of Sinai Academy[5] discovered that his great-great-grandfather was a gadol b'Yisrael. His dramatic hatzlachah in returning to Yiddishkeit is undoubtedly the outcome of heartfelt prayers.*
>
> *Eliezer is a Sinai alumnus who has developed into a true ben Torah. Today, he is a distinguished avreich in Beis Medrash Govoha in Lakewood. A few years ago, Eliezer discovered that he was a descendant of Mordechai Aryeh Varmashenko, otherwise knows as Reb Mottel the Dayan.*

---

2. Ibid., Ch. 14.
3. *With Hearts Full of Faith*, Rabbi Mattisyahu Salomon (Art Scroll/Mesorah Publ.), p. 250.
4. Adapted from an article written by Malkie Lowinger in *Hamodia* Weekend Edition, 17 Elul 5768, September 17, 2008.
5. Sinai Academy is a yeshivah high school in Brooklyn where boys from the former Soviet Union with little or no knowledge of their Jewish heritage are introduced to a life of Torah and *Yiddishkeit*.

Eliezer pored over old sefarim, trying to gather any information about his great-great-grandfather. He made some amazing discoveries. "Reb Mottel," says Eliezer, "received semichah from the Netziv and from Harav Yitzchok Elchonon Spector."

Reb Mottel's mesirus nefesh for Torah was legendary.

Eliezer studied the she'eilos and teshuvos of the Netziv, and discovered one segment where the Netziv had differed with Reb Mottel. Eliezer probed deeply into the matter. "I learned the same Gemara," he says, "and was able to propose a possible responsa to the Netziv's questions." For Eliezer, this discovery has instilled a renewed sense of pride in his heritage. "I now feel, more than ever, that I have a family legacy and it's my duty to maintain it for future generations."[6]

We must continue to pray, continue to add our own pleas to the millions of words of prayer that have built up over the ages. When the right time comes, our pleas will crash through the barrier, sweeping our nation forward into the era for which we have prayed so long.

Take It With You

▸ *Prayers for the redemption feature prominently in our thrice-daily recitation of the Shemoneh Esrei.*

▸ *Years of prayer accumulate until the time is right for redemption.*

▸ *We continue to pray for redemption and when the time is right, we will witness the answer to our prayers.*

---

6. Eliezer has a sixteen-page *teshuvah* in *Oros Me'ofel*, a series of *sefarim* of *chidushei Torah* by Sinai Academy alumni.

> **14 Kislev —**
> **14 Adar —** Dedicated to Meira, Yedidya, Atara, Akiva,
> and Yehuda Fortinsky
> From Mommy and Abba
> **14 Sivan —**
> **14 Elul —**

THE QUALITIES OF A
PRAYER ANSWERED

DAY 74

15
Kislev

15
Adar

15
Sivan

15
Elul

O*nly God can help us now."*
It sounds like a statement of desperation, a last-resort strategy proposed when all else has failed. In reality, however, it is a simple statement of truth, which applies to every situation from the dramatic to the mundane. In fact, it is the only strategy in any situation.

Prayers that arise from that spirit have the power to redeem us, as the Torah illustrates in the following desperate scene at the Reed Sea:[1]

> *Pharaoh approached. The Jewish people raised their eyes and behold — the Egyptians were journeying after them and they were very frightened and they cried out to Hashem.*

In response to their hopeless plight, Rashi states, the "very frightened [Jews] cried out to Hashem" and they "grasped the handicraft of the Patriarchs," a phrase that refers to the three, regular daily prayers. Rav Yerucham Levovitz[2] raises the question of why the Jews' desperate prayers, recited in a moment of despair, are compared to the "handicraft of the Patriarchs."

His answer reveals the true core of any prayer a person utters, whether in good times or in times of trouble. For the Patriarchs, there was no difference in the emotional content of desperate prayers and their regular prayers, for they keenly felt that they were dependent upon Hashem's kindness and protection from minute to minute.

Standing at the Sea of Reeds, the Jews experienced this same revelation: that God was not their last resort, but

1. *Shemos* 14:10.
2. *Daas Torah, Beshalach* 14:10.

rather, their *only* resort. Their prayers were the embodiment of *emunah* — the belief that the God of Israel is the only Power that exists.[3]

However, in our environment of relative comfort and security, it may be difficult for one to reach that level of *emunah* while praying, when we do not feel ourselves to be at the precipice of disaster.

The Gemara offers an alternative tool:[4]

> *It was revealed to Rebbi that Rav Chiya's prayers had the ability to elicit a direct response from Heaven and could bring the Final Redemption. Rebbi invited him to lead the congregation in prayer, and as he prayed, his words were fulfilled. When, during Shemoneh Esrei, he said, "Mashiv haruach" (He [Hashem] makes the wind blow), the wind blew. When he said, "Morid hageshem" (He makes the rain descend), it began to rain.*
>
> *When Rav Chiya was about to say, "Mechayei meisim," (He restores life to the dead), the world shook in anticipation of the imminent resurrection of the dead.[5] At this point, the angels in Heaven leaped into action, sending a distraction to the congregation to prevent Rav Chiya from finishing the prayer.*

The message derived from this story is that prayer *can* hasten redemption.[6] Rav Chiya's prayer nearly succeeded in bringing Mashiach even before the time was ripe. The factor that gave Rav Chiya's prayer its transformational power[7] was the purity of his intentions.[8] His prayer was aimed solely at the goal of relieving the pain of the *Shechinah* and not, as in the vast majority of our

---

3. See *Ritva on Maakos* 24a, s.v. *Ba Chabakuk*. See also *She'eilos U'Teshuvos HaRashba*, Vol. 5, *Siman* 55; and *Matnas Chaim, Yomim Nora'im*, p. 187.
4. *Bava Metzia* 85b.
5. *Maharsha* ibid.
6. *Sifsei Chaim, Moadim*, Vol. 3, p. 347, s.v. *Agaddos Chazal*.
7. Ibid., p. 351, s.v. *Rebbi Chiya*.
8. *Emes L'Yaakov, Shemos* 26:15, in the name of the *Gra*. See *Sefer Chassidim, Siman* 131.

▸ *In every
situation
at every
moment,
only God
can help us.*

▸ *It was this
awareness
of God's
control of
everything
that gave
the Jews'
prayers at
the Sea of
Reeds the
power to
redeem
them.*

▸ *The fact
that we
do not
always see
answers to
our prayers
can blind
us to their
true
potential.*

prayers,[9] at relieving our own pain in exile.[10] According to *Michtav MeEliyahu*,[11] the objectives of such a prayer can be achieved only when one's underlying, sincere goal is to reveal God's honor.[12]

Rav Chiya had the power to accomplish this in on his own. We, by purifying our intentions and strengthening our reliance on God, can likewise do it. Every sincere prayer for redemption brings it closer.[13]

---

9. Rav Chaim Voloziner, cited in *Talelei Oros* on *Eichah* 1:2; *Siddur HaGra, Pesichah* to *Tefillas Rosh Hashanah*.

10. See *Beis Elokim, Shaar Tefillah*, Ch. 17, for additional explanations.

11. Vol. 2, p. 90, s.v. *Ikar geder*.

12. Ibid.; see also ibid., Vol. 3, p. 67, s.v. *Zehu omek*, where Rav Dessler states: "The length of the exile runs parallel to the degree that Hashem's honor is hidden. Therefore, *tefillah* hastens the Final Redemption, as we find in Egypt: 'And the Children of Israel groaned...and they cried out. Their outcry...went up to God' (*Shemos* 2:23). The key to bringing the *Geulah* through prayer is to draw closer to Hashem and peel away the layers that distance us from Him."

13. See *Mesillas Yesharim*, Ch. 19, s.v. *V'im yomar:* "A person may ask: 'Who am I, will my prayers bring about the ingathering of the exiles and the burgeoning of the Redemption to come?' The answer is as stated in *Sanhedrin* 37a: 'Each person should say: The world was created for my sake.' "

15 Kislev —
15 Adar —
15 Sivan —
15 Elul —

HASTENING THE FINAL REDEMPTION

DAY 75

*I*t is a time of war. A family hides in a bomb shelter, gradually running out of food and water. The father must stay with his family to protect them from the chaos outside. The mother must remain with her infant. Only the son, a 12-year-old boy, has the wherewithal to leave the shelter in search of food.

Imagine the father's dread as he bids his son good-bye. Then, imagine the joy and gratitude he would experience if he were to discover that his son was assisted every step of the way by a kind-hearted neighbor who saw that he required help. Surely, when the opportunity arose, the father would do anything he could to repay that neighbor.

16
Kislev

16
Adar

16
Sivan

16
Elul

The above story provides one window of insight as to why giving *tzedakah* is such a profuse source of merit and protection for the Jewish people. God, our Father, sends each beloved soul out into a dangerous world to fulfill its mission. When one Jew helps another, guiding him past life's pitfalls, our Father's gratitude knows no bounds. The Rambam[1] explains that showing compassion for the needy and downcast evokes a reciprocal compassion from Heaven,[2] thus hastening the Final Redemption.[3]

Giving charity[4] offers a unique abundance of personal

1. *Hilchos Matnas Aniyim* 10:2.
2. See *Klei Paz*, Part 3.
3. See *Eliyahu Zuta*, Ch. 1; see also *Shabbos* 139a.
4. The actual giving of money or an item of value is classified as

benefits to the giver, as well. The Gemara states that giving charity can save a person from an unusual death[5] and from Gehinnom.[6] In fact, the Gemara[7] teaches that charity is equivalent to all the mitzvos.

Ultimately, charity saves the Jewish nation, not only the individuals who comprise it: "Zion shall be redeemed through justice and her returnees through *charity*."[8] For by giving charity, a Jew is performing the utmost emulation of God, whose very essence is to provide for His world. The Maharsha[9] observes that a person's acts of charity help to bring the Final Redemption, which in turn brings worldwide recognition of God's constant charity in sustaining His creation.[10]

In view of the great importance of Jewish unity as a prerequisite for redemption, charity performs another essential function. It binds the Jewish people together in a web of caring and compassion. *Ksav Sofer* concludes:[11] "*Tzedakah* hastens the Final Redemption because…it shows how great peace is amongst us."

"Observe justice and perform *charity*, for My salvation is soon to come," states the prophet Yeshayah,[12] again linking charity to redemption. *Ben Yehoyada*[13] notes that the verse also links charity to "justice," as is the case in the previous verse cited above. The juxtaposition teaches that charity is a source of merit only when the funds have been

---

charity, but the effort one extends, in the pauper's favor, is counted as kindness. See *Ahavas Chesed* III, Ch. 7.

5. *Bava Basra* 10a. See *Tosafos* ibid., s.v. *V'eizu.*

6. *Gittin* 7a: "Whoever shares some of his possessions and devotes them to charity is saved from the judgment of Gehinnom"; *Bava Basra* 10a; *Yalkut Shimoni, Mishlei, Remez* 945.

7. *Bava Basra* 9a. See *Tosafos*, s.v. *She'neemar; Maharsha* ibid. and *Maharal* ibid. for various explanations of this teaching.

8. *Yeshayah* 1:27. *Metzudos* ibid. explains that Jerusalem will be rebuilt in the merit of the mitzvah of charity. See *Maharsha* to *Sanhedrin* 98a, *Ben Yehoyada* to *Shabbos* 139a and to *Bava Basra* 10a.

9. *Bava Basra* 10a.

10. See *Ahavas Yonasan* on *Parashas Eikev* and *Beis HaLevi al HaTorah, Parashas Beshalach* (both cited in *Talelei* Oros on *Eichah*, pp. 367-368) for an alternative explanation.

11. *Derush* for the Month of Teves, 5606, s.v. *U'mah.*

12. 56:1.

13. To *Bava Basra* 10a, s.v. *U'mah she'kasuv.*

honestly acquired by the giver.

Today, as economic strain exacts a toll on our community, God presents us with ample opportunities to give charity with our justly earned assets. It may be that this opportunity, clothed in the guise of challenge, is the most potent protection God can give us for the turbulent times ahead.

Take It With You

▸ *In showing compassion to one's fellow Jew by giving charity, we arouse God's compassion for us.*

▸ *Giving charity emulates God's constant giving to His creation.*

▸ *Charity must be given with honestly acquired money.*

▸ *God gives us opportunities to give in order to enable us to earn protective merit in times of imminent danger.*

16 Kislev —
16 Adar — May today's learning be a זכות for our family
Dedicated by Rabbi & Mrs. Elliot Hecht and family, Queens, NY
16 Sivan —
16 Elul —

WHEN OPPORTUNITY COMES KNOCKING

W hen a needy person knocks, some might respond inwardly, "Oh, no, another burden to assume, another sad story to hear."

Yet, as we learned, such an occurrence might be placed in one's path for one's own benefit. The Gemara illustrates such a situation:[1]

> On the day of his daughter's birth, the stargazers informed Rabbi Akiva that on her wedding day, a snake would bite her and she would die.[2] Despite the family's worries, a suitable match was found when she reached marriageable age, and a wedding date was set.
>
> On the night before the wedding, Rabbi Akiva's house was buzzing with excitement. People were cooking, baking, welcoming guests, and rushing to complete the preparations. The bride, who would be fasting the next day, was advised to get to bed early. She was given a meal and sent to a quite corner of the kitchen to eat peacefully.
>
> As she sat down, she noticed a poor man at the door. He called out in a barely audible voice: "Please give me something to eat. I haven't eaten in a long while." Because everyone was busy with the wedding preparations, no one heard him — except Rabbi Akiva's daughter. She gave her meal to the poor man.
>
> She then went to her room. Just before lying down

---

1. *Shabbos* 156b.
2. See *Rambam, Hilchos Avodah Zarah* 11:8, as to whether relying on stargazers is prohibited, and *Megadim Chadashim* on *Berachos* 64a, who discusses how Rabbi Akiva accepted the words of the stargazers.

to sleep, she removed a golden hairpin from her hair, and stuck it into the wall next to her bed for safe-keeping. In the morning, she pulled the pin from the wall, and a dead, poisonous snake came out with it. She had pierced the snake when she placed the pin in the wall the previous night. Had she not stuck the pin in the wall, the snake surely would have killed her, just as the stargazers had predicted.

When Rabbi Akiva heard what happened, he asked his daughter, "What good deed did you do last night that you were worthy of such a close escape?"

She told her father about the poor man and how she — the only one who heard his plea — had given him her meal.

Rav Lopian[3] highlights the seemingly remarkable coincidences leading to the daughter's salvation: The poor man went to this particular house, exactly when no one else could hear him, on the eve of the wedding when the household was hectic with activity. Obviously, this was engineered from Above, to give Rabbi Akiva's daughter the opportunity to earn the merit that would nullify her preordained fate. She grasped the opportunity, thus saving her own life.

For the Jewish people charity operates in this manner as well, says Rav Lopian. When misfortune looms over the nation, God provides an opportunity to perform a mitzvah that will engender the merit to shield us.

These special opportunities do not come labeled, "Warning: Ignore at Your Own Risk." Rav Lopian advises that, "You never know when those times arrive and what those opportunities are." Whenever a mitzvah appears in a person's path, he can regard it as a special gift from God to help him escape some predestined misfortune.[4]

Says Rav Lopian: At that very moment when a person faces misfortune, when he can be saved only by a special Divine protection, God might send him a special opportunity to earn the protection he so desperately needs. This

3. Cited in *With Hearts Full of Faith*, Rabbi Mattisyahu Salomon (Art Scroll/Mesorah Publ.), p. 60.
4. See *Makkos* 23b, s.v. *R' Chananyah ben Akashia Omeir.*

Take It With You

▸ *By giving charity, one can acquire the merit to avoid a predestined misfortune.*

▸ *God sends opportunities for us to earn this protective merit, just when it is needed.*

▸ *One can never know when that need has arisen, and therefore, all opportunities to be charitable should be pursued.*

is the opportunity embedded in the struggles preceding the *Geulah*. We can help one another through the difficulties, and thereby engender the Divine protection that will guide us safely into a newfound era of redemption.

STRATEGY 6: INCREASE TORAH STUDY

CHAPTER 11:
THE UNIQUENESS OF TORAH

A TRUE COMPASS

DAY 77

18
Kislev

18
Adar

18
Sivan

18
Elul

Many great philosophers and historians have written about the impact of the Torah upon the entire world. The ideals that Western civilization holds dear — the rule of law; the dignity of human life; the value of education, charity, morality, family, and communal service — all have their roots in our Torah. No matter what political or social trends come into vogue, the Torah stands firm, providing a guidepost that cannot be dislodged. We, the Jewish people, have accepted the mission of carrying this banner through the centuries.[1]

But what is it about Torah study that endows it with the power to hasten the Final Redemption?[2] If it is simply the Jewish people's compliance with God's will that creates this effect, then it would seem that almost any mitzvah would be equally propitious.[3]

Rav Hutner[4] states that the Torah and the ultimate redemption both turn darkness into light. In our world, there is darkness because God's presence is obscured behind the veil of nature. In the times of Mashiach, God's light will be clear for all to see. We will understand completely that God controls everything, and the "natural events" we take for granted will show themselves to be as much God's work as the splitting of the Reed Sea.

Within man himself, the darkness is the evil inclination. Although a person desires to do God's will, the evil inclination clouds his ability to distinguish right from wrong

---

1. See *Emes L'Yaakov, Bereishis* 1:22, 9:25.
2. *Zohar* III:270a; *Eliyahu Zuta,* end of Ch. 14; see *Even Sheleimah* 11:3.
3. *She'eilos U'Teshuvos Yechaveh Daas,* Vol. 4, *Siman* 48.
4. *Pachad Yitzchak, Succos, Maamar* 53, *Os* 19, p. 151.

and good from evil.[5] This confusion engulfs a person in a constant state of darkness, for which the remedy is the light of Torah. As the Gemara relates:[6] "God says: I created the evil inclination and I created the Torah as an antidote." As the bearers of the Torah, the Jewish people have been given the gift of morality — a true compass for distinguishing right from wrong. By bearing aloft this torch of morality for the world, we spread God's light and move the world closer to its redeemed state.

Chazal[7] teach that the angels protested Hashem's gift of the Torah to mankind, claiming that its holiness was suited only to Divine realms. Moshe Rabbeinu was able to convince them that the Torah's mitzvos and prohibitions were (at least on a basic level) directed to human beings — do not steal, do not kill, do not speak improper words, etc. Nevertheless, the angels still argued that there was no place for the holy amid the profane.

The *Darchei Mussar*[8] explains that Moshe Rabbeinu was able to convince them that the Torah was as essential to life on this planet as the air we breathe, that the Torah was the ultimate, indispensable element that would sustain the functioning of God's Creation. Not only was it necessary for our survival, but also, it was the only means by which we could repair our relationship with God when we, as fallible mortals, would inevitably stray. By learning Torah, we attach ourselves to God, and fulfill our role of maintaining God's presence in the world.

To Jews, the Torah is *mayim chaim*, refreshing, life-restoring, living waters. It is an "elixir of life" that brings healing to the world.[9] And it is our prized possession .

---
5. *Rambam, Hilchos Geirushin* 2:20.
6. *Kiddushin* 30b.
7. *Shabbos* 88b.
8. P. 332.
9. *Kiddushin* 30b.

18 Kislev —
18 Adar —
18 Sivan —
18 Elul —

Take It With You

▸ *The Torah is the source of morality, human dignity, charity, and all the other pillars of civilized society.*

▸ *By learning Torah, a person kindles the light of morality against the darkness of the evil inclination.*

▸ *By learning Torah, a person attaches himself to God and strengthens His presence in the world.*

▸ *Torah learning helps to intensify the light of redemption.*

LETTING THE LIGHT SHINE IN

DAY 78

19
Kislev

19
Adar

19
Sivan

19
Elul

No matter how much time one spends learning Torah, and no matter what form a person's learning takes, Torah learning leaves its mark on a person as nothing else can.[1] When you open a *sefer*, you are opening a window into yourself and allowing some of God's light to shine in.[2] Negative traits such as arrogance, anger, or overindulgence in physical pleasure can block the "window," but the holiness of Torah is still there, seeking a place to seep into a person's *neshamah* and bring it closer to its Creator.

Furthermore, learning itself, separate from any practical application, possesses spiritually uplifting power. This vital fact is revealed in the words the Jewish people said upon acceptance of the Torah:[3] "*Naaseh v'nishmah*, We will do and we will hear." The *Beis HaLevi*[4] explains that if they had responded in the natural order — we will hear (learn) the Torah, and then fulfill it — learning would be construed only as a preparation for doing mitzvos. The fact that the statement is reversed means that learning is a mitzvah in its own right.[5]

Torah learning, infused with love for each precious word, constantly generates merit toward redemption.

---

1. *Nefesh HaChaim, Shaar* 4, Ch. 33; *Shem Olam*, Vol. 2, Ch. 5; *Ohr Gedalyahu, Bereishis*, p. 5.
2. *Michtav MeEliyahu*, Vol. 3, p. 67. See *Alshich*, end of *Parashas Nitzvim*, s.v. *Ki hamitzvah hazos*.
3. *Shemos* 24:7.
4. To *Shemos* 24:7; *She'eilos U'Teshuvos Beis HaLevi*, Introduction to Vol. 1.
5. See *Emes L'Yaakov* on *Kiddushin* 29b, which states that studying Torah is unique from other commandments of the Torah in that a minor is required to study Torah so that when he becomes bar mitzvah, he immediately understands how to properly perform mitzvos.

This cause and effect can be derived from the prophet Malachi's words:[6] "Behold, I send you Eliyahu the prophet before the coming of the great and awesome day of Hashem." *Metzudas David*[7] observes that this verse is preceded by the words:[8] "Remember the Torah of Moshe My servant," implying that in the merit of Torah, God will speed the Final Redemption. The *Zohar*[9] confirms the link between learning Torah and redemption, stating that by virtue of Torah, the Jewish people will return to the Holy Land and be gathered in from exile.[10]

At the end of Moshe Rabbeinu's life, God commanded him to write the Torah, to teach it to the people, and to place the scroll beside the Ark.[11] Chofetz Chaim[12] comments that this commandment, the final one listed in the Torah, follows the words:[13] "But I will surely have concealed My face on that day because of all the evil that it did…" The juxtaposition teaches that the Torah will save the Jews from distress even in a generation where Hashem's face is hidden, as it is now. Therefore, the Chofetz Chaim advises:[14]

> *If you were to ask what is appropriate to do to bring Mashiach, I would say…each one of us, according to his abilities*[15] *— if he can learn Mishnah, he must set a time each day…and learn his [appropriate] amount of Mishnah. Similarly, if he can understand Ein Yaakov,*[16] *Midrash, etc., he should learn that which he is able. Certainly, if he can also learn Gemara and halachah,*

---

6. 3:23.
7. Ad loc.
8. Malachi 3:22.
9. Ibid. v.22.
10. See *Eliyahu Zuta*, end of Ch. 14, which states that Israel will be redeemed in the merit of ten people sitting and learning *b'chavrusa* (with a study partner). See *Yeshuos Yaakov*, note 4.
11. *Devarim* 31:19.
12. *Chofetz Chaim al HaTorah, Devarim* 31:19, p. 281.
13. *Devarim* 31:18.
14. *Zachor L'Miriam*, Ch. 18, s.v. *V'haya im*.
15. See *Chofetz Chaim al HaTorah, Vayikra* 25:26; *Maasai L'Melech*, p. 171.
16. *Ein Yaakov* is a compilation of all the Aggadic material in the Talmud together with commentaries.

Take It With You

▸ *Learning Torah has an incalculable value apart from its practical applications.*

▸ *Torah learning has the power to redeem even at a time when God's presence is hidden.*

▸ *By learning as much as one is able, for every available moment, one is instrumental in hastening the redemption.*

he is required to set aside time to learn them.

Imagine if a medical research institute announced that if everyone would make a daily donation to fund its projects — each according to his ability — a cure for cancer would be guaranteed. Certainly everyone with even a nickel to offer would dig into his pockets and give. Those with more to give would be thrilled to know that they would soon be instrumental in curing a virulent, feared disease.

The Chofetz Chaim is telling us that we, too, have the power to conquer a dreaded disease — that of exile. Our currency is our Torah learning, and if we will only give each day according to our means, the cure is assured.

TRULY A PLEASURE

DAY 79

*T*raining for the marathon, the runner committed himself to a grueling practice sched-
ule. He had to muster all his self-discipline
*to rise early every morning and face hours of running
in the rain, cold or heat. But once he was out there,
running with all his strength and skill, he entered a
mind-set in which time and fatigue fell away.*

*In contrast, were he to jog half-heartedly around
the track, he would soon feel bored and tired. By fulfilling his obligation wholeheartedly, he experienced
the exquisite sweetness in his exertion.*

20
Kislev

20
Adar

20
Sivan

20
Elul

A Jew and his Torah learning are like the runner and his
marathon. The power the Torah possesses to lift us above
the tangled web of mundane life is in direct correlation
to the toil we put into it. A Jew is commanded not only to
study Torah, but "*la'asok,* to engross himself," in his studies.[1] Only then will he hit the "zone" in which time and
fatigue fall away, as his connection to God fuels his ascent.

God's mandate that we study Torah, thereby imbuing
our lives with spirituality and knowledge of the mitzvos, is
a commandment of which every observant Jew is aware.
It is therefore understandable that the first blessing on
Torah study is expressed in words typical for *birchos hamitzvos* — blessings on a mitzvah: "...Who has sanctified us
with His commandments and has commanded us..."

What is not as clear, however, is why the last blessing on the Torah employs the wording used for *birchos*

---

1. From the formula of the morning Blessing of the Torah; see *Berachos*
11b.

hanehenin — blessings on objects of enjoyment:[2] "...Who selected us from all the nations and gave us His Torah."

The form of the blessing hints at the profound pleasure a Jew can derive from immersing himself in Torah. A broad spectrum of sources teaches that Torah, like the manna given to our ancestors in the Wilderness, provides each person with the precise taste that satisfies him. One is a discussion in the Gemara[3] regarding which day of the month of Sivan should be designated as the Yom Tov of Shavuos, which marks the giving of the Torah. Not only is the exact date unclear, but so is the exact location of Mount Sinai, where this world-changing drama took place.

Rav Moshe Feinstein commented[4] that these ambiguities illustrate that there is no specific place, date, or individual upon whom Torah learning is incumbent, and therefore, there is no time, place, or person to whom it is unavailable. The concept that "the words of the Torah are in the language of man,"[5] teaches us that the Torah is written so that each person can understand it on his own level.

> *Photo archives from the Warsaw Ghetto show a door of an inn that read, "Society of Wagon Drivers for the Study of Talmud in Warsaw." This referred to coachmen who seized a few moments from their work to gather in a group to "nosh" (grab a tasty morsel of) a page of Talmud...These were not intellectuals, concerned only with the intricacies of scholastic dialectics; they were deeply religious men thirsting for spiritual refreshment, and they found it, as countless generations of Jews before them, in the study of Torah.*[6]

When the true value of Torah enters a person's heart, it becomes not only his obligation, but his longing and his joy. It becomes an exertion that re-energizes, rather

---

2. Similar to blessings for food (i.e., *borei pri ha'eitz*).
3. *Yoma* 4b.
4. Heard from Rabbi Yisroel Reisman, *Pathways of the Prophets*, "The Torah Speaks to Everyone," May 11, 2002.
5. See *Berachos* 31b; also see *Ibn Ezra, Shemos* 13:17.
6. Aish.com, "What Is Torah," by Rabbi Maurice Lamm.

than drains, the spirit of the learner.[7] It is in that spirit that learning initiates a deep communion with God and a powerful sanctification of His Name.

------

7. However, see *Sanhedrin* 26b, which states that Torah weakens the strength of man. *Maharsha* ibid. explains that Torah and the many mitzvos weaken men so that their strong-willed nature becomes subdued and their hearts humbled. See also *Rav Bartenura* on *Avos* 2:2, s.v. *She'yegias she'neihem; Shaarei Teshuvah*, end of *Shaar* 4:11; *Zohar HaChadash* 10a; and *Pesach Einayim* on *Sanhedrin* 26a for additional explanations.

YIRAS HASHEM: THE ESSENTIAL INGREDIENT

21 Kislev

21 Adar

21 Sivan

21 Elul

*O*ne person learns Torah diligently and becomes extremely knowledgeable, and yet, he remains a difficult, uncaring individual. Another person learns Torah diligently and becomes a tzaddik.

If Torah is the great beacon of light, how can one who learns it remain a difficult, uncaring individual? Awe of God is the distinguishing factor, for without it, knowledge is just intellectual acrobatics. It has no power to imbue a person with the real wisdom that enables him to discern right from wrong, holy from impure, just from unjust.

Yiras Hashem is awe — a combination of trepidation and amazement at God's unlimited power. It causes a person to consider: Whose Torah is he learning? Whose mitzvos is he doing? When one focuses on God's unfathomable grandeur, his learning enters his soul filtered through a prism of humility. All he wants is to gain understanding of what God wants of him.

Yiras Hashem is also translated as fear: In all that one does, he maintains an acute awareness of God's watchful presence and makes his decisions based on that awareness. *Yiras Hashem* is the fertile soil; one's learning and deeds are the seeds he sows; wisdom is what grows.

The Gemara[1] teaches that all of a person's spiritual achievements in this world will render him a favorable judgment in the next world only if fear of Hashem was "in his storehouse" throughout his life. *Yiras Hashem* is the preservative that keeps one's Torah learning fresh and wholesome and enables it to become integrated into

---

1. *Shabbos* 31a.

one's being. As Rabbi Chanina ben Dosa states:[2] "Anyone whose fear of sin takes priority over his wisdom, his wisdom will endure. And anyone whose wisdom takes priority over his fear of sin, his wisdom will not endure."

Notwithstanding the essential nature of *yirah*, most people do not want to feel fear. We understand that *yiras Hashem* can save us from sin, much like a pain in one's chest can provide the warning that will save a person from a fatal heart attack. We also understand that the stark awareness of God's presence helps us control our words and actions. Even so, most people find the idea of such close Divine scrutiny to be an uncomfortable mindset. Making it a constant mind-set[3] is therefore even more difficult.

The Maharal explains that when man feels this awe, he subjugates his will to that of God and attains a profound closeness to Him, thereby achieving the goal of creation. Yet, on a deeper level, there is also tremendous comfort in living one's life with fear of God. A person who always senses God's presence likewise always senses His protection. As King David writes in *Tehillim*:[4] "Even though I walk in the valley overshadowed by death, I will not fear evil, for You are with me."

> Five-year-old David can't wait to ride his new bike. Nonetheless, he is scared. The bully from across the street might grab his new bike out from under him. Worse yet, his other neighbor's annoying puppy might chase him.
>
> There's another danger too; Dovid knows he has to stay on the sidewalk, because if his father sees him ride into the street, he'll lose his bike for a whole week.
>
> "Go and enjoy your new bike," his father says. "I will be watching you and checking on you every few minutes, so stay off the street!"
>
> Dovid leaves the house happy. If the puppy or the bully bothers him, his father will protect him. True, he

---

2. *Avos* 3:11.
3. See *Beur Halachah*, Siman 1:1, s.v. 5. *L'hiyos yiras*.
4. 23:4.

Take It With You

- *Yiras Hashem means awe of God.*

- *One will not derive lasting wisdom from his Torah learning without a foundation of yiras Hashem.*

- *We develop yirah by thinking about God's grandeur and by realizing that He is always watching us.*

- *This sense of constant scrutiny is actually our deepest comfort, for it makes us aware that God is always there to protect us.*

has to stay on the sidewalk, but even this, he knows, is for his protection. Being loved, being protected, being watched — it all comes from the same source.

21 Kislev —
21 Adar —
21 Sivan —
21 Elul —

SEEING IS BELIEVING

*W*hen I behold Your heavens, the work of your fingers, the moon and the stars that You have established. What is frail man that You should remember him?...Hashem, our Master, how mighty is Your Name throughout the earth![1]

In the psalm above, King David expressed the essence of *yirah*. The Hebrew word for *"yirah"* (awe), explains *Reb Tzadok HaKohen*,[2] shares a root with the word *"re'iyah"* (seeing). Although God cannot actually be seen, His presence can be felt or intuited. In the above verses, King David looked upon the heavens and saw the grandeur of God's creation, engendering a sense of awe and reverence.

The Rambam[3] advises that one who takes notices the vastness, power, and genius of God's creations will come to *yirah*:

> *When a person contemplates God's great and wondrous acts and creations, obtaining from them a glimpse of God's endless wisdom that is beyond compare, then he will promptly love, praise, and glorify Him, longing exceedingly to know the great Name of God...*

Rav Shlomo Wolbe comments: Rambam says it is not enough to be awed by the wondrous deeds of our Creator. A person must also view himself in comparison to the infinite greatness of God. From this, *yiras Hashem* is born.

Such a comparison was the purpose of the artist who created the pen-and-ink drawing described below:

> *A massive mountain was crowned by a jagged peak. At the foot of the mountain, there were bare trees*

22 Kislev	
22 Adar	
22 Sivan	
22 Elul	

---

1. *Tehillim* 8:4-5,10.
2. *Pri Tzaddik, Rosh Chodesh Tammuz, Os* 2.
3. *Hil. Yesodei HaTorah* 2:2; see *Shemiras HaLashon*, Vol. 2, Ch. 26; see also *Pachad Yitzchak, Yom HaKippurim*, p. 187, s.v. *U'bazeh ba'u.*

Take It With You

- *Yirah* — awe — shares a root with the word "re'iyah" — seeing.

- The connection teaches that we can come to awe of God by observing the majesty of His creation.

- To arrive at true *yirah*, one must also view himself in comparison with God's creation.

- Using observation and intellect, a person can develop a constant sense of *yirah*, fulfilling one of the six constant mitzvos.

whose highest branches reached not even past the sole of the mountain's feet. Beside the grove of trees were two mere specks, represented in by a small dot and a few, comma-like marks. They were the people.

But even a massive mountain is only a speck compared to the earth, and the earth is but a speck in the solar system; man keeps falling further and further away as our mind's eye soars through the cosmos. And all of it, in its unfathomable vastness, is but an emanation of God — a tiny corner of physicality carved out of unknowable spiritual realms. Thus King David wondered, what are we that God deigns to interact with us, that He tends to us and lifts us from our obscure existence? At just the mere mention of God's Name, our souls should quake, as they did in the Yom Kippur Mussaf service in the times of the Beis HaMikdash.

Imagine that you are there as the ineffable Name of God, a Name no one else dares speak, emerges from the Kohen's pure lips, and you, with the great mass of Jews assembled at the Beis HaMikdash drop to the ground, kneeling and prostrating yourselves, shouting, "Blessed is His glorious Name forever!"

Yiras Hashem is one of the six constant mitzvos, which the *Chinuch*[4] states "should never leave a person's thoughts." By using our powers of observation, our imagination and intellect, we can engrave images of God's majesty upon our minds, and thus carry *yirah* with us wherever we go. In that way, the Torah learning we pursue will imbue its wisdom into our hearts, changing our lives and thus changing our world, by hastening the redemption.

---

4. Intro, *Mitzvah* 25, 26, 387, 417, 418, 432.

STRATEGY 7: TESHUVAH: THE ANTIDOTE TO OUR EXILE

CHAPTER 12:
TESHUVAH:
IN OUR TIMES

NOT A SECRET

DAY 82

23
Kislev

23
Adar

23
Sivan

23
Elul

Several decades ago, an uncommon, if not unprecedented, phenomenon emerged in the Jewish world; there arose a palpable longing for the coming of the Geulah. While many earlier generations have harbored the same longing in their hearts, it has often been in response to horrific persecution and poverty, for which redemption was the only foreseeable relief.[1]

Today, however, the majority of Jews live in peace and relative prosperity. Even so, talk of Mashiach's imminence seems more pervasive than ever. Rav Shimon Schwab viewed this as a significantly positive development, but the impatience for the *Geulah*, he said in January 1989, was lacking one vital element:[2]

> ...Being impatient, we forget something very important: the meeting between Mashiach and the Jewish people will not occur through his lowering himself to our level, but rather through our elevating ourselves to his level. This means Mashiach will not come unless we repent.

Therefore, says Rav Schwab[3] it is time to prepare in earnest. Before we pack for our return to the Holy Land, we must endeavor to become a people worthy of being redeemed by Mashiach. That means learning the practical steps we must take to arrive at this level, starting with *teshuvah*.

> "You will return unto Hashem, your God, and hearken to His voice... He will not abandon you nor

---

1. See Prologue.
2. Adapted from *Selected Speeches*, Rav Shimon Schwab (CIS Publishers, Abridged Edition pp. 23-24.
3. *Beis HaSho'eivah*, p. 20.

destroy you..."[4] *Sforno*[5] *explains that this refers to the period just before Mashiach, which the Torah describes as follows:*[6]

Then Hashem, your God, will bring you back from your captivity and have mercy upon you, and He will return and gather you from all the peoples to which Hashem, your God, has scattered you...You shall return and listen to the voice of Hashem, and perform all His commandments that I command you today.

The Gemara[7] teaches that the Jewish people will undoubtedly repent before they are redeemed. As the Rambam writes:[8] "The Jewish people will be redeemed *only* through *teshuvah*." It is only through *teshuvah* that our performance of every other mitzvah, such as Torah learning, Shabbos observance, and *tefillah* will be complete. The question is: Through which means will the people arrive at repentance. [9]

Elsewhere, the Gemara states:[10] "Great is *teshuvah*, for it brings the redemption nearer."[11] The link between the two, says *Mabit*,[12] arises from the fact that the Messianic

---

4. *Devarim* 4:30-31.

5. Ad loc.

6. Ibid. 30:3,8.

7. *Sanhedrin* 97b with *Rashi*, s.v. *B'teshuvah*. See *Midrash Tanchuma*, *Bechukosai*, Ch. 3; *Pirkei D'Rabbi Eliezer*, Ch. 43.

8. *Hilchos Teshuvah* 7:5. See *Ramban, Devarim* 30:11.

9. See *Sanhedrin* 97b: "If they do not repent [on their own] then Hashem will appoint a wicked king over them whose decrees will be as harsh as Haman. *Michtav MeEliyahu*, Vol. 5, p. 295 states that even according to Rabbi Yehoshua in *Sanhedrin* 97b, who does not opine that Hashem will impose a wicked king over the Jews, they will come to do *teshuvah* at the last moment before Mashiach's arrival. See also *Maharsha* ibid.; *Yerushalmi Taanis* 1:1, which states that five merits earned the Jews their redemption from Egypt, and one of them was repentance, which will also occur at the End of Days. See also *Maharal, Netzach Yisrael*, Ch. 45, s.v. *U'b'Midrash*.

10. *Yoma* 86b.

11. See *Maharsha* ibid., which states that there is a predetermined date for the arrival of Mashiach. But if the people repent, the Mashiach will come earlier. See *Chomas HaDaas*, Ch. 13, where the Chofetz Chaim states that if the Jewish people repent fully, they will be redeemed immediately.

12. *Beis Elokim, Shaar HaTeshuvah*, Ch. 18.

▸ *Our
demand for
Mashiach's
speedy
arrival
must
include an
effort to do
teshuvah,
whereby
we will
merit his
arrival.*

▸ *Repentence
is a major
component
of redemp-
tion. The
only ques-
tion is
whether
we will be
driven to it
by frighten-
ing events,
or strive
toward
it out of
desire for
closeness
to God.*

era and *teshuvah* each signify a triumph over enslave-ment. The Messianic era is our salvation from physical ser-vitude[13] — our release from the domination of the nations of the world. *Teshuvah* is the soul's deliverance from its servitude to sin.[14]

The past century has seen horrific events, and we pray that those were the worst of the birth-pangs that the sages foresaw as the prelude to the Final Redemption.[15] We must never lose faith in the Torah that promises our return from exile; neither should we lose faith in the people of Israel, who will undoubtedly arrive at a complete, wholehearted return to God.

---

13. *Rambam, Hilchos Melachim,* Ch. 12.
14. See *Takanas HaShavim,* p. 19.
15. Rav Yechezkel Levenstein (*Ohr Yechezkel, Emunah,* p. 313) stat-ed: "It seems to me that many of the details [that apply to the End of Days] have already occurred during the Holocaust...it was an *eis tzarah,* a time of suffering [of a magnitude] that previously had not existed until our time..."

RARE AND PRECIOUS

DAY 83

*A*group of high school girls were gathered on one Shabbos afternoon around the dining room table of their friend's home. "For sure, the Geulah is coming soon," one girl asserted. "Look at the mess the world is in. It's all the signs Chazal told us to watch for. The economy, the Middle East, all the confusion. It's so bad that it's perfect!"

"Are you joking?" another girl responded. "There's supposed to be teshuvah! How in the world is that going to happen when most Jews aren't even religious? How can the Geulah come without all of us doing teshuvah?"

Indeed, the second girl's observations echo those of the Torah,[1] which indicate that *teshuvah* is necessary in order for the Jewish people to be redeemed with the coming of the *Geulah*.

The Chofetz Chaim[2] resolves the contradiction between the two End-of-Days scenarios — between the low, chaotic state of affairs that characterize the *ikvesa d'Meshicha*, footsteps of Mashiach,[3] and the exalted state of a united Jewish people turning their hearts toward God. He explains that at the time of the redemption, the Jewish people will include two groups. One group will have maintained their spirituality. Though imperfect, they will serve God with their heart and soul. The other group will

24 Kislev

24 Adar

24 Sivan

24 Elul

---

1. *Devarim* 4:27-31.
2. *Tzipisa L'Yeshuah*, Ch. 1.
3. The *Mishnah* (*Sotah* 49b) speaks of *ikvesa d'Meshicha*, "the footsteps of Mashiach," which is the final period of exile before the coming of Mashiach.

be comprised of Jews whose spiritual level is decidedly lacking. Yet, both groups will be instrumental in hastening the Final Redemption.

On the one hand, the role of the Torah-observant groups in ushering in an era of unvarnished spirituality appears to be obvious. On the other hand, it is hard to imagine what role could be played by our generation's spiritually distant, alienated Jewish majority in bringing the world closer to redemption.[4]

> *The teacher promised the class an extra 15 minutes of recess if the students behaved well during a special assembly at which they would be addressed by a guest speaker. Three out of the twenty-five children in the class began whispering and laughing during the speech, and therefore the class lost its special privilege.*

The above scenario is not unusual. What would be highly unusual is if twenty-two children misbehaved, but the teacher rewarded the class based on the three who conducted themselves properly. Yet, that is the principle upon which God will redeem the Jewish people. He will treasure the *teshuvah* of the minority who are striving to serve Him wholeheartedly, and upon that basis, bring redemption to the rest.

Shir HaShirim provides a vivid description of this redemption:[5] "The voice of my Beloved! Behold, it came suddenly to redeem me, as if leaping over mountains, skipping over hills." The Midrash[6] explains that when Moshe told the Jewish people that they would be redeemed from Egypt during the month of Nissan, they replied, "How can we be redeemed? We do not have good deeds... Egypt is full of our idols!" Moshe

---

4. See *Michtav MeEliyahu*, Vol. 3, pp. 222-223, which states that a person who completely lacks virtue, and thus has no grounds for self-deception, understands on some level that without *teshuvah*, there is no hope for him. Hence, the group that is completely adrift in sin can indeed do *teshuvah*, thereby hastening the redemption. See ibid., Vol. 2, p. 81, *s.v. Madreigas hateshuvah*. See also ibid., Vol. 2, p. 87, *s.v. Mitzad zeh*, for a different approach.
5. 2:8.
6. *Yalkut Shimoni, Shir HaShirim, Remez, 986, s.v. Kol dodi.*

responded, "Because Hashem wants to redeem you, He does not look as much at your bad deeds. To whom does Hashem look? To the righteous ones among you."

The "righteous ones" in our day are the Jews who, in spite of all the confusion of this world, in spite of all the excess materialism that pulls people so strongly, in spite of all the lusts and desires that are readily acquired, reject the falsehood and turn to God. To the best of their abilities they cleave to Torah and mitzvos in the midst of the social and spiritual riptide that exists in pre-Messianic times. Their *teshuvah* will suffice to bring the Final Redemption.

Zohar[7] recounts that Rabbi Akiva asked Rabbi Eliezer: "How is it possible that this [sect] will awaken to *teshuvah*, how will all Jews combine to do *teshuvah*? Rabbi Eliezer responded: If one synagogue does *teshuvah*, in their merit all [Jews] in exile will gather [in redemption]."

The fact that so many Jews are disconnected from Torah — and therefore unable to grasp the concept of proper *teshuvah* — need not obstruct the *Geulah*. If those who do observe the mitzvos embark on sincere *teshuvah*, their spirit will prove sufficient. That is because God truly wants to redeem us. As He did when we were redeemed from Egypt, God will overlook the sins of those whose bond with Him was broken by the hardship of exile, and set His eyes instead upon those who, despite every obstacle, have served Him and clung to Him for so long. For the sake of this precious group, "the righteous among you," the world will be redeemed.[8]

Rav Mattisyahu Salomon expounds on the Chofetz Chaim's concept of two groups of Jews:[9]

> *It is clear that in today's days, the person who stands firmly against the influences of the world, even though it is difficult, and studies Torah and performs mitzvos, is considered as if he has accomplished with his teshuvah on behalf of all Jews, and his*

---

7. *Zohar HaChadash, Bereishis* 40a; *Matnas Chaim, Moadim*, p. 223; *Kovetz Sichos Maamar Mordechai*, Vol. 1, p. 26.
8. See *Mesillas Yesharim*, Ch. 13
9. *Matnas Chaim, Kinyanim*, Vol. 1, p. 232, s.v. *Harei mi'divrei*.

▸ *Two con-*
tradicting
scenarios
are offered
as forerun-
ners to the
coming of
Mashiach.
The Chofetz
Chaim
reconciles
these
views, say-
ing that
there will
be a large
group of
Jews who
neglect the
Torah, and
a small
group of
righteous
Jews.

▸ *God wants*
to redeem
us, there-
fore the
merit of
the small
group,
remaining
righteous
in a corrupt
society, will
prove suf-
ficient to
bring the
Geulah.

teshuvah actually hastens the coming of the Final Redemption."[10]

Clearly, the ability of those who observe Torah and mitzvos is of monumental import. The sincere *teshuvah* of this segment of the Jewish people has a direct impact on hastening the redemption.

---

10. The Chofetz Chaim was asked how Hashem would bring Mashiach if the Jewish people had been experiencing deterioration in each succeeding generation. Furthermore (see *Ohr Yechezkel, Darchei HaAvodah*, p. 97), "in our deteriorating generation, is there anyone for whom Mashiach should come?" He responded that the *Geulah* will come based upon the *pasuk* in *Malachi* 3:16, "*Az nidbaru yirei Hashem ish el rei'eihu* — Then those who fear Hashem will talk among themselves" [to strengthen the Jewish people]... and then Hashem will send Eliyahu HaNavi.

Rav Dovid Kviat, in *Succas Dovid*, teaches: At the time of the miracle of Chanukah, the entire Jewish people had not yet repented—it was only a small band that fought the Greeks. The majority of the Jewish people were mired in sin. Yet, following the victory of the Chashmonaim and the miracle of the jug of oil, the nation repented. Just as from the one small jug of oil, the Menorah was able to remain lit for eight days, so, too, did the few Torah-true Jews miraculously save all of Jewry.

24 Kislev — Charlotte Brickman
לע"נ שבע שולא בת משה דוב הלוי ע"ה
By her children, grandchildren and great-grandchildren
24 Adar —
24 Sivan — לזכות חיים ברוך נ"י בן לאה ע"ה
24 Elul — Szrolovits לע"נ שלמה רפאל בן חיים ז"ל

THE HEART OF
THE MATTER

T he small minority of Torah-true Jews is like the heart of the nation, pumping spiritual vitality into all the limbs and organs that have distanced themselves. Because the Jewish people are one body, the health of the nation's heart plays a vital role in determining the health of every organ and extremity.[1] This was the principle put forth by Rav Yisrael Salanter when he would say that time wasted from Torah study in the holy city of Kovno[2] causes Shabbos desecration in the secularized homes of France.[3] If the heart is not healthy, the rest of the body cannot survive.

The Chofetz Chaim's view on *teshuvah* illustrates that this principle can also work for the good.[4] When the "heart" of devoted Jews beats strongly, it energizes the rest of the body. In addition, like a heart, its contents flow outward to the entire nation, subtly carrying the spirit of *teshuvah* into the heart and mind of every other Jew.[5] Even if this superimposed *teshuvah* never results in

25
Kislev

25
Adar

25
Sivan

25
Elul

---

1. See *Tomer Devorah*, which states that "all Jewish souls are linked together, each one has a portion...when one sins he impairs himself and the portion that his friend has." See also *Sifsei Chaim*, Vol. 1, pp. 103-104.
2. Between 1920 and 1939, Kovno (Kaunas), located in central Lithuania, was the country's capital and largest city. It had a Jewish population of 35,000-40,000, about one-fourth of the city's total population. Kovno was also a center of Jewish learning.
3. *Shimusha Shel Torah*, p. 107, cited in *Matzmiach Yeshuah*, p. 77, s.v. *Yeduim divrei*.
4. *Leket Divrei Chizuk*, p. 17 cited in *Matzmiach Yeshuah*, p. 79, s.v. *Adam*.
5. *Divrei Moshe, Parashas Shemini; Ginzei Yosef, Parashas Ki Sisa; Be'er Mayim Chaim, Parashas Vayikra 2; Tomer Devorah; Tzidkas*

a full return to Torah and mitzvos, it nevertheless prods a gentle awakening within every Jew:

> It will be that when all these things come upon you—the blessing and the curse that I have presented before you—then you will take it to your heart among all the nations where Hashem, your God, has dispersed you. [6]

These words of the Torah pinpoint the location of the alienated Jews' first stirrings of *teshuvah* at the End of Days — the heart. Abarbanel[7] explains that these Jews, although unable to repent fully, will engage in *hirhur teshuvah* —contemplating *teshuvah* in their heart — which initiates the *teshuvah* process.

The verses state:[8] "...then you will take it to your heart among all the nations where Hashem, your God, has dispersed you. And you will return unto Hashem, your God..."

The first part, "then you will take it to your heart," refers to those Jews who, because of their upbringing or due to the hardships of the exile, do not practice Judaism. As a result, they cannot perceive the specific sins they have committed. Therefore, their *teshuvah* will be "in their hearts" and not in their mouths [referring to *Viduy*]... They are the majority of Jews who have been dispersed among the nations and who identify themselves with the nationality of their host country. [9]

HaTzaddik, Os 159; *Shemiras HaLashon, Shaar HaTevunah* 5; *Shiurei Daas*, Vol. 1, pp. 152-157; *Iggeres Chazon Ish*, end of *Siman Dinim V'Hanhagos*.

6. *Devarim* 30:1.
7. *Abarbanel* on *Nitzavim*, p. 132, s.v. *Kasav haRan; Mashmia Yeshuah, HaMevaser* 3, *Nevuah* 15:9.
8. *Devarim* 30:1-2.
9. Two college professors, Barry Kosmin and Ariela Keysar, presented the findings of their groundbreaking American Religious Identification Survey (ARIS), "American Jews Show Steady Numbers but Growing Diverse and Secular," at the 15th World Congress of Jewish Studies Conference in Jerusalem on August 6, 2009. The survey concluded that the proportion of American Jews who identify themselves as religious has dropped by more than 20 percent over the past two decades, while the cultural Jewish population has nearly doubled.

Regarding the smaller part of Judaism who identify themselves as Jews… and follow God's Torah, the verse states:[10] "And you will return unto Hashem, your God, and listen to His voice, according to everything that I commanded you today, you and your children, with all your heart and all your soul." They will do *teshuvah* — return and perform the mitzvos and listen to Hashem's voice, since they never left Hashem's Torah.

To them, Hashem promises:[11] "Then Hashem, your God, will bring back your captivity and have mercy upon you." Because this remnant of Judaism has kept the Torah, the verse states that Hashem "will bring back your captivity." They are considered captives in foreign lands. Furthermore, Hashem will "have mercy upon you." Since they suffer by living in foreign lands, they need Hashem's mercy.

When an incomplete "from now on" type of *teshuvah* is all that a person can muster because of his estrangement from Torah, it can suffice for that person at that spiritual level. Says *Michtav MeEliyahu*:[12]

> The lowest level of teshuvah is where one returns by separating from sin from now on, and he has yet to come to full regret [for his sins]…. And when such a teshuvah comes from the depths of his heart, from the point of truth, he is called a "baal teshuvah."[13]

Each form of *teshuvah* is worthy as long as "it is rooted in a desire to change."[14] This single factor is what enables every Jew, wherever he stands in his spiritual life, to play a crucial part in the drama of redemption.

---

10. Ibid. 30:2.
11. Ibid. v. 3.
12. Vol. 2, p. 81, s.v. *Madreigas hateshuvah*.
13. See *Takanas HaShavim*, beg. of *Siman* 9.
14. See *Michtav MeEliyahu*, Vol. 1, p. 20, s.v. *Hinei*.

> 25 Kislev —
> 25 Adar —
> 25 Sivan —
> 25 Elul —

Take It With You

▸ *The Torah promises that at the End of Days, the Jews will do teshuvah and God will return us from captivity and have compassion on us.*

▸ *This applies to those who observe the Torah, since they discern their sins and do teshuvah. Their teshuvah subtly influences those who are distant.*

▸ *Those who are disconnected from the Torah because of the hardships of exile or their upbringing will do teshuvah "in their hearts."*

ATTEMPTING THE POSSIBLE

DAY 85

26
Kislev

26
Adar

26
Sivan

26
Elul

*C*hava looked through her kitchen window into the backyard. There, she spotted 4-year-old Dovid, standing on a picnic table holding five helium balloons in his hand. With a look of steely determination on his pudgy face, he jumped up and down on the table. Over and over, he jumped, landed, marshaled his energy, and jumped again.

"Dovid, what are you doing?" Chava shouted out the open window.

"I'm trying to fly!" he proclaimed.

Had he not believed that five helium balloons possessed enough lift to carry him into the air, he would no doubt have quit his exhausting experiment after a few tries, if he had indeed tried at all. But he was convinced that it could be done, and therefore, he persisted.

It is our task to know that *teshuvah* can be done, for without that knowledge, there would be no incentive to try. Certainly, there would be no incentive to persist when setbacks arise. Only when there is a vision of success spurring us on can we undertake *teshuvah*, or anything at all.

Success is an experience every person has had in some areas of life. Failure, too, is an experience shared by all. Unfortunately, many people allow the failures to cast a shadow over their successes, producing a self-image that is both gloomy and inaccurate. To attempt something new, one needs compelling evidence that he can succeed; otherwise, why try?

The only evidence one can trust is past success. If one pulls those instances out of the shadows, recalls and appreciates those experiences, one's self-image loses its gloomy veneer. The individual recognizes that he has already come a long way in his life; that he has mastered many skills, developed many fine traits; taken upon himself many important commitments and fulfilled them.

Once a person strengthens his belief that he can succeed in general, he still must answer his doubts about succeeding in *teshuvah* specifically. Can he really become more spiritual? Can he actually conquer the physical impulses and indulgences that separate him from God? Can he really change? The answer is an unequivocal "Yes!"

> For the commandment that I command you today is not hidden from you and it is not distant...Rather the matter is very near to you — in your mouth and in your heart — to perform it.[1]

According to the Ramban,[2] the mitzvah depicted in these verses is the mitzvah of *teshuvah* (repentance). The Torah is emphasizing our capacity to repent, telling us that it is "in your mouth and in your heart." Clearly, the Torah is conveying that *teshuvah* is very doable.

> Hashem does not ask a person to perform the mitzvah of building a ma'akeh (railing) around his porch unless Hashem has first given him a house.[3] Hashem does not ask one to wear tzizis unless he first provides him with a garment.[4]

The fact that the Torah demands *teshuvah* of us indeed proves that it is beneficial and doable, for God never demands the impossible.[5] As the Torah proclaims:[6]

---

1. *Devarim* 30:11,14.
2. Ad loc.
3. *Devarim* 22:8; *Chinuch, Mitzvah* 546.
4. *Vayikra Rabbah* 27:2.
5. See *Michtav MeEliyahu*, Vol. 4, p. 23, where Rav Dessler comments that no person is given tests that are too difficult: "All that [Hashem] gives a person in this world, whether intelligence or wealth, are tests for him, to see whether he will become haughty and will take it [intelligence or wealth] for himself or whether he will use it to serve God. And the test of wealth is unlike the test of intelligence. [Hashem] does not give man a task that is so difficult such as two tests [wealth and intelligence] simultaneously."
   However, see *Tzidkas HaTzaddik, Os* 43.
6. *Devarim* 30:14.

Take It With You

▸ *One does not undertake something difficult unless success appears possible.*

▸ *A person must bolster his own image of success by recalling and appreciating times he has experienced it.*

▸ *Success in teshuvah is guaranteed to be attainable, within each person's capacity, because the Torah does not command that which is impossible.*

"Rather, the matter is very near to you — in your mouth and in your heart — to perform it." Ramban[7] explains that "it [*teshuvah*] is near to you at all times and in all places."

_____

7. Ad loc.

THREE-STEP PLAN

L ike a powerful medicine capable of defeating a devastating disease, *teshuvah* must contain the right measure of the right ingredients. Just as a person would not save money by taking an a less effective, "off-brand" of a lifesaving drug, he must ensure that the treatment for his spiritual ills is authentic and full strength.

Rabbeinu Yonah[1] relates that "*Teshuvah* is based on three main components, without which the service of *teshuvah* is not possible...They are, 'regret, abandoning sin, and verbal confession (*Viduy*).'"

• REGRET

Unless a person recognizes that he is doing wrong, he cannot begin to reform. A twinge of guilt is a wakeup call without which the person's conscience remains sound asleep. His guilt prods him to examine why he succumbed and transgressed. Was it social pressure? A desire for pleasure? Or perhaps laziness? He regrets that he succumbed in a moment of weakness, and that opens the door to growth.

True regret is a necessary step in the *teshuvah* process[2] because the kind of *teshuvah* that is based on "feeling sorry" for an action that one does not really believe was wrong does not lead to true growth.[3] There has to be

27
Kislev

27
Adar

27
Sivan

27
Elul

---

1. *Shaarei Teshuvah, Shaar* 1:19.
2. See *Matnas Chelko* on *Shaarei Teshuvah*, p. 21, which states that in order for a person to erase his sin and to make a meaningful verbal confession — the second and third steps — he must first regret what he has done.
3. See *Mesillas Yesharim*, end of Ch. 4.

real remorse in a person's heart.[4] When the person thinks about what he has done, he should feel, without reservations, "I wish I could rewind this film and do it over again differently." [5]

Part of that sense of regret, according to Rabbeinu Yonah,[6] springs from fear; there is an acute realization that God is watching and meting out justice for all that occurs,[7] and that no unrepented sin goes unpunished.[8] The purer sense of regret, however, comes from understanding the impact of a person's misdeeds on his own soul and on his relationship with God. He feels confounded by his own neglect of and cruelty to his pure soul and to his existence in the World to Come. Like a parent who has looked away from his child for that one crucial moment in which the child is injured, he exclaims to himself, "What have I done?" That is the level of remorse that triggers the mechanisms of *teshuvah*.

• ABANDONING SIN

The second step in *teshuvah* is to "forsake it (the sinful action)," to abandon it and make a commitment to engage in that act no more. This is not an "I'll try to do better" commitment, but rather, as the Rambam[9] describes, it is a heartfelt commitment so resolute that God Himself can testify to the purity of the person's intentions.

What is God seeking when He looks into the person's

---

4. *Michtav MeEliyahu*, Vol. 2, p. 79, s.v. *Amnam*.
5. "One who does a sin and is embarrassed by it, God will forgive him" (*Berachos* 12b).
6. *Shaarei Teshuvah, Shaar* 1:10.
7. See *Ramban*, Introduction to *Iyov*, who writes that it is better to suffer the afflictions that Iyov had for seventy years than to be punished in Gehinnom for one small sin that he purposely transgressed.
8. Rabbeinu Yonah ibid. mentions seven things that are involved in having regret.
9. *Rambam, Hilchos Teshuvah* 2:2: "What constitutes *teshuvah*? That a sinner should abandon his sins and remove them from his thoughts, resolving in his heart never to commit them again, as it states: 'May the wicked abandon his ways' (*Yeshayah* 55:7). [He must reach the level where] He Who knows the hidden will testify concerning him that he will never return to this sin again as (*Hoshea* 14:4) states: 'We will no longer say to the work of our hands: You are our gods.'"

heart? Rabbeinu Yonah[10] says that He is looking for the person's firm resolution to shed his "evil ways" — the personality trait, situation, or mistaken belief that led him to do wrong. If the person does not forsake the root of the sin, says Rav Mattisyahu Salomon,[11] he is likely to relapse when faced with the same *nisayon*. This means that a person who cheats in business because of his overpowering love of money must resolve firmly to reform that trait. Otherwise, a resolution to refrain from cheating is doomed to failure.[12]

• VIDUY

A person's mind is a nonstop monologue encompassing thoughts as sublime as remorse and self-improvement, and as mundane as the traffic report. Thoughts flit through one's consciousness helter-skelter, each roosting only until another comes to displace it. Therefore, *teshuvah* must manifest itself in something more than thought.

Viduy, in which a person verbally confesses his sin[13] before God,[14] transfers *teshuvah* from the realm of amorphous thought into reality. Speaking one's feelings has a profound internal impact; for example, telling someone "I'm sorry" is a far more concrete step than simply feeling regret. If a person cannot speak the words "I have sinned" privately before God, he probably has not yet arrived at true introspection.[15] Obviously, we are not tell-

---

10. *Shaarei Teshuvah, Shaar* 1:11.
11. *Matnas Chelko,* on *Shaarei Teshuvah,* p. 27.
12. *Sanhedrin* 25a, *Rashi,* s.v. *V'yachzir aveidah;* 25b, s.v. *D'afilu l'nachri.*
13. This doesn't have to be done in shul, and it doesn't have to be said in Hebrew. Talk to God in at least an audible whisper, not just in your head. Although God knows already, you need to hear it. Tell Him that you are sorry for whatever you did wrong. If your actions harmed another person then you have to make amends and ask forgiveness from the one who was harmed.
14. See *Shaarei Teshuvah, Shaar* 1:40, and *Beis Elokim, Shaar HaTeshuvah,* Ch. 3, s.v. *V'hinei haviduy.*
15. *Viduy* is not a public act; the requirement is for a person to verbally acknowledge his misdeeds to God privately. See also *Midrash Shocher Tov,* Ch. 45, s.v. *Rachash; Rosh, Moed Katan,* Ch. 3, *Siman* 76; *Minchas Chinuch, Mitzvah* 364:1,3; *She'eilos U'Teshuvos Lev Chaim,* Vol. 1, *Siman* 10; *Rav Yosef Engel* on *Kiddushin* 49b; and *Derech Sichah,* Vol. 1, p. 615, s.v. *Shema hirhur.*

Take It With You

▸ *The three main components of teshuvah are regret, abandoning sin, and verbal confession.*

▸ *The regret must be sincere and include an awareness that no unrepented sin goes unpunished.*

▸ *Abandoning the sinful action requires a commitment to never again engage in that action.*

▸ *Once the first two components are in place, Viduy — verbally confessing — transfers teshuvah into reality.*

ing God something He doesn't know. Rather, we "come clean" to elicit God's help in healing our deficiency, and to move forward.[16]

One cannot place a roof upon a house that has no framework. And yet, a house without a roof has no function. In *teshuvah*, regret and forsaking the sin form the framework. If they are not topped by *Viduy*, they will not serve their function. On the other hand, *Viduy* alone is like a roof plopped down upon a house that is supposed to be there, but isn't. Only when the first two steps are in place does *Viduy* establish one's *teshuvah*, eradicating past sins and making way for the Final Redemption.

------

16. See *Rambam, Hilchos Teshuvah* 2:2, which states that without this step there is no *teshuvah*. He derives this ruling in part from the prophet Hoshea's injunction (14:3): "Take words and return to your God." In fact, *Viduy* is counted as one of the 613 commandments of the Torah, from the verse, "And they shall confess their sins which they commit" (*Bamidbar* 5:7).

27 Adar — לעילוי נשמת הרב שמואל צבי בן ר' חיים שראגא
27 Sivan —
27 Elul — Our dear daughter should have continued brachah, hatzlachah, and shalom as she grows as a bas Yisrael. Dedicated by her loving parents, Jennifer and Will Coane

BEFORE IT'S
TOO LATE

*W*hy start making big changes now? Maybe my little flaws and foibles aren't so bad. Maybe it's just my nature, and God won't hold me accountable for things I can't really help. Maybe I'm not really trespassing on a mitzvah at all — just a custom or halachic stringency that has been passed down through the generations. When the Geulah comes, it will all be clear, and then I'll do what I have to do...."

28 Kislev

28 Adar

28 Sivan

28 Elul

People have many rationales for deferring a serious commitment to *teshuvah*.[1] A clear picture of this emerges from the following allegory about a man who has fled from the government due to unpaid taxes:

> The man enters a town and notices numerous signs promising amnesty to all who come to the tax office by their own volition. They will be absolved of the penalties for their outstanding debt and free of fear of retribution. If, instead, he waits to be found by a government agent and brought back unwillingly, he will no doubt have to fully account for his decision to flee from his obligations.

As the allegory above illustrates, the time for *teshuvah* is now. Returning to God on our own accord, out of sincere regret for our departures from His service, ensures us that our *teshuvah* will be accepted completely and our past sins forgiven. If we hold out, relishing our freedom from God's yoke for as long as possible, then when Mashiach

---

1. *Chofetz Chaim, Zachor L'Miriam*, Ch. 4, pp.13-14.

▸ *One can
easily con-
vince him-
self that
teshuvah
can wait, or
that it isn't
necessary.*

▸ *The Chofetz
Chaim
explains
that one
who
believes
he can
wait until
Mashiach
comes to
do teshu-
vah will
lose his
opportu-
nity.*

comes, it will be too late to do *teshuvah*.[2]

A verse in *Mishlei* says:[3] "If you will seek it as if it were money...then you will understand fear of Heaven." The Chofetz Chaim[4] explains that serving God must be treated as a Jew's business. He should therefore be prompt and energetic in undertaking a mitzvah — even one as potentially formidable as *teshuvah*.

Teshuvah is for everyone — the person who has transgressed (even one who has done evil) can rectify his past misdeeds, and a righteous person can strive toward his potential. Through *teshuvah*, a person increases his awe and love of God, gradually arriving at an awareness of even the slightest breach of His will.[5] Each person, at his own level, can elevate himself through *teshuvah*.[6]

By applying ourselves to *teshuvah*, may we merit fulfillment of the blessing recited in the daily *Shemoneh Esrei*, "Bring us back, our Father, to Your Torah, and bring us near, our King, to Your service, and influence us to return in complete repentance before You." And with this complete *teshuvah*, may we merit the speedy arrival of the Final Redemption.

---

2. See *Michtav MeEliyahu*, Vol. 5, p. 295.
3. 2:4-5.
4. *Zachor L'Miriam*, Ch. 5, p.14; *Chovas HaShemirah,* Ch. 8, *Os* 15.
5. *Nesivos Shalom*, Vol. 1, pp. 195-196.
6. See *Tzidkas HaTzaddik, Os* 67,134.

CHAPTER 13:
A NEW DAWN

A BRIGHTER LIGHT

DAY 88

29
Kislev

29
Adar

29
Sivan

29
Elul

*I*n the darkness of night, the watchman used his powerful flashlight to illuminate his path and examine the source of any suspicious noises. But when the sun rose to its full strength, his flashlight was useless, a mere flicker that added nothing to the light of the sun's brilliant rays.

Likewise, in the days of Mashiach, when God's light inundates the world, the brilliant light shed by His miracles and commemorated by our Yomim Tovim will no longer outshine the pervasive brilliance of the entire natural world. The splitting of the Reed Sea will reveal itself to be neither more nor less God's work than the splitting of a seedling as it begins to sprout.

This message was the one that Reb Shraga Feivel Mendlowitz[1] delivered to his students during his last Purim in Bais Medrash Elyon. In the midst of their exuberant singing and dancing, he rose to speak to them about the teaching cited in *Yalkut Shimoni*[2] that with the coming of Mashiach, all the holidays will no longer be celebrated, and only Purim will still be observed. How, he asked the students, could anyone suggest that precepts of the eternal Torah would be suspended?[3]

Reb Shraga Feivel explained that while God's presence is hidden within nature, the hand of God is visible only through miracles that override the laws of nature, such as

1. *Reb Shraga Feivel*, Yonoson Rosenblum (ArtScroll/Mesorah Publ.), pp.119-120.
2. *Mishlei, Remez* 944.
3. In fact, the *Rambam, Hilchos Melachim* 11:1 writes: "In the future, the King Mashiach will arise and restore the Davidic Kingdom to its original state, He will build the Beis HaMikdash, and gather in the exiles of Israel. All the laws of old will be reinstated in his days. Offerings will be brought. Sabbatical and Jubilee years will be observed in accordance with all the mitzvos stated in the Torah."

those surrounding the Exodus from Egypt and the Revelation at Sinai. The Torah's festivals commemorate those miracles. But Purim involves no blatant miracles; its events can easily be interpreted as a series of royal intrigues. Only the teachings of the Sages make us aware that the Purim drama was as much a miracle as the splitting of the sea.

In the times of Mashiach, God's light will be clear for all to see. When we truly understand that God controls everything, His ability to override the laws of nature will come as no surprise. Indeed, the "natural events" we take for granted will show themselves equally to be God's work.[4] Thus, while all the festivals will surely be observed as the Torah prescribes, the "miracles" that they commemorate will no longer be regarded as more extraordinary than "normal" events. The lesson of Purim — that everything is God given and directed — will be the primary lesson of our lives.

The Chofetz Chaim[5] explains that when Yosef reveals his identity to his brothers and declares, "I am Yosef,"[6] God's master plan becomes clear to the brothers. Everything that had happened during the previous twenty-two years suddenly falls into perspective. Likewise, when the time comes for God to reveal Himself and announce, "I am Hashem!" the veil will be lifted from our eyes and we will comprehend everything that transpired throughout history.[7]

In the full light of redemption, we will also recognize how every episode of the exile was the work of the Creator, aimed at bringing the world to perfection. Rav Dessler[8] draws this message from the words of *Shir HaMaalos* said on Shabbos and Yomim Tovim prior to reciting the Grace After Meals: "When Hashem will return the captivity of Zion, we will be like dreamers."[9] When the return to Zion

---

4. See *Sichos Mussar* (Rav Chaim Shmulevitz), *Shaarei Chaim*, *Maamar* 26, p. 111 [5731, *Maamar* 2], s.v. *V'zehu she'amar*.
5. *Chofetz Chaim al HaTorah*, *Bereishis* 48:3, p. 79.
6. *Bereishis* 45:3.
7. See *Midrash Tanchuma*, *Vayeishev* 10, which states that all that happened to Yosef will happen to Tzion.
8. *Michtav MeEliyahu*, Vol. 3, p. 245.
9. *Tehillim* 126:1.

(Jerusalem) comes, the suffering of past oppressions will seem like a dream[10] — a vaporous non-entity leading us to open our eyes to the true reality.

Reb Shraga Feivel noted that this is an awareness one must build within himself now, even before Mashiach's arrival. It is expressed in the verse of *Tehillim* that declares:[11] "The voice of Hashem comes in power, the voice of Hashem comes in majesty." This, he explained, teaches that "every force and all the beauty of nature proclaim, 'There is a Creator!'"

At the heart of all our longing is this one desire: that Hashem's presence, His glory and Divine Providence manifest themselves clearly in the world so that His Name will be sanctified. Everything else — including the physical abundance in the world, the end of suffering and illness, and the removal of all obstructions to our spiritual growth — springs from His singular, all-encompassing presence.

---

10. *Michtav MeEliyahu*, Vol. 1, p. 101, s.v. *Ach kaasher*.
11. 29:4.

---

29 Kislev — With gratitude for yeshuos and refuos past and future בעזהשי״ת
29 Adar — As as z'chus for Ephraim ben Shira Rus נ״י
29 Sivan —
29 Elul —

MAKING IT TO
THE FINISH LINE

DAY 89

*A*traveler set out on the road in a wagon. Fearful of nighttime marauders, he chose to sleep during the day and remain awake at night. He would awaken just as the moon began to rise, and fall asleep with the first glimmer of sun. When he arrived at his destination, he asked the wagon-driver why his route, which was known for its scenic beauty, had been so dark and dismal. The driver answered, *"The scenery was beautiful. The sun shone every day, but you never saw it, because you slept through it all."*

30 Kislev

29-30 Adar

30 Sivan

29 Elul

Like this traveler, the Dubno Maggid[1] expounds, the Jewish people have many times throughout history "slept through" a potential time of redemption. As many commentators[2] describe, there are times when Mashiach can arrive in a moment — "*achishenah*," suddenly. There is an "illumination" up above in Heaven for redemption. However, we, on earth, did not prepare the "receptacle" to receive the great "light" from above.[3] Had the Jewish people remained "awake" and vigilant, they could have brought Mashiach during those times.

As a verse in Yeshayah states:[4] "Said the watchman, 'Morning is coming, but also night. If you really desire it repent and come.'" The prophet laments the fact that the

---

1. As cited in *Ohr Gedalyahu, Vayikra*, p. 82, fn. 8. See also *Ohel Yaakov, Parashas Emor*, p. 116.
2. *Sanhedrin* 98a. See *Abarbanel* in *Yeshuos Meshicho*, Part 2, *Iyun* 1, Ch. 1, p. 39; *Turei Even* on *Rosh Hashanah* 11b, s.v. *B'Tishrei*; and the *Chasam Sofer* in *She'eilos U'Teshuvos Chasam Sofer*, Vol. 6, *Siman* 98, s.v. *V'hinei*.
3. *Ohr Gedalyahu, Bereishis*, p. 129, s.v. *V'inyan zeh*.
4. 21:12.

▸ *There are times when Mashiach can arrive in the mode of achishenah — suddenly.*

▸ *Mashiach is ready to be revealed at a moment's notice.*

▸ *The Jewish people have at times missed the opportunity to greet Mashiach because they were asleep — unaware of their potential to hasten the Geulah.*

▸ *Through our actions we can forge a connection to God and thereby hasten the redemption.*

Jewish people did not "repent and come" because they were asleep — unaware of their potential to hasten the Final Redemption. This verse elucidates our obligation to do our part, to be awake and alive to the active role we must take in hastening the blessing of the Final Redemption.

The implication is clear: Mashiach can come *any* day, even before the predetermined date: As *Tehillim declares*:[5] "*This day* if you will listen to His voice!" Every generation has a special *keitz* of its own, for, as stated, Mashiach is alive and present in every generation, albeit concealed.[6] He is ready to be revealed at a moment's notice.[7]

That the *Geulah* will come — this is God's promise; that our generation is indeed capable of achieving *teshuvah* we have shown to be true. By revitalizing our devotion to *tzipisa l'yeshuah*, unity with our fellow Jews, honoring Shabbos, *tefillah*, charity, Torah learning, and *teshuvah* — we can forge a connection to God that will enable the Jewish people to hasten the Final Redemption, and hopefully to greet *Mashiach Tzidkeinu* in our times.

---

5. 95:7.
6. See *Even Sheleimah* 11:9, which states that every generation has its own special *keitz*, subject to Israel's merit.
7. See *Sanhedrin* 98a.

> **30 Kislev —**
> **29-30 Adar —**
> **30 Sivan —** In honor of Esti Holczer and Dubby Gruen
> for completing the sefer "Positive Word Power"
> twice within one year.
> We are so proud of you!
> **29 Elul —**

The V'Ani Tefillah Foundation

The V'Ani Tefillah Foundation's (VAT) mission is to increase awareness of the importance and power of tefillah and to provide education, inspiration and tools for more sincere, powerful and effective tefillah. Since its inception in 2005, VAT has successfully put forth numerous tefillah programs and initiatives, which have had an impact on millions of tefillos around the world from tens of thousands of people. Below is a list of some of the many programs available from the V'Ani Tefillah Foundation:

....

BOOKS: 'PRAYING WITH FIRE 1' — *A 5-MINUTE-LESSON-A-DAY FORMAT*
'PRAYING WITH FIRE 2' — *A 5-MINUTE-LESSON-A-DAY FORMAT*
'YEARNING WITH FIRE' — *A 5-MINUTE-LESSON-A-DAY FORMAT*

....

• Impact: Inspiring over 90,000 Worldwide

Over 90,000 people were inspired by the first volume of 'Praying With Fire', as of Elul, 5770. 'Praying With Fire' contained 89 daily lessons, in a 5-minute lesson-a-day format. Praying With Fire 2 (released in Elul 5768 — September, 2008) contains 118 daily lessons that take only 5 minutes a day to learn.

PWF: Chapters Include:

• The immeasurable Power of Tefillah •Achieving Personal Growth Through Tefillah • Gaining a Proper Understanding of Kavannah • 13 Practical Strategies to Achieve True Kavannah • Finding Answers to Unanswered Prayers • And much more!

PWF 2: Chapters Include:

• Emunah & Tefillah: The Antidote to Fear and Terrorism • Emunah & Bitachon: The Foundation of Prayer • 8 Practical Strategies To Strengthen Emunah and Bitachon • Building Your Relationship With Your Creater • 14 Practical Strategies To Getting Prayers Accepted • The Power of Praying For Others • And much more!

ASERES YEMEI TESHUVAH TEFILLAH INITIATIVE
5765 (2005), 5766 (2006), 5768 (2008):

- **Impact: Inspiring Hundreds of Thousands Worldwide**
  In 5765\2005 ; 5766\2006, and 5768 \2008 over 100,000 Booklets (each time) with inspiring 10-day excerpts from 'Praying With Fire' and 'Praying With Fire 2' were distributed free each year to 250 cities in 10 countries around the world. By distributing these booklets, thousands each year gained a new appreciation of the power of each prayer to stir the Heavens and alter the fabric of their daily lives during the most important time of the year for tefillah.

ASERES YEMEI TESHUVAH 5768 –
THE POWER OF PRAYING FOR OTHERS

- **Impact: Inspiring Tens of Thousands To Pray For Others Worldwide**
  In 5768\2008 over 100,000 Booklets with inspiring 10-day excerpts from 'Praying With Fire 2' were distributed free to 250 cities in 10 countries around the world. In addition to the 'The Power of Praying For Others' booklet, a bookmark to be inserted in a siddur was distributed which gave people the opportunity to list names of those to daven for during Shemoneh Esrei.
  The merit of praying for another Jew is so immense that the Gemara (Bava Kamma 92a) states that anyone who prays for mercy on behalf of his fellow when he himself is in need of that same thing, he is answered first. In fact, every individual who prays for members of the community—his prayers are a thousand times more valuable than if every individual had merely prayed for himself, says Michtav M'Eliyahu.
  In addition to distributing the booklet and bookmark, a phone number and database was be set up to match those with similar needs, to pray for each other.

SHUL TEFILLAH INITIATIVE

- **Impact: Over 120 shuls have participated in the shul Tefillah Initiative.**
  Now is the time for our shul to join the over 120 shuls who have already participated in the shul Tefillah Initiative. The Shul Tefillah Initiative works with the whole shul together to strengthen collective tefillos in each shul. The Tefillah Initiative entails learning the 89 five-minute lessons-a-day of Praying With Fire – Volume 1 or 2, shul-wide. A Shabbos is designated

to launch the program and a siyum is scheduled for the end. Each shul receives 'PRAYING WITH PASSION' – a free (email) weekly newsletter with inspiring information and insights about a unique portion of the daily tefillah, as well as PDFs of flyers and posters encouraging participation, a calendar with the learning dates for their community.

- **Project I.G.N.I.T.E – with NCSY/OU**
  - **Impact: Over 700 NCSYers read Praying With Fire and many participated in national contest.**

  This project provides inspiration for NCSYers to grow in Tefillah by learning 'Praying With Fire', the 5-minute lesson-a-day program. Participants also are encouraged to pray shacharis, mincha and maariv, as well as reciting "personal tefillos." In addition, the weekly Tefillah newsletter "PRAYING WITH PASSION" was made available. NCSYers were able to pray with more kavannah –using colorful engaging bookmarks and pamphlets supplied by the V'Ani Tefillah Foundation.

SCHOOL-WIDE TEFILLAH INITIATIVES

- **Emunah Through Tefillah Initiative**
  - **Impact: Strengthening Thousands of Students Around The World In Emunah**
  - This program helps students from high school grades and above build and strengthen their Emunah through Tefillah.

- **Project I.G.N.I.T.E**

  This project provides inspiration for students around the globe to pray with more kavannah by providing colorful engaging bookmarks and pamphlets to help improve kavannah in tefillah. Also included in this program are the learning of 'Praying With Fire', the 5-minute lesson-a-day program.

OTHER WORLDWIDE TEFILLAH INITIATIVES

- **Shliach Tzibbur Guide**

  This guide provides a number of important Halachic points to guide the Shliach Tzibbur in properly discharging his duties.

- **Tefillin Awareness Project**

  Thousands of men in almost 40 shuls in various communities benefited in properly fulfilling the mitzvah of tefillin.

- **'Count Up To Purim' Tefillah Initiative**
  This special initiative, available to schools and shuls, inspired thousands around the world to empower their tefillos through enhancing kavannah in tefillah during the week counting up to Purim

- **Yom Kippur Shul Initiative**
  Encouraged thousands to abstain from unnecessary speech on Yom Kippur.

- **2007, 2008 and 2009 Aseres Yemei Teshuvah Worldwide Broadcast: With Rabbi Yisroel Reisman**
  People in over 30 locations around the globe received chizuk during this most important time of year.

- **Jerusalem Tefillah Initiative**
  This special initiative, available to schools and shuls, emphasizes the importance of beseeching Hashem to have more mercy over Jerusalem.

- **VAT Tefillah Lecture Series**
  'Praying with Fire' author travels to communities, shuls, and schools to inspire them about the importance and power of prayer and emunah.
  Summer Tefillah Projects 2007

- **5-minute Lesson-A-Day Program**

- **Summer Teleconference Series**
  Inspiring weekly teleconference shiur by the author of 'Praying With Fire' followed by a question-answer session.
  Future VAT Tefillah Projects

- **Creation of Elementary School Tefillah Curriculum**
  - To impart the concepts and underpinnings of tefillah at the child's level.
  - To provide a solid understanding and appreciation of the practical aspects of tefillah for children.

- **Tefillah Inspiration Phone Line**
  A specially dedicated phone message by popular Magidei Shiur providing daily inspirational messages on prayer with several menu options

- **Tefillah Newsletter**
  Will provide information about tefillah, including inspiring stories, relevant halacha and hashkafah, an 'Ask the Rabbi' column, and interesting relevant questions and issues posed to and by our readers.

- **Audio Visual Material**
  The V'Ani Tefillah Foundation, BE"H has already begun to produce several audio and audio-visual materials on the daily prayers and Tehillim.

....

For more information about these or any of our other initiatives,
please contact us at **201.837.0354**, or fax to 201.837.7774,
or e-mail info@prayingwithfire.org

The V'Ani Tefillah Foundation
1616 E. 29th St.
Brooklyn, NY 11229

This volume is part of
THE ARTSCROLL SERIES®
an ongoing project of
translations, commentaries and expositions
on Scripture, Mishnah, Talmud, Halachah,
liturgy, history, the classic Rabbinic writings,
biographies and thought.

For a brochure of current publications
visit your local Hebrew bookseller
or contact the publisher:

Mesorah Publications, ltd.

4401 Second Avenue
Brooklyn, New York 11232
(718) 921-9000
www.artscroll.com